THE CONFEDERATE NAVY:

A PICTORIAL HISTORY

by Philip Van Doren Stern

DA CAPO PRESS

Library of Congress Cataloging in Publication Data

Stern, Philip Van Doren, 1900—
    The Confederate Navy: a pictorial history / by Philip Van Doren
Stern. — 1st Da Capo Press ed.
        p.   cm.
    Originally published: Garden City, N.Y.: Doubleday, 1962.
    Includes index.
    ISBN 0-306-80488-3 (pbk.)
    1. Confederate States of America. Navy. 2. United States — History
— Civil War, 1861–1865 — Naval operations. I. Title.
E596.S8   1992   92-19258
973.7′57 — dc20   CIP

First Da Capo Press edition 1992

This Da Capo Press paperback edition of *The Confederate Navy* is
an unabridged republication of the edition published in New York
in 1962.

06 07 08 09 10   04 03 02 01 00

Published by Da Capo Press, Inc.
A member of the Perseus Books Group

ACKNOWLEDGMENTS

Many people have generously contributed their time and specialized knowledge to make this book possible. With keen appreciation for their help, the author wishes to thank the following institutions and the persons mentioned. LIBRARY OF CONGRESS: Dr. David C. Mearns, Dr. Percy Powell, John De Pory, Milton Kaplan, Willard Webb; NATIONAL ARCHIVES: Forest L. Williams, Josephine Cobb, Elmer Parker, Elbert L. Huber; SMITHSONIAN INSTITUTION: P. K. Lundeberg; DEPARTMENT OF THE NAVY: Rear Admiral E. M. Eller, Captain F. Kent Loomis, Commander D. D. Overby, Commander Penhard Hendler, H. A. Vadnais, Jr.; U. S. MARINE CORPS: Major James C. Gasser, Lieutenant Colonel Robert M. Walker; U. S. NAVAL ACADEMY: Captain Wade De Weese; U. S. MILITARY ACADEMY: Richard E. Kuehne; FRANKLIN D. ROOSEVELT LIBRARY: Herman Kahn; HARRY S. TRUMAN LIBRARY: Milton F. Perry; NATIONAL PARK SERVICE (Vicksburg): Edwin C. Bcarss; DEPARTMENT OF STATE: Carl Bode, Phillips Brooks; DEPARTMENT OF JUSTICE, ADMIRALTY AND SHIPPING SECTION: Captain Morris G. Duchin; CORCORAN GALLERY OF ART: Hermann Warner Williams, Jr., Henri Dorra; THE MARINERS MUSEUM: Harold S. Sniffen, Robert H. Burgess, John L. Lochhead; FORT MONROE CASEMENT MUSEUM: Dr. Chester Bradley; HENRY E. HUNTINGTON LIBRARY: Dr. John E. Pomfret, Dr. Allan Nevins, Mary Isabel Fry, Helen Mangold, Marion Chevalier, Herbert C. Schulz, Carey S. Bliss, Erwin K. Morkisch; RICE UNIVERSITY: Dr. Frank Van iver; UNIVERSITY OF CALIFORNIA: Dr. Brainerd Dyer, Dr. Jay Monaghan; WHITTIER COLLEGE: James M. Merrill; WILLIAMS COLLEGE: Dr. James P. Baxter, III; TULANE UNIVERSITY LIBRARY: Dorothy Whittemore; UNIVERSITY OF TEXAS: Frank H. Wardlaw; UNIVERSITY OF GEORGIA: Dr. E. M. Coulter; UNIVERSITY OF ALABAMA: William Stanley Hoole; LOUISIANA STATE MUSEUM: C. E. Frampton; THE CONFEDERATE MUSEUM: India W. Thomas, Eleanor S. Brockenbrough; VALENTINE MUSEUM: Mrs. Ralph Catterall; THE NEW-YORK HISTORICAL SOCIETY: James J. Heslin; CHICAGO HISTORICAL SOCIETY: Paul Angle, Mrs. Paul M. Rhymer; GEORGIA HISTORICAL SOCIETY: Walter Hartridge, Lilla M. Hawes; SAVANNAH PUBLIC LIBRARY: Elizabeth Hodge; ATLANTA HISTORICAL SOCIETY: Colonel Allen P. Julian; BROOKLYN PUBLIC LIBRARY: Corinne Shepard, Louise Turpin; NEW YORK PUBLIC LIBRARY: Leon Weidman; GOODSPEED'S BOOK SHOP: M. J. Walsh.

ENGLAND. PUBLIC RECORD OFFICE: E. K. Timings; BRITISH MUSEUM: Frank Francis, C. M. Dodd, B. Schofield; ADMIRALTY: P. W. Kemp; H. M. CUSTOMS AND EXCISE: R. C. Jarvis; UNIVERSITY OF LONDON: J. G. Edwards, Michael Howard; NATIONAL MARITIME MUSEUM: G. P. B. Naish; CONFEDERATE RESEARCH CLUB: Patrick J. Courtenay, Thomas Green.

FRANCE. ARCHIVES NATIONALES: Jacques Meurgey de Tupigny; BIBLIOTHÈQUE NATIONALE: Julien Cain; Mlle. Gaston-Cheraud, M. Bruno.

DENMARK. ROYAL NAVAL MUSEUM: Bredo von Munthe af Morgenstierne; SOCIETY FOR NAVAL HISTORY: Captain R. Steen Steensen; A. P. Møller Co.: Morten P. Hoogland.

In addition to those listed above, thanks are also due to the following individuals for their helpful cooperation: Robert V. Bruce, Bruce Catton, Hamilton Cochran, Mrs. Frances Cole, Sheffield Coles, Katherine Fowler, James D. Horan, Miss Marianne M. Laird, Betty Lass, Alex A. Lawrence, E. B. Long, Robert F. Marx, James F. Mathias, Henry Allen Moe, Ken Parks, Howard C. Rice, Mrs. Theodore Douglas Robinson, Colonel William Morrison Robinson, Jr., Archibald Roosevelt, William Sloane, Ray D. Smith, Helmer L. Webb, and Miss Frances Leigh Williams.

Picture Credits

Where more than one picture is credited on a page, they have been listed from top to bottom and from left to right as a, b, c, etc.

Atlanta Historical Society: 181a.

Author's Collection: 20a, 23, 24b, 25b, 31, 42a, 42b, 42c, 43a, 46b, 65a, 65b, 70a, 70b, 83a, 90, 97a, 101a, 111b, 120, 131b, 135a, 138b, 139a, 156, 162–163, 182a, 182b, 183b, 183c, 186b, 195, 197b, 202b, 204a, 211b, 229, 250–251, 251.

Battles and Leaders of the Civil War: 34, 48b, 55, 71a, 71b, 81a, 82a, 83b, 83c, 84b, 87, 98a, 98b, 124b, 136a, 189, 190, 191, 194a, 197d, 201a, 201b, 218a, 219a, 220b.

British Battleships by Dr. Oscar Parkes, Seeley Service & Co., Ltd., London: 43b.

Caisse Nationale des Monuments Historiques, Paris: 223a.

Cammel-Laird's, Liverpool: 35a.

Century Magazine: 114a, 126b, 127b, 127c.

Confederate Museum, Richmond, Va.: 57c, 114b, 151a.

William Fehr, Cape Town: 154–155a.

Franklin D. Roosevelt Library, Hyde Park, N.Y.: 51, 211c, 230c, 245a.

Harper's Weekly: 12, 19a, 19b, 20b, 25a, 25c, 25d, 26c, 28–29, 40–41, 48c, 49b, 59b, 62, 64, 72, 73a, 75a, 76, 79, 85b, 91, 92–93, 94, 99a, 109, 112–113, 118a, 122–123, 129a, 132, 133, 134, 134–135, 136b, 136c, 138a, 141a, 141b, 145a, 152a, 152b, 153, 160b, 164, 169, 172a, 172b, 173a, 176, 177a, 180a, 182c, 183a, 184, 185, 197e, 198a, 198b, 202c, 205a, 206–207, 208b, 211a, 214a, 214b, 225b, 227c, 230a, 239b, 240, 242b, 243a, 249b.

Henry E. Huntington Library, San Marino, Cal.: 254a.

The Illustrated London News: 15, 18a, 18b, 30, 36a, 45a, 45b, 46a, 47a, 47b, 47c, 52b, 56, 60a, 60b, 60c, 60d, 61, 66–67, 68, 86–87, 95a, 110a, 117, 127a, 130–131, 142–143a, b, c, 144a, 145b, 146–147, 146a, 147a, 148a, 149, 154b, 155, 158a, 159, 165, 166, 167a, 170–171, 180c, 181b, 186, 187a, 192, 193b, 200, 203, 215, 226a, 226c, 227a, 228–229, 228b, 234–235, 248b, 253a.

Illustretet Tidende, VI, 1864, Copenhagen: 246.

L'Illustration, Paris: 129b, 220a.

Imperial War Museum, London (Crown copyright reserved): 161.

Courtesy of John G. Johnson Collection, Philadelphia: 194b.

Courtesy Friedrich Jorberg, Berlin: 162b.

Leslie's Weekly: 22, 26d, 53a, 53b, 69, 75b, 78–79, 85c, 95b, 96a, 99b, 100, 104–105, 124–125, 146b, 168, 183d, 201c, 205b, 216b, 226b, 237, 238a.

Library of Congress: 18c, 21, 26a, 26b, 32, 33, 39a, 52a, 54, 73b, 74a, 74b, 88, 93, 106a, 107b, 108, 108b, 108c, 118b, 137, 144b, 160a, 177b, 208a, 225a, 230b, 236–237, 238b, 239a, 242a, 244a, 244b, 253b.

Liverpool Public Library: 36–37, 158b.

The Mariners Museum, Newport News, Va.: 24a, 27, 35b, 48a, 80b, 81b, 89, 110b, 111a, 174, 175, 178a, 193a, 197a, 217b, 231, 232–233, 248a, 249a.

Mississippi Agricultural & Industrial Board: 107c, 254b.

Le Monde Illustré, Paris: 59a, 84a, 96–97, 173b, 209, 222, 223b, 224, 248c.

National Archives, Washington, D.C.: 14, 16, 17, 19c, 57a, 57b, 58, 139b, 157, 199, 202a, 210, 212, 217a, 219b, 227b, 232, 245b, 245c, 247.

National Portrait Gallery, London, copyright: 33a.

New-York Historical Society: 49c, 71c.

New York Public Library: 39b, 101c, 180b.

Official Records of the Union and Confederate Navies: 38, 107a.

Official U. S. Navy Photo: 85a, 101b, 115, 116, 121, 126a, 128, 140, 178b, 178d, 188, 197c, 198c, 213, 216a, 221, 243b, 250, 252.

Public Record Office, London (Crown copyright reserved): 167b, 167c, 187b.

Scientific American, 1861: 44a, 44b, 49a.

Smithsonian Institution: 70c, 102–103, 218b.

Submarine Library, Electric Boat Division, General Dynamics Corp., Groton, Conn.: 178c.

U. S. Naval Academy Museum, Annapolis: 80a, 196.

Valentine Museum, Richmond, Va.: 148b, 148c, 150a, 150b, 151b, 179, 241.

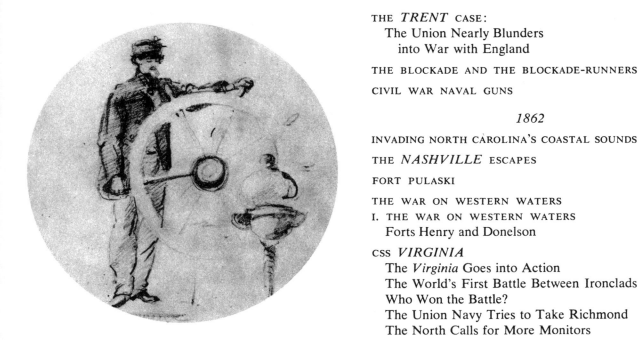

CONTENTS

INTRODUCTION

This book has grown out of a larger work—still in progress—which will deal with the high-seas operations of the Civil War navies, Union and Confederate. Research for the larger volume has taken me to many libraries, archives, and museums. While looking for material in them, I came across so many remarkable little-known pictures illustrating the activities of the Confederate Navy that I decided to put them into a book which would cover briefly the activities of that Navy on inland waters as well as on the high seas.

When I began this book, I thought that it would be fairly easy to do because it was supposed to have many pictures and relatively little text. But the need for more explanatory matter soon became apparent, and the number of words increased accordingly. This change in plan made the task more difficult, for very few books had been written about the Confederate Navy to serve as a guide. The only full-length general work on the subject is John Thomas Scharf's *History of the Confederate Navy* (Baltimore, 1887). The author had the advantage of having been in both the Confederate Navy and Army, but he wrote his 800-page book before the great mass of documents printed in *Official Records of the Union and Confederate Navies in the War of the Rebellion* were made available from 1894 to 1922. As a result, Scharf's text has many errors and omissions. He also tends to emphasize those aspects of the naval war with which he had had some personal contact and gives little space to those with which he was unfamiliar. For instance, he compresses the whole story of the Confederate raiders and the European-built ironclads into 32 pages. Yet one must be grateful for what Scharf did to make a record of what his contemporaries told him, for their priceless recollections would otherwise have been lost.

The other important large work written by a Confederate participant is James Dunwoody Bulloch's *The Secret Service of the Confederate States in Europe* (London and New York, 1884). As the title indicates, it deals only with the European phase of the conflict.

It soon became evident that I would have to rely heavily on the 30 volumes of *Official Records,* on the thousands of pages of evidence presented in the so-called *"Alabama* Claims," and on the narratives of the men who served in the navies for detailed information to accompany the pictured ships and battles. In some cases I had to go beyond these to manuscript sources.

This volume and the one that is to follow were made possible by the grant of a fellowship from the John Simon Guggenheim Memorial Foundation which enabled me to go to England, France, and Denmark to examine records there. And a grant from the Henry E. Huntington Library permitted me to spend some time in San Marino, California, to inspect the Thomas H. Dudley papers. Since Dudley was the United States Consul in Liverpool, where he served as a secret agent in charge of the spies who were keeping watch on the building of the Confederate ships in British ports, his day-to-day record is invaluable.

Readers may want to know why I decided to tell the Confederate side of the story rather than that of both Civil War navies. I have no partisan leaning toward the Confederacy, but I think that its Navy, which was a miracle of improvisation, is far more interesting than that of its Northern rival, which finally prevailed because of sheer weight of ships, arms, wealth, manpower, and greater means of all kinds.

The Union Navy, with the exception of the various types of monitors it adopted, contributed little to naval development. Its growing might was based on what was long known or on what had recently been done in France or England. Although Union Navy chieftains were not as firmly opposed to technical progress as their counterparts in the Union Army, they decided to stick to conventional weapons because they understandably hesitated to make changes in the middle of a war. So they refitted existing merchant ships with existing guns or built new ships after old designs and armed them with guns that had been invented before the war. Then they sent this makeshift fleet out to blockade the ports of the Confederacy. Until the Union had enough ships to wall off the coast, blockade-runners slipped merrily past them with munitions from Europe. There was no question of fighting at this early stage of the war, for the South had no navy then. She tried to induce shipowners to arm their vessels and operate them as privateers under letters of marque issued by the Confederate Government, but this was a stopgap measure—and not a very successful one.

The Confederacy quickly began to organize a navy by any means it could. It seized Northern vessels lying in its ports; it built ships at home and abroad; and it bought them from anyone who would sell. In its desperate need, it soon went far beyond the mere acquiring and arming of ships for naval warfare. It is axiomatic in the history of armed conflict that a weaker nation will inevitably resort to guerrilla tactics, to unorthodox methods of fighting, and, if its people are clever enough, to inventing new weapons and ways of striking back at their more powerful opponent.

The old adage that necessity is the mother of invention soon proved to be true. Under the pressure of urgent need, the South, which had far less experience with mechanical things than the more industrialized North, suddenly became an innovator of the tools of war. In a very short time the Confederacy was ready to send ironclads into action; it pioneered in the development of electrically-exploded underwater mines, and produced the first underwater craft that sank an enemy warship. The CSS *Hunley* was a crudely built submarine, powered by men turning cranks to operate a propeller, but it sent the USS *Housatonic* to the bottom on February 17, 1864.

And the Confederate Navy not only created new ideas, it also revived workable old ones. Reaching back into history, it equipped some of its ships with sharp-pointed beaks or rams like those used on the oar-propelled galleys of an earlier day. They had been effective when the muscle power developed by hundreds of rowers could drive them deep into the side of a wooden vessel but had fallen into disuse during the age of sail when ships were slow and difficult to maneuver. With steam, rams again became effective weapons—as the USS *Cumberland* found out at Hampton Roads the day before the *Monitor* arrived.

And with steam available to give quick mobility for pursuit and attack, the Confederacy could send out commerce-raiders like the *Florida,* the *Alabama,* and the *Shenandoah* to range the far corners of the world and drive its opponent's merchant vessels from the seas for more than a generation to come. Sail alone would have carried these cruisers on their distant voyages, but they needed steam for overtaking and capturing the fastest ships afloat.

But for all the foresight and inventiveness of its leaders, the Confederate Navy was destined to lose, for the odds against it were too great—10 to one in men and even more than that in ships and guns. Yet some of its men-of-war went on fighting long after the land forces of the Confederacy had surrendered. The names of its more famous vessels will be remembered as long as naval history is read. The ironclad *Virginia* (often misnamed and misspelled the *Merrimac*), the *Alabama,* and the primitive little *Hunley* surely deserve a place in the annals of the world's navies.

In order to tell the story of the Confederate Navy, I frequently had to depend upon Union sources for background information and pictures because Confederate material is regrettably slight and—on some subjects—nonexistent. In comparison with the Union Navy, the Confederate Navy was much smaller in ships and personnel. Therefore, relatively few records of its operations were made, and of those that were made, many perished with the ships or were later lost or destroyed. An examination of *Official Records* will show that the space devoted to the Union is far greater than that devoted to the Confederacy. But this was not because its Northern editors were unduly biased in favor of their own cause. To the contrary, Confederate documents were so scarce that the compilers had to search diligently for them. As a result, the number of Confederate letters and reports in *Official Records* is actually larger in proportion to those available than it is with Union material.

The editors requested former Confederate officials to lend them their confidential files and were thus able to print many valuable and important papers that had never before been made public. These may be found in the three final volumes (Part Two) of *Official Records*. For the sake of history, it was fortunate that this was done, for in some cases the original manuscripts have since disappeared.

Official Records forms a vast repository of firsthand information about the Civil War navies, but sometimes the references are tantalizingly fragmentary. For instance, an example of the Union's interest in underwater warfare appears in a few brief entries as "*Alligator,* U.S. submarine torpedo boat," but they tell little and then stop. References are more numerous to Matthew Fontaine Maury's brilliant scheme for organizing a mosquito fleet that would have been a forerunner of the PT boats of the Second World War. Maury wanted the Confederate Navy to build a hundred fast steam launches so small squadrons of them could make hit-and-run attacks on the Federal ships that were blockading Southern ports. A few launches were actually built, but the fleet as such never came into being. It was difficult to find a hundred experienced daredevil officers to command the boats, and the success of the ironclad, as proved by the *Virginia* at Hampton Roads, induced Richmond to concentrate its available funds on building more big armored ships.

Another clever idea that was far in advance of its time was proposed by a young officer in the Federal Navy. He was Alfred Thayer Mahan, who wrote, a generation later, *The Influence of Sea Power Upon History* and other works that were avidly studied by the top command of the world's navies. When Raphael Semmes began destroying Northern commerce with the first Confederate raider (the *Sumter*), Mahan submitted a plan to Washington for catching the dangerous cruiser that was eluding all pursuit. "A sailing ship," he wrote, "might be equipped with a heavy pivot gun and a light house built over it, such as are often seen on merchant ships." The disguised gunboat was to carry a hundred men or more for possible use in boarding. Mahan offered to lead the enterprise himself if the Navy "should not wish to risk a better man." He persuasively pointed out how small the possible loss was in case of failure: "A useless ship, a midshipman, and a hundred men," he said in calculated understatement.

But the Federal Navy had little use for new ideas from midshipmen, so it ignored Mahan's suggestion. It was carried out during the First World War when the British sent their seemingly harmless "mystery" ships to sea to entice German submarines within range of their powerful hidden guns.

I not only had to draw upon Union sources for much of the background information but had to depend on them almost entirely for the illustrations. Except for pictures from a few foreign sources like *The Illustrated London News,* nearly all the pictorial material is of Northern origin. Civil War pictures made by Confederates are scarce, and those of naval interest are scarcer still. A few good ones were made by the South's most talented artist, Conrad Wise Chapman. Photographs of Confederate naval scenes are even rarer than drawings and paintings.

The reason for the great disparity between the richness of Northern pictorial material and the poverty of Southern is simple. The North had illustrated newspapers like Harper's *Weekly* and Leslie's *Weekly,* while the Confederacy, except for *The Southern Illustrated News,* did not. And even this Southern paper, which featured pictures, printed very few and of indifferent quality. The highly successful Northern weeklies could afford to keep artists in the field. So could the powerful *Illustrated London News* which sent Frank Vizetelly to the Confederacy to cover the war. It was through such Northern artists and photographers as Matthew Brady and Alexander Gardner that we got our great wealth of pictorial material on the Civil War. The South, unfortunately, could not provide much.

Since artists who worked in newspaper offices far from the scene of action had very little to go by, they often filled in missing details from their imaginations. I have tried to correct their more egregious errors by pointing them out in the captions. Generally speaking, however, the wood engravings of the time are remarkably accurate. This is especially true of ships, for the larger papers employed special artists who could draw any kind of vessel as skillfully as a naval architect.

It is regrettable that the Civil War battles fought on water should be almost forgotten while those waged on land are endlessly studied, analyzed, and described. Perhaps this is because there were so few men in the Civil War navies. When those navies were at their peak at the end of 1864, only 5213 officers and men were serving in the Confederate Navy, and about 51,500 in its Union counterpart. This is a pathetically small number compared with the millions who fought in the armies. As a result, naval veterans were scarce during the period after the war when the memoirs and the histories were being written. Thousands of volumes of Civil War literature deal with the land battles, whereas all the books about its naval affairs—including a complete set of *Official Records*—can easily be shelved against the wall of a small room.

Perhaps as people get tired of refighting Shiloh or going over familiar ground at Gettysburg, they may want to learn more about the men who pioneered on the first power-driven ships of war that took part in a major conflict. These short-lived ships and their equipment, which was rapidly made obsolete by technical progress, are so little known to modern readers that they have to see what they looked like in order to understand how they operated. This book, illustrated with more than 390 contemporary pictures of the ships and men of the Civil War navies, is intended to serve as an introduction to an enormously complex and still largely unexplored subject. But it should provide the reader with enough basic information to enable him to investigate the naval history of the Civil War still further. And it is well worth investigating, for it has dozens of heroic exploits, much hard fighting, and many colorful incidents, all of which took place on ships which have vanished as completely as the triremes of ancient Rome. Here, in the largest collection of pictures ever published of these once formidable navies, will be found the likenesses of the gallant ships and men who fought on the rivers and bays of America and on the oceans of the world.

PHILIP VAN DOREN STERN
Brooklyn, New York
November 7, 1961

THE CONFEDERATE NAVY:
A PICTORIAL HISTORY

THE OPENING GUNS OF THE WAR A signal shot arching over Charleston Harbor at 4:30 A.M. on April 12, 1861, marked the beginning of actual hostilities in the Civil War. Here the Confederate bat-

1861

tery at Fort Johnson shells still-uncompleted Fort Sumter. Cummings Point is at the right while Fort Moultrie and the Floating Battery are at the left of the central target.

January 1, 1861, saw one Southern state already seceded. South Carolina had left the Union on December 20, 1860, and was soon to be followed by ten other states. But at that time the still-unformed Confederacy had no army (except state militia) and no navy, whereas the North had a regular army of 16,000 men and a navy of 42 ships in commission, even though most of them were obsolete and widely scattered across the world. The North also had an operating government, diplomatic and trade relationships with foreign countries, well-established credit, and laws and tax collectors enabling it to raise millions of dollars for an emergency.

1861.

JANUARY								JULY						
Sun.	M.	T.	W.	T.	F.	Sat.		Sun.	M.	T.	W.	T.	F.	Sat.
..	..	1	2	3	4	5		..	1	2	3	4	5	6
6	7	8	9	10	11	12		7	8	9	10	11	12	13
13	14	15	16	17	18	19		14	15	16	17	18	19	20
20	21	22	23	23	25	26		21	22	23	24	25	26	27
27	28	29	30	31	..	..		28	29	30	31	..	..	..

FEBRUARY								AUGUST						
..	..	..	..	..	1	2		..	..	..	..	1	2	3
3	4	5	6	7	8	9		4	5	6	7	8	9	10
10	11	12	13	14	15	16		11	12	13	14	15	16	17
17	18	19	20	21	22	23		18	19	20	21	22	23	24
24	25	26	27	28	..	..		25	26	27	28	29	30	31

MARCH								SEPTEMBER						
..	..	..	..	..	1	2		1	2	3	4	5	6	7
3	4	5	6	7	8	9		8	9	10	11	12	13	14
10	11	12	13	14	15	16		15	16	17	18	19	20	21
17	18	19	20	21	22	23		22	23	24	25	26	27	28
24	25	26	27	28	29	30		29	30	..	..	..	..	..
31	..	..	..	..	..	..								

APRIL								OCTOBER						
..	1	2	3	4	5	6		..	..	1	2	3	4	5
7	8	9	10	11	12	13		6	7	8	9	10	11	12
14	15	16	17	18	19	20		13	14	15	16	17	18	19
21	22	23	24	25	26	27		20	21	22	23	24	25	26
28	29	30	..	..	..	..		27	28	29	30	31	..	..

MAY								NOVEMBER						
..	..	..	1	2	3	4		..	..	..	..	..	1	2
5	6	7	8	9	10	11		3	4	5	6	7	8	9
12	13	14	15	16	17	18		10	11	12	13	14	15	16
19	20	21	22	23	24	25		17	18	19	20	21	22	23
26	27	28	29	30	31	..		24	25	26	27	28	29	30

JUNE								DECEMBER						
..	..	..	..	..	..	1		1	2	3	4	5	6	7
2	3	4	5	6	7	8		8	9	10	11	12	13	14
9	10	11	12	13	14	15		15	16	17	18	19	20	21
16	17	18	19	20	21	22		22	23	24	25	26	27	28
23	24	25	26	27	28	29		29	30	31	..	..	..	..
30	..	..	..	..	..	..								

JEFFERSON DAVIS, President of the Confederate States of America, West Pointer, Army officer in the Mexican War, and Secretary of War from 1853 to 1857, had much greater experience in military than in naval affairs. But he knew how essential it was to protect the Confederacy's inland waterways and keep sea lanes open.

The inauguration of Jefferson Davis as President of the Confederate States of America.

A NATION IS BORN

A new nation was born on the North American continent when the Provisional Government of the Confederate States of America was established at Montgomery, Alabama, on February 4, 1861. Only six states participated in the initial proceedings—South Carolina, Mississippi, Florida, Alabama, Georgia, and Louisiana. Texas had seceded from the Union four days before—too late to send delegates.

Events moved swiftly—as they had to under the press of circumstances. On February 9 Jefferson Davis of Mississippi and Alexander Stephens of Georgia were elected President and Vice-President. Davis was inaugurated on the eighteenth; he announced the formation of his Cabinet almost immediately. On February 21 the Confederate Navy began its official existence with fifty-four-year-old Stephen R. Mallory as its head. Born in Trinidad, the newly appointed Secretary of the Navy had grown up in Key West, then as now an important naval base. Elected to the United States Senate in 1851, Mallory had been made chairman of the Committee on Naval Affairs in 1857 and since that time had been in touch with technological developments throughout the world. His biographer, Joseph T. Durkin, says that "Mallory, in 1861, was a capable and earnest small-town official trying with no small degree of confidence to fill a post that a statesman of unique and preeminent qualities, with a thorough grasp of naval history and unusual administrative gifts, would have found a fair field for his powers. But he possessed one important quality that sometimes raises the average man to greatness—he was filled with a passion for learning his job. . . . He had not sought the post but, once saddled with it, began, somewhat to his own surprise, to enjoy the challenges it offered."

Although many people in the South still hopefully believed that the new nation would be allowed to maintain its independence without having to fight for it, preparations for a possible war were begun. Since the Confederacy had no warships or private yards equipped to construct them, it had to buy existing vessels or have them built in other countries.

Many Southern officers were leaving the United States Navy at this time and were coming to Montgomery to offer their services to the nascent republic. Among them was the brilliant and daring Raphael Semmes, then fifty-two years old. Born in Maryland,

Semmes had been appointed a midshipman in the United States Navy in 1826, nineteen years before the Annapolis Naval Academy was founded. During his eleven-year training period before he was made a lieutenant, he served on many ships and saw most of the world. He was in command of the brig *Somers* (famous for the mutiny of 1842) when she sank in a gale in 1846. Despite the loss of the ship, the Naval Court of Inquiry praised Semmes for his skillful seamanship. He saw service on both land and sea in the Mexican War. During the long period of inactivity that followed, he moved his family to Mobile, practiced law, and wrote a book about his experiences in Mexico.

Semmes used the long hours aboard ship to educate himself. There he studied law, oceanography, meteorology, navigation, literature, and became proficient in writing and speaking.

In February 1861 he wrote to a Southern congressman saying that he was "listening with an aching ear and beating heart for the first sounds of the great disruption . . . at hand." Soon afterward he received a letter from C. M. Conrad, chairman of the Confederate Congressional Committee on Naval Affairs, asking him to come to Montgomery. Semmes immediately resigned from the United States Navy and arrived in Alabama before Mallory became Secretary of the Navy. President Davis interviewed the man who had just resigned as a commander in the Federal Navy and given up a good post in the Lighthouse Service in Washington. Davis was so impressed with Semmes that he sent him to the Northern states to buy materials of war and hire skilled mechanics. Semmes said of his mission: "The persons alluded to were to be mechanics skilled in the manufacture and use of ordnance and rifle machinery, the preparation of fixed ammunition, percussion caps, etc. So exclusively had the manufacture of all these articles for the use of the United States been confined to the North . . . that we had not even percussion caps enough to enable us to fight a battle or the machines with which to make them."

It must be remembered that Virginia had not yet seceded at this time, so the Confederacy could not count on having the services of the great Tredegar Iron Works or the Bellona Foundry in Richmond. And the Norfolk Navy Yard, which was to be the source of so

STephen R. Mallory, Secretary of the Confederate Navy

many large-caliber guns for the Confederacy, was still in Union hands. In the states that had already seceded, it was literally true that there was "not a rolling-mill capable of turning out a 2½-inch iron plate, nor a workshop able to complete a marine engine." This lack of facilities for building steam engines for its ships was to plague the South from the beginning to the end of the war.

After his arrival in New York Semmes said: "I found the people everywhere not only willing but anxious to contract with me. I purchased large quantities of percussion caps in the city of New York and sent them by express without any disguise to Montgomery. I made contracts for batteries of light artillery, powder, and other munitions, and succeeded in getting large quantities of the powder shipped. It was agreed between the contractors and myself that when I should have occasion to use the telegraph certain other words were to be substituted for those of military import to avoid suspicion.

"I made a contract, conditioned upon the approval of my Government, for the removal to the Southern states of a complete set of machinery for rifling cannon with the requisite skilled workmen to put it in operation. Some of these men, who would thus have sold body and soul to me for a sufficient consideration, occupied high social positions and were men of wealth. I dined with them at their comfortable residences near their factories, where the music of boring

out cannon accompanied the clatter of the dishes and the popping of champagne corks; and I had more than one business interview with gentlemen who occupied the most costly suites of apartments at the Astor House in New York City. Many of these gentlemen, being unable to carry out their contracts with the Confederate States because of the prompt breaking out of the war, afterward obtained lucrative contracts from the Federal Government and became, in consequence, intensely *loyal*."

Soon after Mallory assumed office, he wrote to Semmes in New York, instructing him to purchase several steamboats light enough to navigate the shallow waters along the Confederate coasts. Semmes looked for suitable ships but could find none that satisfied his high standards. It was unfortunate that he was so particular, for some of the vessels he rejected were soon bought or chartered by the Federal Navy which armed them for use against the Confederacy.

When Semmes returned to the South late in March on one of the passenger steamers plying between New York and Savannah, the ship carried a United States flag at the peak and a Confederate flag at the fore. Such tokens of amity, however, were soon to vanish from the sea.

Semmes was not the only one authorized by the Confederate Government to obtain ships and munitions in the spring of 1861. Agents were sent to Philadelphia, Baltimore, and Canada, while a board of officers went to New Orleans on March 17 to try to purchase steamers there and fit them out as ships of war. The Confederate Army sent Major Caleb Huse to Europe to obtain weapons and ammunition. And then, on March 16, in order to attempt to win European support for the Confederate cause, a civilian mission was instructed to go to England and the Continent.

Diplomatic and naval affairs were inextricably bound together throughout the Confederacy's existence. It was important for the new nation to obtain recognition and actual assistance—if possible—from England and France. They were major shipbuilding countries, the only ones equipped to turn out ironclads as well as wooden vessels. And England's heavy ordnance for naval and coast defense use was famous throughout the world. Since cotton weaving was important in the economy of both nations, they were largely dependent upon the South for supplies of this essential raw material. The Confederacy was counting on their vital need for her main cash crop to win them to her side.

The three Commissioners were instructed to emphasize the fact that the Confederate Government was imposing very light duties on imports—so light that they could be said "to closely approximate free trade." This was intended to appeal to England's free-trade policy as a manufacturing nation. And they were to explain to other European nations that the seceded states had only "reassumed the powers which they [had] delegated to the Federal Government" and that they had "merely exercised the sovereignty . . . possessed since their separation from Great Britain." These commercial and legal arguments were expected to carry great weight when presented to the chancelleries of Europe. But the cautious leaders there wanted to wait and see if the new nation could maintain its independence in the face of the strong opposition which the Federal Government was likely to put up to resist the South's efforts to break away from the Union.

And the selection of the men who were chosen to be sent abroad was, to say the least, unfortunate. The late Frank L. Owsley, scholarly Southern historian, said in his *King Cotton Diplomacy* that "the three men were about the poorest choices possible. . . . William L. Yancey, of Alabama, who was to head the mission, was internationally known as a champion of slavery. . . . To dispatch as chief of the diplomatic mission a man who advocated a militant attitude on the slave trade was extremely naïve or extremely arrogant and, whether the one or the other, very disregardful of the strong antislavery sentiment of both England and France. . . . Pierre A. Rost was a former judge, born in France but reared in Louisiana. His qualifications as a diplomat are doubtful. . . . As for A. Dudley Mann, it is difficult to see just what Davis could have had in mind in sending him abroad; surely it was not to get him safely out of the country so as to render him harmless as is sometimes said about the sending abroad of William L. Yancey. Mann was harmless either at home or abroad."

Bumbling as the Confederacy's first efforts in foreign diplomacy were, they at least indicated a keen awareness of the need for European support. And the Montgomery Government showed itself to be foresighted in other ways. On February 21, 1861, its Committee on Naval Affairs made recommendations for the defense of New Orleans, Mobile, Pensacola, Savannah, and Charleston; cost estimates for naval operation were prepared in March; and the search for ships and weapons was pushed vigorously forward. All these moves were made before the outbreak of actual warfare on April 12, when Sumter was fired upon.

Half a dozen revenue cutters and a few coast-survey ships and lighthouse tenders belonging to the United States Government were seized in Southern ports. They were small and not of much use in a war, but the

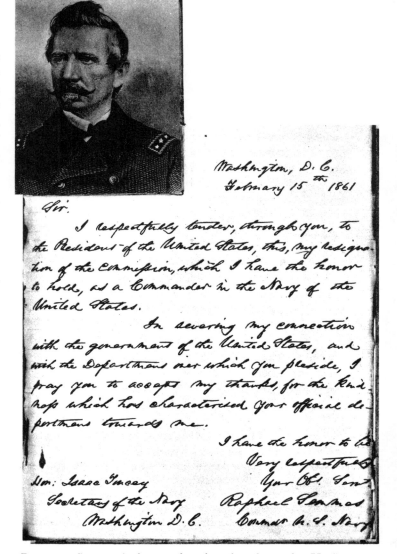

RAPHAEL SEMMES's letter of resignation from the U. S. Navy. It was addressed to Isaac Toucey, who was still Secretary of the Navy under the Buchanan administration.

best of them were pressed into service as armed vessels. An appeal was made on January 14, 1861, to Southern officers who were about to resign from the United States Navy, asking them to bring their ships with them. But the appeal was ignored, and the South did not obtain a single ship in this way. It got only two vessels from the Federal fleet—the twenty-four-year-old side-wheeler *Fulton,* which had been laid up at Pensacola, and the burned-out hulk of the *Merrimack,* which was set on fire and sunk when the North abandoned the Norfolk Navy Yard. A few privately owned passenger steamers were purchased to be converted into warships, and flatboats and barges were acquired to be made into floating batteries and fire ships. But the Confederates knew that their best chance of getting first-rate naval vessels was in Europe, and they concentrated their efforts there.

The First Mission to Europe

On March 16, 1861, Yancey, Mann, and Rost were instructed to go to Europe to try to gain recognition for the Confederacy from England, France, Belgium, Spain, and Russia. They were also authorized to negotiate commercial treaties with those countries. They left Montgomery and were on the high seas when war broke out, so that word of what had happened at Fort Sumter did not reach them until they arrived in England.

Early in May the Commissioners sought and obtained two interviews with Lord John Russell, the British Foreign Secretary. Pierre Rost went to Paris where he sounded out the Count de Morny, who was close to Emperor Napoleon III. Neither the British nor the French made any commitments or even promises, but the self-deceived Commissioners reported hopefully to Robert Toombs, Confederate Secretary of State, that they were of the opinion that "England in reality is not averse to a disintegration of the United States, and both of these powers will act favorably toward us upon the first decided [military] success which we may obtain."

There were many "decided successes" for the Confederacy in the early part of the war. First and Second Manassas, the repulse of McClellan's attack on Richmond, Fredericksburg, and Chancellorsville were all Confederate victories, but the favorable action so confidently predicted by the three Commissioners never came.

While the Confederacy was winning victories on the battlefield, the Union was actively establishing the Federal Government's prestige in Europe. Its agents worked behind the scenes to swing public opinion toward the Northern cause; and its Ministers brought pressure to bear on foreign governments to maintain a hands-off policy toward the war in America. The Union had the money, the diplomatic connections, and the war machinery to do this. Northern newspapers circulated freely abroad, and Northern speakers were sent to Europe to address public meetings.

Against these efforts the Confederates could pit only ingenuity, quick thinking, and whatever propaganda measures they could afford. They were not always fortunate in the choice of men they sent abroad. This first mission accomplished nothing and soon had to be replaced.

WILLIAM LOWNDES YANCEY, born in Georgia but brought up in an antislavery household in upstate New York after his widowed mother remarried, became an active secessionist when he returned to the South to settle in Alabama. He was largely responsible for the breakup of the Democratic Party at its National Convention in Charleston in April 1860, thus making possible the election of a Republican President—an event which brought on secession and war. Yancey resigned from the Confederate mission to Europe in 1862 and returned to Alabama to die in 1863.

AMBROSE DUDLEY MANN, born in Virginia and educated at West Point, served in Europe for the United States Government for many years and was Assistant Secretary of State from 1853 to 1856. But his career in foreign affairs had not been a distinguished one, and he came to England with unfavorable reports already filed against him. British consuls in Southern cities, who kept the Home Office well informed, had portrayed Mann unfairly. He was verbose, pompous, and indecisive, but his character was not as bad as the consuls had charged. He remained in Europe for the rest of his life.

PIERRE A. ROST, the least known of the Confederate Commissioners, was born in France but was brought to America at an early age. In Louisiana, where Rost grew up, his French undoubtedly took on a non-Parisian accent. Chosen because of his Gallic background for service in France, Rost was not successful there. It has been said that his faulty accent and boundless optimism hurt him with the cynical rulers of the Third Empire. He was sent to Madrid in August 1861 to seek recognition for the Confederacy; failing to obtain it, he resigned in May 1862.

Early Confederate Ships

As the Southern states seceded, they confiscated Northern ships in their harbors and in some cases bought and paid for ships belonging to Northern as well as Southern owners. A few guns were put aboard them, and with these makeshift vessels a Southern fleet was ready for action even before the Confederate Navy began operating. Some of the states encouraged privateering for a short while, but state-owned ships should not be confused with privateers, which are privately owned vessels cruising under national authorization.

The story of the state naval ships which operated for a short time early in 1861 is an unwritten chapter in Confederate history. No complete list of them has ever been made, for they had such brief careers and changed name and ownership so often that they are difficult to trace. Most of them were quite small; many were sailing vessels without steam power; all were poorly equipped for naval fighting. Some later became privateers, but the majority were transferred to the Confederate Navy as soon as it was able to man them.

This mosquito fleet saw little action while its vessels were still under state ownership. A handful of small South Carolina ships bravely guarded Charleston Harbor when a Federal squadron was expected to sail in to reinforce Fort Sumter. And some of these little armed ships prowled the coastal waters looking for stray Yankee vessels and succeeded in taking a few as prizes. Two Louisiana State ships fought in the Battle of New Orleans in April 1862 (SEE PAGE 96).

A partial list of these state ships follows:

SOUTH CAROLINA *General Clinch, Lady Davis, Gordon, Nina, Petrel*

GEORGIA *Everglade* or *Savannah, Huntress*

ALABAMA *Lewis Cass*

LOUISIANA *General Quitman, Governor Moore*

TEXAS *Dodge*

Virginia and North Carolina did not secede until after Sumter, but they too had state-owned ships for a while.

VIRGINIA *Arrow, Empire, George Page* or *City of Richmond, McClellan, Northampton, Roanoke, Teaser, United States, Yorktown*

NORTH CAROLINA *Beaufort, Ellis, Raleigh, Winslow*

At the beginning of the war the South was short of postage stamps, paper currency, and other official printed matter. This blank, issued by the United States Government for registering ships, was converted into a Confederate document by writing in the word "Confederate" for "United."

The *Lady Davis,* a steam tug originally called the *James Gray* and renamed after Jefferson Davis's wife, was one of the tiny South Carolina fleet guarding Fort Sumter.

The *Marion* was seized by the state of South Carolina but was restored to her New York owners who sold her to the Federal Government. She was then used to enforce the blockade of the Southern coasts.,

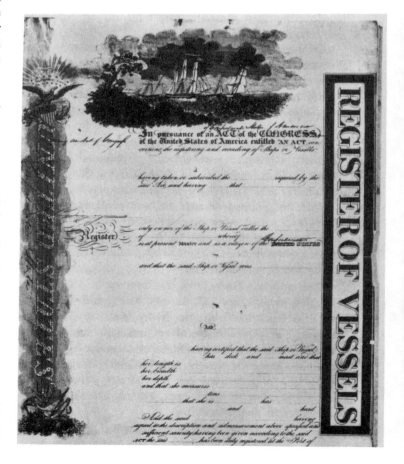

Fort Sumter as it looked while occupied by Anderson's garrison of 86 men and officers.

THE FIRST SHOTS

Charleston, where secession began, was also the scene of the first shots fired in the war. Major Robert Anderson had been sent there by the United States Army to head the garrison in Fort Moultrie on the northern side of the harbor. When South Carolina seceded on December 20, 1860, Anderson, realizing that land-based Fort Moultrie could not be held against attack, moved the garrison six days later into Fort Sumter, a large, nearly completed masonry fort built on an island at the entrance to the harbor.

His move incensed the people of Charleston, who felt that the Federal Government had no claim on the forts around the harbor after South Carolina had declared herself independent. They were determined to resist any effort to send supplies or reinforcements to Sumter.

In Washington, however, resistance to the idea of Southern resistance was growing. Lieutenant General Winfield Scott, head of the Army, urged that recruits with arms and provisions be sent secretly to Sumter. At first he planned to use the powerful sloop-of-war *Brooklyn;* when some question was raised about the deep-draft ship being able to cross the bar at the entrance to the harbor, a light-draft paddle steamer, *Star of the West,* was chartered.

This ship left New York on January 5, 1861, after stopping to pick up 200 recruits, arms, and provisions for three months from the Army base at Governors Island. The *Star of the West* reached the coast of South Carolina during the night of January 8–9. When daylight came, the troops were ordered to stay below while the ship headed up the narrow channel that brought it close to shore near Morris Island, where a red palmetto flag was flying.

The *Star of the West* was carrying an American flag as she neared the shore in the early dawn light.

When a cannon shot was fired across her bows from a masked battery in the sand hills, her captain hastily ordered a huge garrison flag to be displayed. But this did not stop the Charleston Citadel cadets who were manning the guns in the shore battery. They fired several times until one of their shots struck the steamer in the fore-chains about two feet above the waterline, narrowly missing a sailor who was heaving a lead to test the depth of water. Another shot passed over the pilothouse; then one came so close that it went between the smokestack and the vigorously moving walking beam.

The captain, seeing the guns of Fort Moultrie ahead, and noting that a steamer towing what he believed to be the armed cutter *Aiken* was heading for his ship, ordered her turned around. More shots followed the retreating steamer as she went back over the bar, touching several times as she crossed it to seek the safety of the open ocean. The Charleston steamer fol-

A Confederate battery fires on the *Star of the West* as she runs close to shore while coming up the channel.

lowed her for some time to make sure she did not turn back.

The *Star of the West* arrived in New York Harbor on January 12—a bitterly cold day. After the soldiers were taken off by steam tugs, the ship docked at the foot of Warren Street. Those allowed to enter the dock enclosure saw an egg-shaped dent "showing that the ball struck . . . obliquely . . . from the stern toward the bow. . . . Its force was considerably spent." The first shot of the Civil War to make its mark had been fired.

The day after the firing on the *Star of the West,* the Charleston *Mercury* ran a fiery editorial: "South Carolina may be proud of her historic fame and ancestry. . . . The haughty echo of her cannon has . . . reverberated through every hamlet of the North. . . . And if . . . blood they want, blood they shall have. . . . For, by the God of our fathers, the soil of South Carolina *shall be free!*"

Negro workmen mount Confederate cannon on Morris Island near Fort Sumter.

The interior of the ironclad floating battery used by the Confederates against Fort Sumter. Note powder in bags being handed up from below (lower left).

The Guns Roar Out in Charleston Harbor

During the period between the firing on the *Star of the West* and the outbreak of war on April 12, there had been a change in the United States Presidency on March 4, when Democrat James Buchanan was replaced by Republican Abraham Lincoln. By that time seven Southern states had left the Union.

Relations between the North and the South rapidly worsened, especially in South Carolina, where Anderson's occupation of Fort Sumter was bitterly resented. Matters came to a head early in April when word reached Charleston that another attempt was to be made to relieve the garrison, this time by several Federal Navy vessels. The little fleet was delayed by a storm at sea, but when its first ships arrived off Charleston Bar during the early morning of April 12, they were just in time to see a 10-inch mortar shell from Fort Johnson curve across the sky at 4:30 A.M. as a signal for the bombardment of Fort Sumter to begin. From the various forts and batteries around the harbor 30 guns and 17 mortars concentrated their fire on the vast pile, smashing brick walls, and eventually setting fire to some of the interior buildings.

Only 48 of Sumter's intended 140 guns were ready for use. These began to reply at 7 A.M., sending solid shot at the well-protected Confederate batteries. Fort

Moultrie was buried under sandbags, and its gun embrasures were covered by cotton bales which were moved away when a cannon was ready to fire. Near Sullivans Island a large ironclad floating battery was anchored. This was the first use of metallic armor for watercraft in American naval warfare—the first of many Confederate firsts to be. (SEE PAGES 42–49, 80–85, 174–79.) The iron covering of the floating battery proved to be impervious to 32-pounder shots which the guns at Fort Sumter fired at it for an hour and a half. It was hit many times, but "the shots were seen to bounce off its sides like peas." The success of this ironclad battery undoubtedly influenced Confederate naval policy, as will be seen.

During the night of April 12–13, the Confederates thought that the Federal fleet lying off the harbor might attempt to send reinforcements to Sumter. And the men in Sumter thought that the Confederates might try to take the fort by an attack by men in small boats. It was a tense night, during which the mortars around the harbor kept up a slow but regular fire that prevented sleep and kept everyone on edge. When daylight came, hot shot were dropped into the fort, setting fires which blazed so fiercely that they could not be brought under control. A huge column of dark smoke rising over the fort could be seen by men on the Federal ships waiting outside the harbor.

The Federal fleet remained inactive because its operations had been bungled by the new Secretary of State, William H. Seward, who had persuaded the President to detach its most important ship, the *Powhatan,* and send her to the relief of Fort Pickens. This was done so secretly that the Navy Department did not know about it. As a result, the other Federal vessels were kept waiting for a ship that was well on its way to Florida. And the gale at sea had prevented the arrival of three steam tugs which were supposed to tow boats filled with sailors past the Confederate batteries at night. Even if the tugs had arrived they would have been of no use, for the boats had been put on the *Powhatan.*

On the morning of April 13, while officers on the Union naval ships were still debating about what they should do, a steamer flying a flag of truce came out of the harbor with a U. S. Army officer from Sumter who informed them that Anderson was ready to evacuate the fort. One of the Federal ships then took the garrison to New York to be received as heroes.

Oddly enough, during the 34-hour bombardment in

The floating battery: details of exterior construction.

which about 4000 shells were fired at Fort Sumter, no one was killed, and only four men were slightly wounded. On Sunday morning, April 14, while evacuation ceremonies were being held, the premature discharge of one of the guns being fired in 100-gun salute killed a Union soldier and injured several others. The dead gunner, Private Daniel Hough, was the first casualty of the Civil War.

MAP OF CHARLESTON HARBOR

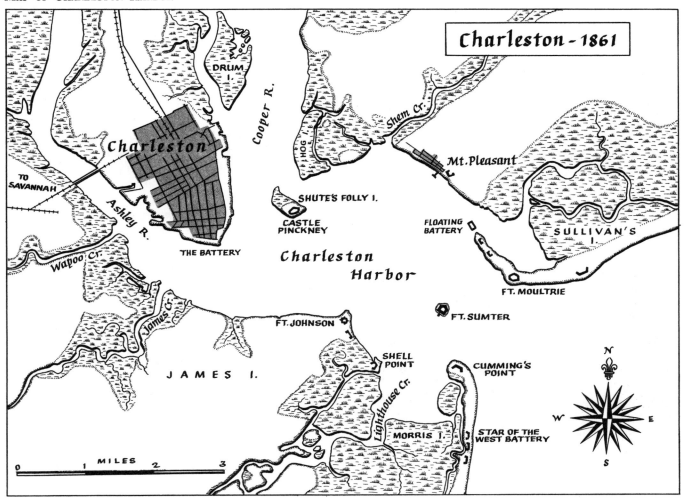

The Norfolk Navy Yard goes up in flames.

The Burning of the Norfolk Navy Yard

Events moved swiftly in both the South and the North after the surrender of Fort Sumter. On April 15, President Lincoln called for 75,000 volunteers "to repossess the forts, places, and properties which have been seized"; on April 17, Virginia seceded from the Union; on the same day, President Davis issued a proclamation offering letters of marque and reprisal to the owners of private ships; on April 18, the U. S. Arsenal at Harpers Ferry was abandoned and burned; on April 19, Lincoln replied to Davis' proclamation by issuing one blockading the Southern coasts from Texas to South Carolina; on April 20, Confederates seized the Norfolk Navy Yard.

The great Norfolk naval base was a rich prize. Many of the officers, as well as nearly all the local mechanics and workmen, sympathized openly with the South. Its aged Commandant, C. S. McCauley, who had been more than fifty years in the service, did not

The ruins of the Norfolk Navy Yard, photographed several years later after the Confederates had also abandoned and burned it.

know what to do. One of the finest ships in the yard was the steam frigate *Merrimack,* brought there for repairs. Orders to transfer her to Philadelphia had been sent to the yard before Sumter was fired on. Crews of men had worked on her day and night to get her ready, but she was still waiting for her guns when Virginia seceded.

As soon as this happened, a Virginia state navy was organized, and its senior officer, Captain Robert B. Pegram, was sent to Norfolk to assume control of the Navy Yard. Washington also hurried officers to Norfolk to hold the important base. The USS *Cumberland* and several other ships were stationed there to guard Federal property.

Confederates sank several old hulks in the river channel, not, however, entirely blocking it. Demonstrations were made outside the yard which led its elderly commandant to believe that it would be impossible to hold the well-protected base. Virginia Navy officers arrived late on April 18 with two volunteer companies. They were far outnumbered by Union men on the ships and in the yard. But the Federal Navy officers, believing that they would be overwhelmed, began evacuating the base on April 20. They scuttled many fine ships, set buildings on fire, and tried to blow up the dry dock before they left. Among the ships sunk was the *Merrimack* which also burned.

The Confederates inherited about 1200 heavy guns, 2800 barrels of powder, thousands of shells, cannonballs, and small arms; many valuable machines, tools, steam engines, and various pieces of equipment. Some was damaged, but much was in good condition or salvageable. This windfall enabled the Confederacy to arm and equip many ships and batteries. The guns were distributed throughout the South to be used during the next four years.

The Confederate naval battery at Manassas Junction in the summer of 1861. The guns came from the Norfolk Navy Yard.

The Big Guns

The heavy guns from the Norfolk Navy Yard stood the Confederacy in good stead. But they were not the only ones inherited from the Union. Others were found in the various forts, arsenals, and warehouses which the Southern states took over as they seceded.

The Civil War marked a revolution in gun design just as it did in ships. Rifled guns, however, were less useful at sea than on land be-

A Confederate Marine gunner at Manassas.

cause naval guns had to be fired from a heaving deck, so direct fire was seldom used for distant shots. Ricochet firing was used instead. For this, a round projectile fired from a smooth-bore gun was better than an elongated shell. It skipped over the water without losing direction while a rifled shell might tumble and go wild.

Naval battles of earlier times were fought at very close range. So, in fact, were many Civil War naval battles. But long-range firing was coming into its own; so were much larger calibers (up to 20 inches for seacoast guns) and far heavier projectiles. In addition to solid cannonballs, chain shot for cutting rigging, explosive shells, grapeshot, shrapnel, and canister were used by both navies. Projectiles were sometimes heated red-hot in special furnaces and then shot at wooden ships or buildings to set them on fire. Fuses for shells to be ricocheted over water were protected against getting wet by a special cap.

William H. Russell, correspondent of the *Times* of London, inspects a 10-inch Columbiad at Fort Pulaski.

A sandbag battery at Pensacola with its guns bearing on Fort Pickens.

JEFFERSON DAVIS,
President of the Confederate States of America.

To all Who shall see these Presents---Greeting:

Know Ye, That by virtue of the power vested in me by law, I have commissioned, and do hereby commission, have authorized, and do hereby authorize the _____ or vessel called the _____ (more particularly described in the schedule hereunto annexed,) whereof _____ is Commander, to act as a private armed vessel in the service of the CONFEDERATE STATES, on the high seas, against the United States of America, their Ships, Vessels, Goods and Effects, and those of their citizens, during the pendency of the War now existing between the said CONFEDERATE STATES and the said United States.

This Commission to continue in force until revoked by the President of the CONFEDERATE STATES for the time being.

Schedule of Description of the Vessel.   Given under my hand and the Seal of the CONFEDERATE STATES at
                                                Montgomery, this _____ day of
Name, _____   _____ A. D. 1861.
Tonnage, _____
Armament, _____
No. of Crew, _____
                    BY THE PRESIDENT:
                                                _____
                                                Secretary of State.

A commission blank for authorizing a privateer to operate under the Confederate flag.

The *Savannah*, the Confederate privateer that made legal history and gave her name to a celebrated admiralty case. This picture shows her flying an American flag after being captured.

PRIVATEERS

A privateer, as the name indicates, is a privately owned armed vessel operating against enemy shipping by the authorization of a sovereign government. The certificate of authorization is called a letter of marque and reprisal.

United States privateers had been remarkably successful during the War of the Revolution and of 1812 when its privateers had been far more numerous and effective than its official Navy ships. They brought the war to the coasts of the British Isles and made a greater impression upon their people than the continental armies fighting far away in America did. The United States had therefore been unwilling to abandon the right to resort to privateering when the practice was outlawed among most nations by the Declaration of Paris in 1856.

Privateering may seem now to be a primitive method of waging war, but in 1861 many people still remembered the privateers of 1812. Since the Confederacy was not involved in the ruling of the Congress of Paris, it had a legitimate right to issue letters of marque, and its urgent need for armed ships made it do so. On April 17, two days after President Lincoln had called for 75,000 volunteers, President Davis invited shipowners to apply for letters of marque. (Privateering was also authorized by some of the Southern states.) In retaliation, on April 19, Lincoln issued his first proclamation of blockade which carried a warning that anyone molesting a United States ship, its per-

Harper's *Weekly* suggested that ships sent to capture privateers should carry their own gallows.

The *Quaker City*, a Yankee privateer which operated without a commission early in the war.

The yacht *America* as rigged in 1851 when she won the first International Cup Race.

sons, or cargo, would be punished as a pirate. The punishment for piracy was death.

But the threat did not prevent shipowners from applying immediately for letters of marque. Applications came not only from Southern cities, but from Liverpool, where a proposal was made to outfit an armored ship and use it to set New York City on fire. It was also rumored that offers came from Northern owners. Applications were so numerous that the Montgomery *Confederation* reported on May 7 that 3000 had been received.

The first privateers had easy pickings, for Yankee captains were still following their usual coastal routes. It took time for the Union blockade to be enforced. When it grew stronger, Confederate privateers could not bring their prizes into port. Many privateersmen then became blockade-runners, while their ships were often acquired for naval use by the states or by the Confederate Government. Within a year, most of the privateers had vanished from the ocean. They were replaced by commerce-raiders like the *Sumter, Alabama, Florida,* and *Shenandoah,* which were owned and operated by the Confederate Navy.

The first letter of marque granted (on May 18, 1861) was to the *Savannah,* a small schooner which had been a Charleston pilot boat. Armed with an 18-pound swivel gun and manned by a crew of 20, the little ship ventured out on June 2. The next morning her captain saw a Yankee brig, promptly captured it, and was following his prize into port when another ship came in sight toward evening. He turned back to chase the stranger, which, to his surprise, kept coming on. The inquisitive stranger fired a warning shot at the *Savannah.* Still not knowing what kind of vessel he was dealing with in the growing darkness, the captain fired the 32-pounder at his pursuer. More shots were exchanged, two of which went through the priva-

teer's sails. The *Savannah* was forced to surrender. The stranger turned out to be the U. S. Navy brig *Perry.*

When the 21 men from the *Savannah* reached New York they were accused of piracy. Jefferson Davis sent a letter of protest to Lincoln on July 6, saying that the Confederate Government would "deal out to the prisoners held by it the same treatment and the same fate as shall be experienced by those captured on the *Savannah.*" Before long he had to repeat this threat of retaliation—not for the sake of the men from the *Savannah* but for another privateersman condemned to death for piracy. A number of the highest Union officers held as prisoners of war in the South were chosen by lot to receive the same treatment as the privateers jailed in the North. For each one actually executed, a Union officer was to die. This "eye for an eye" policy aroused a great deal of protest, but it worked. Not a single privateersman was executed, and those held in common jails were transferred to military prisons and given better treatment.

Another vessel to make Confederate history, although not a true privateer, was the famous yacht *America,* which had won the first British-American cup race in 1851. She had been purchased by a self-styled English "Lord," who brought her to Charleston just after Fort Sumter surrendered. She then became a dispatch boat for the Confederate Navy under the name *Camilla.* In June 1861 she took Lieutenant James H. North and Colonel E. C. Anderson to London to buy ships and weapons. After that she became a blockade-runner until the spring of 1862, when she was found mysteriously sunk in Florida's St. Johns River. The Federal Navy raised her for use as an armed schooner. The solidly built pleasure yacht outlasted nearly all her contemporaries, and was at Annapolis until 1942, when her ancient timbers collapsed under a heavy fall of snow.

THE MELANCHOLY FATE OF
THE CONFEDERATE PRIVATEER *PETREL*

Another privateer unfortunate enough to tangle with a Federal warship was the former Charleston revenue cutter *Aiken*, renamed *Petrel*. She carried two guns; her nemesis, USS *St. Lawrence*, had 52. When they met on

July 28, 1861, the temerarious little schooner fired
first. She fired just three shots; then her bigger adversary
sank her. She went down with four men drowned and
36 taken prisoner.

THE FIRST CONFEDERATE RAIDER

SEMMES *and the* SUMTER

By mid-April 1861 the Confederate Government and the individual states had acquired a few small and not very important ships. (It must be remembered that privateering was not authorized until April 17 and was not confirmed by the Confederate Congress until May 6.) The need for oceangoing cruisers to destroy enemy commerce was understood so early that on April 22, Raphael Semmes arrived in New Orleans to take command of the *Habana,* a passenger steamer between that city and Cuba. He said: "I found her only a dismantled packet ship . . . as unlike a ship of war as possible. Still, I was pleased with her general appearance. Her lines were easy and graceful, and she had a sort of saucy air about her which seemed to say that she was not averse to the service of which she was about to be employed."

Semmes personally supervised the extensive work needed to transform the passenger steamer into the commerce-raider CSS *Sumter.* She was stripped down to what was to be her gun deck, and this was strengthened by heavy supporting beams. It took two months to make the alterations and arm her with "an 8-inch shell gun . . . pivoted amidships and four light 32-pounders of 13 cwt. each in broadside." The outfitting of the *Sumter,* like nearly all Confederate undertakings of a technical nature, was a miracle of improvisation. Nothing went easily, and almost nothing was ever on time. But on June 18, Semmes was able to run down the river past Forts Jackson and St. Philip to watch for a chance to escape the blockading squadron barring his way to the Gulf.

The two main outlets of the Mississippi were closely guarded by the *Brooklyn* and the *Powhatan,* both fast, powerful Union warships. It was June 30 before the way seemed open. Semmes hurried to sea only to find the *Brooklyn* waiting for him about eight miles away. The chase began. At first it appeared to be hopeless, for the Federal ship was reputed to be able to do 14 knots to the *Sumter's* ten. They were just beyond the reach of the *Brooklyn's* guns when they cleared the bar. Then began a combination sail-and-steam race in which Semmes outpointed his pursuer. Actually the *Brooklyn* was nowhere near as fast as 'tween-decks gossip had made her out to be.

The *Sumter* escaping the *Brooklyn*. Actually the ships were never that close.

Once they were safely away, Semmes sent his crew into the rigging to cheer the Confederate flag and then invited the officers to his cabin for a glass of wine to celebrate the occasion.

The *Sumter* quickly proved to be a dangerous raider. She made her first capture on June 3, when she overtook the *Golden Rocket* from Maine. The ritual for destruction was as follows: After sending a warning shot across the hunted ship's bows to stop her, an officer with boarding party went by boat to interrogate her captain and examine the ship's papers in order to make certain she was of American registry. Once that was determined, the captured vessel was doomed. The crew was taken on board the *Sumter,* and coal, sailing gear, chronometers, and any food or water that might be needed were also taken off. Then the torch was applied. Here is Semmes's own description of the burning of the *Golden Rocket:*

"The flame was not long in kindling, but leaped full-grown into the air in a very few minutes after its first faint glimmer had been seen. The boarding officer . . . had applied the torch simultaneously in three places—the cabin, the mainhold, and the forecastle; and now the devouring flames rushed up these three apertures with a fury nothing could resist. The burning ship, with the *Sumter's* boat in the act of shoving off from her side; the *Sumter* herself, with her grim black sides lying in repose like some great sea monster gloating upon the spectacle, and the sleeping sea (for there was scarce a ripple upon the water) were all brilliantly lighted. The indraught into the burning ship's holds and cabins added . . . new fury to the flames, and now they could be heard roaring like the fires of a hundred furnaces in full blast. The prize ship had been laid to with her main-topsail to the mast, and all her light sails, though clewed up, were flying loose about the yards. The forked tongues of the devouring element, leaping into the rigging, newly tarred, ran rapidly up the shrouds, first into the tops, then to the topmast-heads, thence to the top-gallant, and royal mast-heads, and in a moment more to the trucks; and whilst this rapid ascent of the main current of fire was going on, other currents had run out upon the yards and ignited all the sails. A top-gallant sail, all on fire, would now fly off from the yard, and sailing leisurely in the direction of the light breeze that was fanning rather than blowing, break into bright and sparkling patches of flame, and settle . . . into the sea. The yard would then follow, and not being wholly submerged by its descent into the sea, would retain a portion of its flame and continue to burn as a floating brand for some minutes. At one time, the intricate network of the cordage of the burning ship was traced as with a pencil of fire upon the black sky beyond, the many threads of flame twisting and writhing like so many serpents that had received their death wounds. The mizzen-mast now went by the board, then the foremast, and in a few minutes afterward, the great mainmast tottered, reeled, and fell over the ship's side into the sea, making a noise like that of the sturdy oak of the forests when it falls by the stroke of the axeman."

The *Sumter* made 18 captures and burned seven of them before she was laid up in Gibraltar on January 18, 1862, for repairs. She was then sold to an English group to be used as a blockade-runner. Her captain assumed command of the famous *Alabama* in August 1862.

Just before laying up the *Sumter* in Gibraltar,
Semmes captured two merchantmen in sight of that English port.

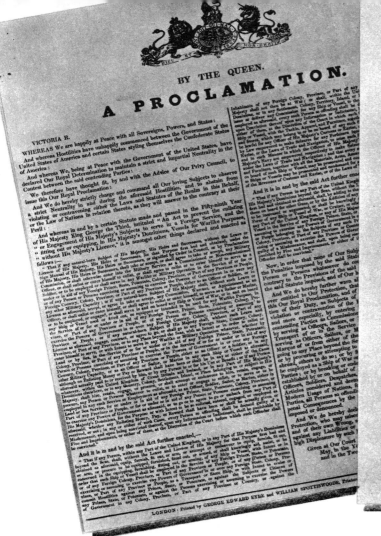

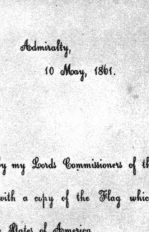

Admiralty,
10 May, 1861.

Sir,

I am commanded by my Lords Commissioners of the Admiralty, to transmit to you herewith a copy of the Flag which has been adopted by the Confederate States of America.

It is intended that the Seven Stars in the upper Canton should be increased in number, in the event of new States being added to the Confederacy.

I am,

Sir,

Your most humble Servant,

Signed W. G. Romaine.

ENGLAND AND THE CONFEDERACY

Strong ties of common ancestry and long tradition existed between the Confederacy and the mother country, England. Some Southerners even thought that the Confederate States should become British territory again. Each had much that the other needed: England obtained more raw cotton from the South than from any other source, while the Confederacy needed diplomatic recognition, ships, arms, and financial and moral support from England. That was why the Montgomery Provisional Government's first move was to send the three Commissioners, Yancey, Mann, and Rost abroad even before war broke out.

When word of the firing on Fort Sumter reached England, the British Government, acting through Queen Victoria, issued a Proclamation of Neutrality on May 13, 1861. This document and the hands-off policy which emerged from it in Parliamentary debate forbade English subjects to enlist on either side in the war in America. It also prohibited the sale of ships of war. It allowed vessels of either side to enter British ports, but they could not alter or improve their equipment while there. Privateers were "regretfully" permitted to operate and were not to be treated as pirates. The Northern blockade of 3500 miles of Southern seacoast would be respected only if it was enforced— but the British were very skeptical about the Union's ability to do so. And—most important of all—the proclamation recognized the Confederacy as a belligerent even though it withheld recognition of independence as a nation, presumably until such independence was fully established and proved likely to endure.

Since this Proclamation of Neutrality was made pub-

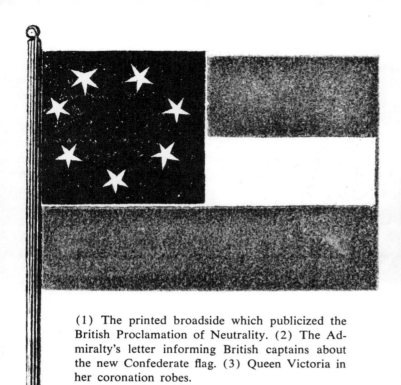

(1) The printed broadside which publicized the British Proclamation of Neutrality. (2) The Admiralty's letter informing British captains about the new Confederate flag. (3) Queen Victoria in her coronation robes.

lic on May 14, the day Charles Francis Adams, United States Minister to the Court of Saint James's, arrived in London, he was understandably put out about it and quickly tried to mend fences by bringing skillful and unrelenting pressure on the British Government. He also did his best to influence popular opinion by cleverly manipulated propaganda efforts.

During all four years of war, a backstage drama was played out in England while Union and Confederate officials and secret agents did their best to win over the British Government and people.

The North had enormous advantages over the South in playing the life-or-death diplomatic game. The American flag was known all over the world. Flown on a ship, it immediately identified that vessel's nationality. But the Confederate flag was naturally unknown at the beginning of the war. In order to acquaint the captains of British ships with the appearance of this strange new flag, the Admiralty sent out letters enclosing a colored copy showing the Stars and Bars as it looked when it had been adopted on March 4, 1861.

Although the British were not averse to seeing the upstart American republic dismembered and therefore made less powerful, they were determined not to become involved in the struggle between the North and the South. Nor did they want to see the war spread to other nations. They were fortunate in having a first-

rate man in Washington at the time. Lord Lyons, the British Minister to the United States, did a great deal to preserve his country's neutrality and did not appear to favor either side. The Queen and her husband, Prince Albert, were also resolved to keep the peace. Many wealthy British people openly favored the Southern cause; so did most Army and Navy officers. As a result, Confederate officials were well received, but England made no promises and did not commit herself. This pleased neither the South nor the North, but it kept the British out of trouble.

But Britain, as one of the great trading nations of the world, placed no restrictions on the sale of arms, ammunition, uniforms, and other war materials to the Confederacy, the Union, or anyone else who wanted them. Only the sale of armed ships of war was forbidden by the Proclamation of Neutrality and the Foreign Enlistment Act. This fine legalistic distinction was to cause the Confederacy much trouble because it was open to various kinds of interpretation—and the interpretation varied with the fortunes of war and was modified in accordance with Britain's ever changing but always realistic foreign policy.

And British foreign policy, as it affected the Confederacy, was shaped largely by Lord John Russell, then sixty-nine years old but untiring and energetic. He was Bertrand Russell's grandfather.

JAMES DUNWOODY BULLOCH
Confederate Naval Agent
in Europe

The Quest for Confederate Ships in Europe

The Yancey-Mann-Rost mission had gone to Europe in March 1861. Its purpose was mostly diplomatic, but it was also supposed to obtain any information that might be useful to the Confederacy. The Commissioners, however, knew nothing about ships. When Fort Sumter was fired on, James Dunwoody Bulloch, one of the most capable shipping experts in America, was in New Orleans. He immediately telegraphed to the Confederate Government in Montgomery, offering his services. Bulloch was then captain of a New York mail steamer, the *Bienville*. When some New Orleans people wanted to buy the ship for the Confederate Navy, he told them that he had no authority to sell and felt obligated to return the vessel to her New York owners. The matter was referred to President Davis by telegraph. He replied: "Do not detain the *Bienville;* we do not wish to interfere . . . with private property."

Bulloch sailed to New York, surrendered the ship to her owners (she was promptly made into a transport vessel for Union troops), and went to Montgomery by train. As soon as he arrived, Mallory told him that he was to go to Europe. He went by train to Detroit and Montreal, where he took a steamer that landed him in Liverpool on June 4, 1861. He was to be associated with that city for the rest of his life.

The Confederacy was fortunate in having Bulloch's services. He knew ships and shipping as few people did. As a former United States Navy officer he was acquainted with naval customs and needs. And he could be entrusted with the vast sums of money that were put at his disposal in Europe. Shortly after he arrived, he ordered construction begun at Liverpool on a ship which was first called the *Oreto* and then the *Manassas*. She eventually became famous as the Confederate commerce-raider *Florida*. A few months later, Bulloch authorized the Laird yard in Birkenhead

to start building a ship that was to become even better known than the *Florida*. In the dockyard she was called the No. 290 (and for a short time, the *Enrica*), but she was to carry the name *Alabama* to the far corners of the world.

After the Civil War, the United States claimed large sums of money from Great Britain as compensation for her alleged responsibility for damages done to American shipping by Confederate commerce-raiders. The long drawn-out legal case, usually referred to as "The *Alabama* Claims," was settled in 1872 by an International Tribunal, which awarded the United States $15,500,000 in gold. The many volumes of documents issued for the Tribunal are among our chief sources of information about the cruisers owned and operated by the Confederate Government. As listed for the Tribunal the ships involved were: The *Sumter;* the *Nashville;* the *Florida** and her tenders, the *Clarence,* the *Tacony,* and the *Archer;* the *Alabama** and her tender, the *Tuscaloosa;* the *Georgia**; the *Tallahassee**; the *Chickamauga**; and the *Shenandoah.** The vessels starred were actually built in Great Britain.

Bulloch built or bought the *Florida, Alabama,* and *Shenandoah,* which were by far the most successful and most celebrated of all the Confederate cruisers. The claims filed for damages done by these three ships alone amounted to $12,498,033.

The little-known, quiet, and unassuming former naval officer whose vast network of conspiracy extended from Liverpool to most of the major cities and ports of the civilized world was worth far more to the Confederacy than most of its best-known generals, but Bulloch has never been given enough credit for what he did. Almost entirely forgotten for several generations, he is only now beginning to receive the attention he has long deserved.

He was not the only one sent to Europe to buy ships for the Confederacy. It was just that his were the ships that counted most. Among the others sent to Europe to obtain ships for the Confederacy were George N. Sanders, who was later to play a prominent part in secret service activities in Canada, several regular Confederate naval officers like James H. North, Samuel Barron, George T. Sinclair, and Matthew Fontaine Maury, the distinguished oceanographer. At one time there were so many Confederate agents in Europe that they worked at cross-purposes. Internal dissension, petty jealousy, and rivalry for rank and recognition hampered their effectiveness. And when funds in Europe ran low, each man tried to get whatever money was available for his own project.

Since British neutrality prohibited ships from being armed for war in England, certain legal devices had to be used. The *Florida* and the *Alabama* set the pattern by being launched without guns; they were then armed at sea with equipment brought to them at an appointed rendezvous by other British ships.

The *Florida*, the first Confederate commerce-raider ordered in Europe by Bulloch.
She is easily identified by her twin smokestacks and rakish masts.

The original builder's model of the *Alabama*, most famous of all Confederate raiders.
Under the command of Raphael Semmes, she ranged the world.

JOHN LAIRD
of Birkenhead.

The Lairds Build Confederate Ships

The *Florida* was built in the yards of W. C. Miller and Sons in Liverpool. Bulloch's next and most successful ship, the *Alabama,* was built across the river in the Birkenhead Ironworks, a well-known yard owned by John Laird and his sons John, Jr., and William. They had been building iron ships since 1829 and had established an international reputation for the high quality of their work. At this time John Laird was standing for Parliament and had turned the active management of the firm over to his sons.

Bulloch said of the Lairds' work on the *Alabama:* "She was built of the very best materials, copper-fastened and coppered, and was finished in every respect as a first-class ship. I was satisfied in every particular with the manner in which the builders fulfilled their contract, and I believe she was as fine a vessel, and as well-found, as could have been turned out of any dockyard in the kingdom, equal to any of Her Majesty's ships of corresponding class in structure and finish, and superior to any vessel of her date in fitness for the purposes of a sea rover with no home but the sea, and no reliable source of supply but the prizes she might take."

The *Alabama* did not get to sea easily, however. The ever vigilant American consul at Liverpool, Thomas H. Dudley, hired spies and private detectives to find out more about the mysterious No. 290 in the Laird yard. As the ship took shape it became obvious that she was well suited to being a fighting cruiser. Since Dudley had to prove that the new ship was intended for use for warlike purposes, he was eager to find evidence that that could be used against her.

Bulloch, however, had taken the precaution of getting legal advice from the eminent Liverpool solicitor, Mr. F. S. Hull, who guided him through the complicated provisions of the Foreign Enlistment Act which was intended to prevent Her Majesty's subjects from violating British neutrality in the American war. According to Hull, "The mere building of a ship within Her Majesty's dominions . . . is no offence, *whatever may be the intent of the parties,* because the offence is not the *building* but the *equipping.*"

Bulloch therefore made sure not to put any guns, gun carriages, hand weapons, or other materials of war on the *Florida* or the *Alabama.* He went to other English firms to buy guns and equipment and obtained two small ships to deliver them to the unarmed cruisers at sea. The *Florida* was outfitted in the Bahamas, the *Alabama* in the Azores.

While these two ships were still on the ways on either side of the Mersey, Bulloch bought a nearly new steamer, the *Fingal,* secretly loaded her in Scotland with 13,000 British-made Enfield rifles, vast stores of ammunition, several pieces of artillery, uniforms, and medical supplies which had been purchased by agents working for the Confederate Army. The *Fingal*

Birkenhead Ironworks as they looked when the *Florida* and the *Alabama* were built there.

was the first blockade-runner to be owned by the Confederate Government, and she carried what was probably the largest shipment of purely military and naval supplies ever to be brought into the Confederacy. Privately owned blockade-runners found it more profitable to carry civilian luxury goods.

Since the *Fingal* was to sail under the British flag "for obvious reasons," it was necessary to have a certified British captain in nominal command even though Bulloch was to be in full charge of the ship himself. Bulloch's efforts to load the ship secretly were of no avail. The United States was not able to prevent the shipment, but its consul in London sent a full report of the *Fingal's* cargo, a detailed description, and a sketch of the vessel which was to be photographed and distributed to captains of the Union blockading fleet so they could recognize her if they saw her.

The *Fingal* sailed from Greenock, Scotland, on October 10, 1861, for Holyhead, where Bulloch was to board her. She entered the harbor during the night of October 14–15 in a heavy gale and ran down and sank an Austrian coal brig lying at anchor. Bulloch hastily got on board, instructed Fraser, Trenholm and Co., the Confederate financial agents in England, to compensate the brig's owners, and was out of the harbor before daybreak.

The *Fingal* was short of drinking water, so Bulloch took her to the island of Terceira in the Azores for food and fresh water. His brief stay in this quiet place

gave him the idea of using it later as a rendezvous for the *Alabama* and her supply ship. He then headed for Bermuda where he met the CSS *Nashville,* then on her way to England, and got a local Savannah pilot from her.

The United States consul at Bermuda tried to get the British authorities to stop the *Fingal* but was unable to do so. She left there on November 7 for Savannah. Bulloch then called his British crew together, told them the ship's actual destination, and offered to put anyone ashore at Nassau who did not want to go with him. He explained that so long as the *Fingal* was flying a British flag she would not have the right to return the fire of a Federal ship if it stopped her. But he then said that he had a bill of sale in his pocket and could take "delivery from the captain on behalf of the Confederate Navy Department at any moment."

He then asked the crew if they would go along with him and defend the ship if necessary. When they all said yes without hesitation, he ordered four guns to be brought up and mounted. He also got small arms and ammunition ready and prepared to fight his way into Savannah if he had to.

It is odd that Bulloch, who was so careful to stay within the British law when he had ships built for other captains, deliberately broke the law by carrying arms and ammunition on the *Fingal* when he took her out. But this was early in the war.

His description of bringing his ship into Savannah

37

is one of the classics of Civil War literature. In his book, *The Secret Service of the Confederate States in Europe,* he wrote:

"We felt a cool damp air in our faces, then a few big drops of moisture, and we ran straight into as nice a fog as any reasonable blockade-runner could have wanted. There was not a light anywhere about the ship except in the binnacle, and that was carefully covered. . . . Not a word was spoken, and there was not a sound but the throb of the engines and the slight 'shir-r-r' made by the friction of the ship through the water, and these seemed muffled by the dank vaporous air. . . .

"We ran cautiously in by the lead . . . the object being to get in-shore of any blockaders that might be off the inlet. We supposed the ship to be drawing fifteen or sixteen feet . . . when we . . . stopped the engines. The fog was as thick as, and about the colour of, mulligatawny soup, and the water alongside looked . . . darkish brown. From the bridge it was just possible to make out the men standing on the forecastle and poop. We could not have been in a better position for a dash at daylight.

"While we were thus lying-to and waiting, every faculty alert to catch the slightest sound . . . there burst upon our ears a shrill prolonged quavering shriek. The suddenness of the sound . . . was startling. . . . I may safely say it was unearthly. None of us could conceive what it was, but all thought that it was as loud and as piercing as a steam whistle, and that it must have been heard by any blockader within five miles of us. In a moment the sound was repeated, but we were prepared, and it was this time accompanied by a flapping and rustling noise from a hencoop in the gangway. . . .

"Several men ran to the spot. Freemantle thrust his arm into the coop, drew out an unhappy fowl, and wrung off its head with a vicious swing. But it was the wrong one, and chanticleer crowed again defiantly. 'Try again,' came in an audible whisper . . . but Freemantle's second effort was more disastrous than the first. He not only failed to seize the obnoxious screamer, but he set the whole hennery in commotion. . . . At last the offending bird was caught. He died game and made a fierce struggle for life; but Freemantle managed to catch him with a firm grip by the neck, and fetching a full arm-swing as if heaving a twelve-pound lead, the body fell with a heavy thud upon the deck, and we were again favored with a profound stillness.

"By this time daylight began to break. . . . I went aloft to look out for . . . the inlet. . . . In less than half an hour I could see the bushy tops of the tall pine trees, then their straight slender trunks, then the brushwood, and finally the pale yellow streak of sand which formed the foreshore."

Bulloch got the *Fingal* safely into Savannah with her much-wanted cargo of armaments, but he could not get her out. He went on to report to Richmond while the ship waited to be loaded with cotton. Meanwhile, the Federal blockading fleet closed in on Savannah. Bulloch spent weeks trying to elude the blockaders but finally had to give up. He left Wilmington on the blockade-runner *Annie Childs* and was back in Liverpool on March 10, 1862—just as the *Florida* was getting ready to sail.

The *Fingal* then underwent a complete change of character. The fast, oceangoing blockade-runner was cut down to her deck and covered over with wood and armor to convert her into an ironclad ram with 6- and 7-inch guns and a spar torpedo at the bow. Renamed the *Atlanta,* with her armor weighing down a deep-draft hull, she drew nearly sixteen feet of water, which made her difficult to handle (SEE PAGE 138).

A SPY DRAWING OF THE *FINGAL*
The United States Consul in London sent this sketch of the *Fingal* made by "our man in Greenock" to Washington so the blockade-runner could be identified by the Federal fleet. It showed the Confederate ship as she looked when she left Scotland on October 11, 1861.

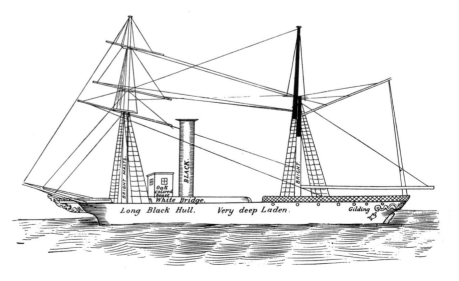

The *Freeborn* and the *Pawnee* attack a Confederate battery at Mathias Point.

WAR ON THE POTOMAC

When Virginia seceded on April 17, 1861, there was good reason to believe that troops from that state might seize Washington. A struggle began for control of the essential Potomac River. The Confederates had only a few small ships, but they salvaged guns from the ruins of the Norfolk Navy Yard and built batteries on the heights along the river. By mid-May, the Union had organized a Potomac River Flotilla, while the Confederates had constructed earthworks near the important railroad terminal and landing wharf at Aquia Creek, 45 miles below Washington. This was then reinforced by other batteries on the hills behind it.

When Confederate guns at Alexandria fired on passing river traffic, a joint Union Navy and Army expedition was sent to take over the town on May 24. (It was then that Lincoln's young friend, Colonel Elmer Ellsworth, was killed.) Virginians resented this invasion of their state and redoubled their efforts to build more batteries along the river. The heavier land-mounted guns could fire farther and more accurately than those on the ships, and the shot-resistant, earth-protected batteries were vulnerable only to shells that landed inside them. They could be taken by a resolute attack from the rear, but the Union had no troops to spare.

At the end of May, the Confederate battery at Aquia Creek, commanded by Captain W. F. Lynch, formerly of the United States Navy, was attacked by the Potomac Flotilla led by Commander J. H. Ward. He had invented a new gun carriage which he was eager to try in action. Heavy shelling went on for two days; nine shots struck the *Freeborn* without causing any casualties. Shells from the ship exploded on shore, destroying houses and tearing up railroad track but actually doing relatively little damage. The Confederates set fire to the wharf after removing everything of value from it.

On June 24 another Flotilla ship sent a party of men to burn the riverside home of Dr. A. B. Hooe, who was accused of harboring Confederate soldiers. Three days later, when the Flotilla attacked a Confederate battery at Mathias Point, Commander Ward was killed by a rifle bullet fired from the shore. He was the first Federal Navy officer to die in the war. His death accidentally spoiled a daring attempt to capture the *Pawnee* a few days later when Richard Thomas Zarvona, disguised as a heavily veiled French lady, boarded the passenger steamer *St. Nicholas* with a band of men carrying arms concealed in trunks. They seized the ship and planned to use her to surprise the *Pawnee*. But the *Pawnee* was in Washington at that time; she had gone there so her officers could attend Ward's funeral.

Commander J. H. Ward is killed by a rifle bullet while about to fire one of the *Freeborn's* guns.

ABOVE: Some of these ships were in the water by October.

BELOW: Six of the 23 Union gunboats which were hastily built of wood in the summer of 1861.

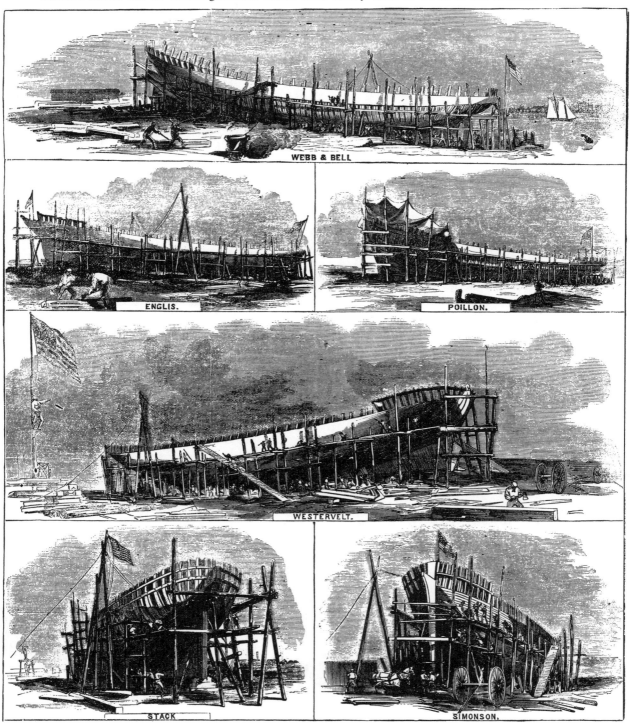

WEBB & BELL

ENGLIS.

POILLON.

WESTERVELT.

STACK

SIMONSON.

THE UNION NAVY PREPARES FOR WAR

Under the guidance of Secretary Gideon Welles, the Union Navy sprang to action. New ships were ordered, while passenger steamers, ferryboats, freighters, tugboats, and practically anything that would float were purchased or chartered to be converted into ships of war. The "paper" blockade of Southern ports had to be made real, and the coastal cities of the North had to be protected against possible attack from the sea.

The North had the yards, the mills and foundries, the trained mechanics, the experience, and the wealth to create a powerful Navy in a short time. Wood was used for the first ships because there was plenty of it, and builders knew how to work it, but Welles saw that ironclads would be needed. In his report to Congress on July 4, 1861, Welles recommended the appointment of a board of three competent officers to investigate the situation. Less than a month later, Congress appropriated $1,500,000 to build "one or more armored . . . steamships or floating steam batteries." An advertisement calling for offers of plans

was published on August 7 with the requirement that the contractors' proposals be submitted in 25 days.

By September 16, the board was able to report that the Union's first three ironclads had been ordered. One was a conventional 220-foot frigate to be made of wood plated with heavy armor. This was to be the Philadelphia-built *New Ironsides*. The officers on the board evidently felt easy about this ship, which was designed along familiar lines. They were less sure about the second one, which was to be constructed at Mystic, Connecticut (SEE PAGE 49), on the rail-and-plate principle. They demanded a guarantee from her builder, for they were afraid that she might not be able to "float her armor . . . and have stability enough for a sea vessel." They were even more apprehensive about the third ironclad, a small floating battery with a revolving gun turret. This one was designed on a novel plan which they said seemed "to render the battery shot and shell proof," but at the same time they were afraid that "her properties for

Cannon being made at Cold Spring, New York. This long-established foundry could turn out 25 heavy guns and 7000 shells a week.

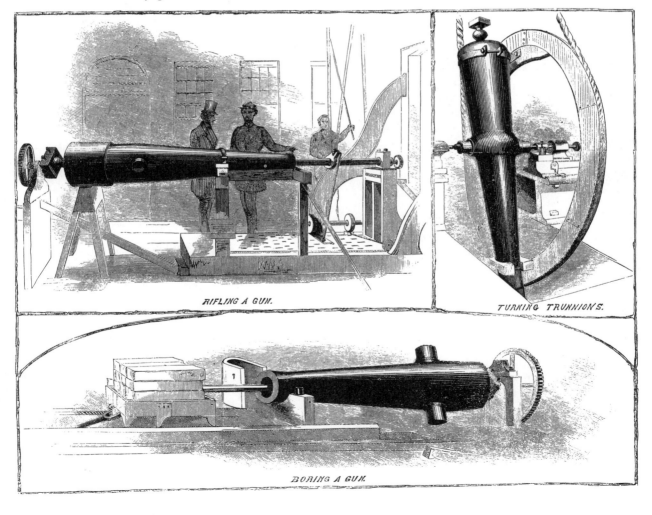

RIFLING A GUN.

TURNING TRUNNIONS.

BORING A GUN.

the sea [were] not such as a seagoing vessel should possess." They were right on both counts. The little ironclad proved to be invulnerable against the projectiles of the day, but she was so unseaworthy that she had to be towed from port to port. In the calm waters of a bay, she was all her designer claimed. He was a Swedish-born inventor named John Ericsson, and he called his novel ironclad the *Monitor*.

IRONCLADS:
The Evolution of the Revolution in Naval Warfare

1807. BLOODGOOD'S TOWER. Ideas for armored naval circular gun platforms go way back. In 1798 plans for an enormous floating circular citadel were submitted to the French Directory; in 1805, a Mr. Gillespie of Scotland published an account of a "movable turning impregnable battery"; and in 1807, Abraham Bloodgood of New York invented this circular revolving floating battery which "would bring all its cannon to bear . . . as fast as they could be loaded."

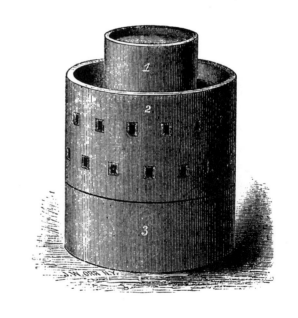

1841. TIMBY'S TURRETS. In 1841, Theodore R. Timby, also of New York, showed a model of this revolving battery to the United States War Department, which rejected it. Timby, however, went ahead with elaborate plans for a huge revolving turret for use either on land or sea. A cross section is shown at the top of the opposite page. It was to turn on roller bearings like the Coles turret. A master artillerist with a telescope sits in the central observation tower.

1854. ERICSSON'S FIRST TURRET. After the success of the *Monitor*, Ericsson was annoyed by English claims that Cowper Coles had invented the first practicable turret. In reply, he sent a letter to Gideon Welles with a copy of a proposal for an armored turret which he said he had submitted to Emperor Napoleon III on September 26, 1854. A careful search of the archives of the French Ministry of Marine in modern times, however, has failed to find any record of such a document.

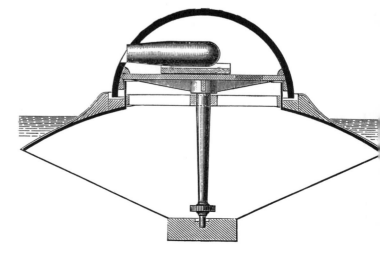

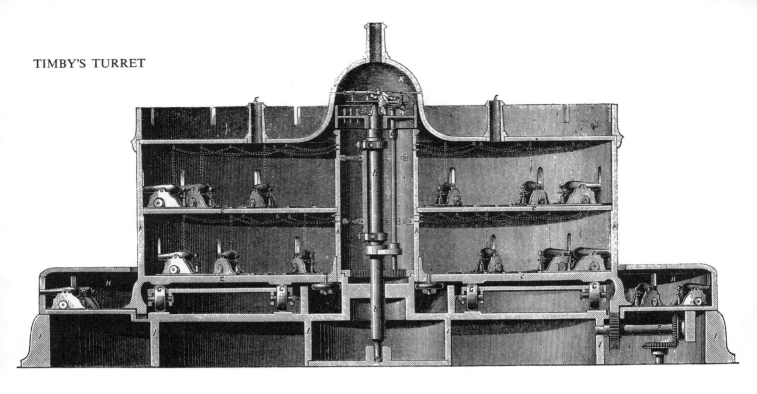

Revolving Gun Turrets

Ericsson's design was novel because it brought into being the first armored gun turret ever to go into action. The idea, however, was not new, as the inventor modestly admitted, saying that "a turret . . . turning on a pivot for protecting apparatus intended to throw warlike projectiles is an ancient device; I believe it was known among the Greeks. Thinking back, I cannot fix any period of my life at which I did not know of its existence."

Ericsson was not the only one working on armored gun turrets. In England, Captain Cowper Coles, RN, had already projected warships with eight or ten turrets, but the Admiralty had turned down his radical designs. The Coles turret turned on roller bearings, while Ericsson's revolved on a central pivot. Coles's was moved by hand power, Ericsson's by steam. The Confederate Navy soon ordered ironclads with Coles's turrets—the famous Laird rams (SEE PAGE 158). Neither Ericsson nor Coles was the first to suggest building armored ships. Crude attempts at protecting vessels by makeshift coverings had been made for centuries, and the wooden naval ships of previous wars had been constructed with enormously thick walls which could stop solid round shot. But in 1824 the French

(SEE PAGE 158)

COLES'S TURRET

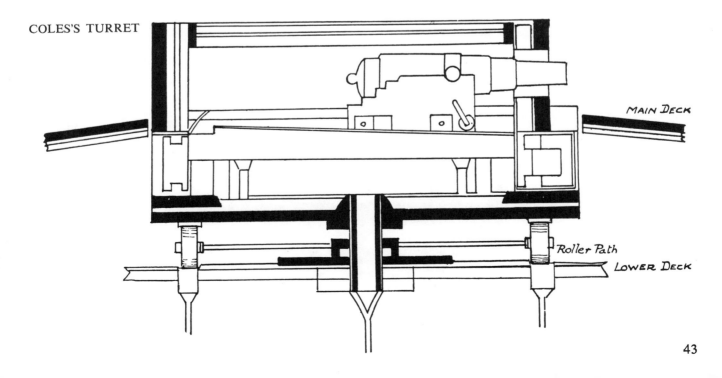

MAIN DECK

Roller Path

LOWER DECK

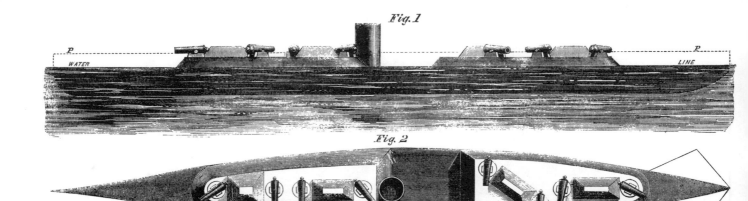

Fig. 1

P   WATER   LINE   P

Fig. 2

THE STEVENS FLOATING BATTERY. This never-completed early ship had many unusual features: an iron hull, twin engines, forced draft, great speed, guns loaded by crews protected by the ship's armor, and the ability to sink down low in the water during action. RIGHT: Cross section showing slanted armor and deep hull.

e   c   e
WATER   a   LINE
Fig. 3

Paixhans gun, which fired a shell that penetrated the timbers of wooden ships and blew them apart, compelled the chiefs of the world's navies to take at least a mild interest in doing something to protect their vulnerable fleets. The French used armored batteries in 1855 during the Crimean War; soon afterward they began to build ten ironclad ships starting with *La Gloire,* launched in 1859. They were followed by the British with the *Warrior* (launched at the end of 1860) and a series of other ironclads.

Long before these early European ironclads were started, two American inventors, Robert L. Stevens and his brother Edwin, of Hoboken, New Jersey, had proposed building an ironclad steam-powered battery in 1841. Congress gave them the necessary authorization, but actual construction did not start until 1854. New interest was aroused in the Stevens battery in 1861, but work dragged on for years. The long-delayed ironclad never got into the water and was finally broken up for scrap in 1881.

Just as the Confederates were the first in America to use armor for watercraft when they fitted out the floating battery used against Fort Sumter (SEE PAGE 22) so were they the first anywhere to put an ironclad ram into action. This was the turtle-shaped *Ma-*

nassas, which was built on the hull of a New England icebreaker, the former *Enoch Train.* The strange-looking craft carried only one gun; it had a long, sharp snout backed by 20 feet of solid wood, and was covered by thin iron plates. The *Manassas* started as a privateer but was quickly pressed into service by the Confederate Government which sent her down the lower Mississippi to attack four Union ships. When she drove a hole in the hull of the USS *Richmond* at 3:45 A.M., October 12, 1861, she committed the first act of war ever struck by an ironclad ram. She damaged but did not sink the big Union man-of-war. Later she took an active part in the defense of New Orleans (SEE PAGE 96). Although Americans were the first to send ironclad ships into action, Europeans were further advanced in the techniques of building them. French naval architects, particularly Dupuy de Lôme, designer of *La Gloire,* pioneered with the basic ideas for oceangoing armored ships. The race between France and England to replace their unarmored ships accelerated the development of the ironclad in Europe. The leading British shipyards had been building iron-framed commercial ships for years. And Brit-

A sketch of the *Manassas* made at Algiers, Louisiana, while she was being converted into an ironclad ram. Although she looks like a submarine she was not submersible; her cigarlike shape was intended to deflect projectiles. She carried a crew of 33, was 143 feet long, and drew only 11 feet.

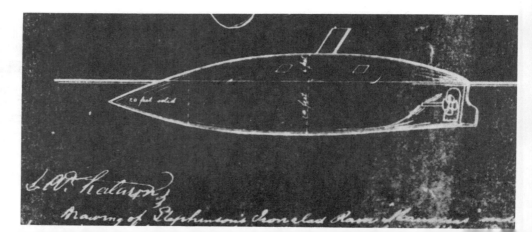

44

The first seagoing ironclad—France's *La Gloire*, a wooden frigate with a complete belt of 4½-inch armor.

THE FIRST SEAGOING IRONCLAD SHIPS

The iron-framed British *Warrior*, with sides protected by 4½-inch armor; stern and bow unprotected.

A giant hydraulic press built in London in 1861 curving armor plate. It worked on cold metal and was operated by the controls handled by the man at the right.

The iron-framed hull and armor of the *Warrior*. The 4½-inch armor was backed by two layers of teak 8 and 10 inches thick placed with the grain crossed.

ish rolling mills and metalworking establishments could turn out the heavy material needed to build and clad warships in armor. They had powerful hydraulic rams that could bend iron plates up to 9 inches thick into any shape desired. Plates 6 feet wide could be run through such a machine, which could also twist, shape, or punch holes by exerting a pressure of 1200 tons on the thick iron plates.

Although the French had long been conducting experiments to test the strength of armor, the British tackled the problem with a true engineering approach. They established a new body of knowledge by using experimental methods. They fired actual shots at sections of armor and also conducted careful laboratory tests on samples of metal taken not only from their own mills but from foreign mills as well. In this way they were able to keep informed about the strength of armor plate being made in the few countries that could then work heavy metal. William Fairbairn, one of their naval engineers, writing toward the end of the Civil War, said that "it is questionable whether the Americans have yet arrived at the same state of perfection in the construction of their ironclads as that which has been attained in this country and in France." And he then promptly added that French iron was "not so well manufactured as that employed for similar purposes by the [British] Admiralty." Fortunately, no naval combat by ships of these three nations took place to prove or disprove his statements. But the Confederacy profited by being able to get some of the powerful British naval guns through the blockade. And when they wanted ironclads they went to England first.

When the British fired their experimental shots to test the effect of projectiles on armor plate they built a mock-up section of an existing or projected ship and put it on a float anchored 1000 yards off shore. Then they fired an explosive shell at it from a rifled Armstrong gun. The big projectile smashed into the armor, blew a huge hole through the 4½-inch iron, and tore out an even larger cone-shaped opening in the 18-inch solid teak backing behind it. The results of these experiments called for ever stronger armor as guns grew more powerful.

The British Government made no secret of its experiments with armor but allowed them to be widely publicized in order to advertise the might of its navy and its manufacturers' engineering skill. Knighthoods were awarded to successful gun designers like William Armstrong, and British businessmen grew rich on profits their shipyards, foundries, mills, and machine shops made from contracts placed with them because of the worldwide fame they had gained from doing work that was up to the standards of the British Navy.

Experiments against a replica of the *Warrior's* armor conducted at Shoeburyness at the mouth of the Thames. ABOVE: When the 600-pound shell struck. BELOW: A section of the target showing the damage done.

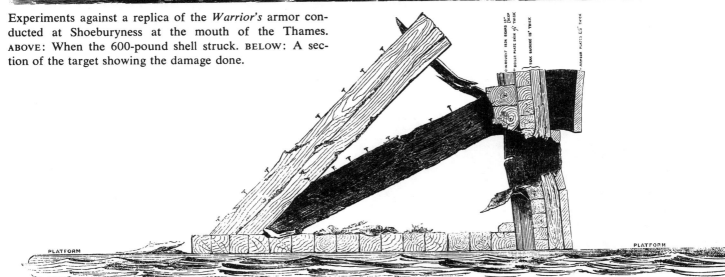

The hole made through the target by a 600-pound explosive shell.

The First American Ironclads

When the Confederates seized the Norfolk Navy Yard on April 20, 1861, the Union Navy tried to destroy everything before they abandoned this important base. The fine screw steam-frigate *Merrimack,* launched in Boston in 1855, was sunk by opening its sea valves. Flaming warehouses set the ship on fire, and she burned to the water's edge. The Confederates raised the hulk in order to salvage the engines.

A report by Secretary Mallory dated March 29, 1862, gives what is probably the most authentic account of the conversion of the burned-out hull into the history-making ironclad *Virginia.* In an earlier report dated May 10, 1861, Mallory had already urged the building of a Confederate ironclad and had directed John M. Brooke, CSN, to design one. After Brooke made his drawings, Chief Engineer William P. Williamson and Naval Constructor John L. Porter were called to Richmond for consultation. Porter brought with him "a model of a flat-bottomed, light-draft propeller, casemated battery with inclined iron-covered sides and ends." Out of this meeting came the idea of using the hull and engines of the former *Merrimack* for the *Virginia.* It was the only chance of getting an ironclad built in a short time. Since no data was available for making the correct armor, the planners "were compelled to determine the inclination of the plates and their thickness and form by actual experiment." Work on the ship began on July 11, 1861. The Tredegar Works in Richmond flattened railroad tracks until they were 8 inches wide and 2 inches thick. These were placed in two crossed layers over the inclined sides of the casemate which were made of 20 inches of pine and 4 inches of oak. The ship carried four guns on each side and a pivot gun at each end (SEE PAGE 64). She also had a stubby underwater ram. The massive frigate hull,

THE FIRST PHASE: The *Merrimack* as a 50-gun wooden frigate under sail and steam. Named after the New England river, the final *k* is correct.

END OF THE FIRST PHASE: The *Merrimack* is deliberately destroyed when the Union had to abandon Norfolk Navy Yard in April 1861.

NEW PHASE: Harper's *Weekly* runs an advance picture of the former *Merrimack,* reborn as the Confederate armored ram *Virginia.*

This drawing of the *Monitor*, published six weeks before launching, revealed some of Ericsson's novel ideas.

weighed down by armor, ram, guns, and coal, drew 22 feet when loaded—a fact which confined the ship to deep water. And her wheezy, rebuilt engines made her slow. She lumbered along like a floating castle, but she was as well protected.

Word that she was being rebuilt and armored soon reached the North. On October 3, 1861, the New York *Herald* said that she was being clad in iron; then on November 9, 1861, *The Scientific American* published a sketch based on information given by a mechanic who had worked on the ship. It errs in showing wide-open gun ports which would have exposed the gun crews to fire. And it gives the *Virginia* a high freeboard, which she did not have. Nor was her pilothouse aft of the funnel; it was way up forward with a small peaked armored roof.

Work on the three Northern ironclads had been started by this time. On October 19, Harper's *Weekly* published a picture of the still-unnamed *Galena,* then building in Mystic, Connecticut, and on December 21 printed a sketch of "Ericsson's Steel-Clad Battery," then under construction in Green Point, Brooklyn. The *Monitor* was due to be launched in less than six weeks. Harper's sketch also was wrong; the illustration shows a very high freeboard, although the finished ship had almost none. The revolving turret is too large and too high; the smokestack should be aft of the turret with a small pilothouse forward. Nevertheless, the sketch gave the Confederates many essential details. And the accompanying article revealed the fact that the *Monitor* drew only half as much water as the *Virginia*.

The *Monitor*, built in 118 working days, was the North's reply to the threat of the *Virginia;* it was the only ironclad that could be made ready in time to challenge the Confederate vessel. Ericsson incorporated many novel features in his new creation while the other two Union ironclads, *Galena* and *New Ironsides,* were conventional wooden ships with armor attached. *Galena* had an iron-roofed gun deck, but her sides were protected by iron bars and plates—a system that proved to be inadequate in battle.

The *New Ironsides* was more successful, although her bow and stern were left unarmored like the Brit-

ish *Warrior*. She had the remarkable record of being in action more than any other Union ship. During the summer of 1863 alone she fired 4439 eleven-inch projectiles. She was struck by shot and shell many times but outlasted the war to be destroyed by an accidental fire in December 1866.

These three ships were the North's only ironclads at this early stage of the war. Not until the *Monitor* had been proved in combat did the Union Navy increase production of armored vessels. But the Confederates were already busy trying to get them built in Europe. And the designs for these European ships were far in advance of anything yet seen in America, for the projected Laird rams were to be fast, sea-going armored ships with double turrets.

This advance picture of the *Galena* tells less about the Federal ironclad. Since the design was more conventional, there was less to tell.

Another conventional Federal ironclad—*New Ironsides*.

The seacoasts of the Confederacy.

THE CONFEDERACY'S VULNERABLE COASTS

Physical geography was to dominate many phases of the war—even the war at sea. One notable geographic fact was that all the Confederate states except Arkansas and Tennessee had seacoasts. Major ports, however, were relatively few: of these, Wilmington, Charleston, Savannah, Mobile, New Orleans, and Galveston were the most important. The entrance to Chesapeake Bay was controlled by the Union throughout the war; so were Pensacola and Key West. Approaches even to the good ports were difficult because of shallow water, shifting sandbars, and tortuous channels from which all navigational aids had purposely been removed for the duration. But the 3500 miles of seacoast in the Confederacy had many inlets through which a shallow-draft ship guided by a skillful pilot could enter to exchange a cargo of foreign goods for the cotton Europe needed so badly.

In June 1861 a board of four experts convened in Washington by the Federal Navy Department began to investigate the possibility of invading the Confederacy's coasts and harbors. They had at their disposal the best charts and information the Coast Survey could supply. From their findings emerged a major strategic plan for capturing certain key spots to cut the Confederacy off from the sea. The board temporarily ignored the major ports, which they knew would be strongly defended, and concentrated on less obvious inlets and harbors. For one thing, the Federal blockading fleet was in urgent need of coaling stations where ships could be repaired, take on fresh water and provisions, and give their crews a brief chance to feel solid ground under their feet.

The first place chosen by the board was Hatteras Inlet. This seemingly unimportant opening into Pam-

Union troops land on the beach to attack Forts Clark and Hatteras (at right).

lico Sound had been brought into sudden prominence because Confederate privateers and ships of the North Carolina Navy were sailing out of it to attack Northern shipping. To defend this inlet against Federal attack, Fort Hatteras and Fort Clark had been constructed. These were hastily built earthworks armed with cannon from the Norfolk Navy Yard. Fairly good descriptions of the forts had been given to the Union Navy by captains of ships captured by privateers or wrecked because the Confederates had removed the lantern from the lighthouse.

Neither the forts nor their guns were in a finished condition when a Federal fleet appeared on August 27. The expedition, which had sailed the day before from Hampton Roads, was the first large striking force sent out by the Federal Navy. Every preparation had been made for it to overwhelm the two not very strong Confederate forts. The squadron consisted of seven warships with 158 guns, two transports, and a steam tug. Towed behind this fleet were a number of iron surfboats and several dismasted steamers carrying still more surfboats. The transports had 900 troops aboard. These were under the command of Major General Benjamin F. Butler, a man whose name was to become notorious when he was made military governor of New Orleans.

The next morning the squadron began its attack. The first of the troops—about 300—came ashore in the surfboats with two 12-pounders. It was a difficult landing through rough water, and some of the boats capsized or were swept so high upon the beach that they could not be sent back for more troops. The men who landed had no fresh water or provisions, and their powder was wet. As the sea got rougher, they found themselves cut off from communication with the fleet. Nevertheless, they advanced on Fort Clark.

The fleet covered their movement down the beach by firing at the forts. They poured in a steady hail of shells, driving the garrison from Fort Clark to Fort Hatteras when the former's inadequate supply of ammunition ran out. Union troops then took possession of the abandoned fort.

Late in the afternoon, the Confederate steamer *Winslow* came up on the Pamlico Sound side bringing Flag Officer Samuel Barron and several hundred reinforcements. These were crowded into already overcrowded Fort Hatteras.

The next morning the Federal fleet resumed its bombardment. The ships ran past the fort, firing as they went, and then came around again on a different course to make it hard for the Confederate gunners to get their range. Ammunition was scarce in the fort, and the ships kept far enough away for the few shots fired at them to fall short. It was a one-way battle in which the men in the fort never had a chance. Shells burst over so fast that Barron ordered the men to take shelter. When a shell came through the ventilator of the bombproof, endangering the magazine, a white flag was run up, and the battle was over.

The Federal fleet took 715 prisoners, 25 cannon, and 1000 stands of small arms. Confederate casualties were amazingly light for such intensive fire. Only two dead were found. Thirteen wounded men were among the prisoners; others may have been removed on the *Winslow* which had on board Lieutenant William H. Murdaugh, whose left arm had been shattered. He was the first Confederate naval officer to be "deprived of the use of a limb by the enemy's shot and shell." Except for one man wounded on the hand, there were no Union casualties. The prisoners were taken to Fort Hamilton in New York Harbor, and the captured forts were garrisoned by Federal troops whose stay was to be plagued by mosquitoes which seemed to be particularly large and vicious on the isolated sandspit.

The Federal fleet bombards the Hatteras forts on the second day.

Trouble at Hatteras

Since the Confederates felt that Hatteras was a serious loss, they immediately began to make preparations to regain it. The Federal troops stationed there tried to consolidate their position against expected attack. The Army tug *Fanny* had been left with them to provide water transport; on September 18 it was sent down to Ocracoke Inlet to destroy a fort which the Confederates had built there. (This nearly forgotten steam tug deserves to be better remembered, for it was the first American aircraft carrier. The balloonist La Mountain had used it to make an observational ascent at Hampton Roads on August 3, 1861.)

The fort had been abandoned by the time the *Fanny* arrived on September 16, but the Union commander destroyed 22 guns which the Confederates had spiked and left behind. He also set fire to everything that would burn.

Once this threat from the south had been put out of commission, the occupation party turned its attention to the north, where they had learned that the Confederates were fortifying Roanoke Island (of Lost Colony fame) to use it as a base of operations. Urgent requests to Washington brought reinforcements from the Ninth New York Regiment, the Twentieth Indiana, and a company of regular artillery. The Indiana regiment of 600 men went into camp at Chicomicomico to defend the northern end of the island against a land attack. The useful little *Fanny* was to be their supply ship.

On October 1 the Confederates sent three small armed vessels to attack the camp. When they approached Chicomicomico, they saw the *Fanny* anchored near the shore ready to transfer supplies to a barge. They promptly closed in on her, and there was some spirited firing for a few moments. It was obvious that the *Fanny* could not get away, so her master ordered ammunition and guns to be dumped overboard. Some 30 or 40 boxes went into the water; then officers of the Indiana troops said that "it would be worse for them if taken prisoners" and told their men to stop. The tug was run aground, and most of the Union troops on the island were taken off by the Confederate ships which also got a rich haul of supplies.

Emboldened by this easy success, on October 4 the Confederates sent 3000 men on 20 oddly assorted vessels to attack what was left of the camp. They found the Indiana regiment already on its way down the island. The ships hurried along the beach to get ahead of the marching column and land troops to block the regiment's way on the narrow strip of sand. But the retreating Indianians kept on going through the night

The *Fanny* destroys the Confederate fort at Ocracoke.

Three Confederate steamers capture the *Fanny* at Chicomicomico.

to reach the lighthouse where they were reinforced the next morning by troops sent from the captured forts. About noon the well-armed U.S. steamer *Monticello* appeared on the ocean side and began to shell the Confederates on the shore and the ships beyond them in the sound.

An Indiana private who had been taken prisoner escaped to the *Monticello*. He described the effect of the shelling on the Confederates:

"Two . . . shells fell into two sloops loaded with men, blowing the vessels to pieces and sinking them. . . . Several . . . officers were killed. . . . The enemy were in the greatest confusion, rushing wildly into the water, striving to get off to their vessels."

After that, things were relatively quiet along the sandy beaches for several months. Federal ships tried to block the channels entirely by sinking stone-filled hulks in them. They were to attempt this later in the quieter waters around Charleston and Savannah, but the angry sea at Hatteras could not be curbed. Towing hawsers broke, the hulks sometimes had to be abandoned, and when they were sunk, they would change position when the pounding breakers and swift currents pushed them out of the way. Nothing would stay put there. Hatteras, always the enemy of ships and the men who sail them, could not be subdued. Her lonely, wreck-strewn beaches could be temporarily occupied by marching men who built forts on them, but eventually the ceaseless winds and waves would reduce everything to its natural wild state again.

The camp of the Twentieth Indiana on Hatteras Island.

Fort Walker on Hilton Head returns the fire of the circling Federal fleet.

The Port Royal Expedition

After Hatteras, the Board of Experts in Washington turned its attention to other Southern ports. Its findings were evidently not kept secret, for Harper's *Weekly* published a list of probable target areas on October 26. They were: Wilmington, North Carolina, Charleston and Beaufort, South Carolina, Brunswick and Savannah, Georgia, Fernandina and Pensacola, Florida, Mobile, Alabama, and New Orleans.

The next move was made three days after the Harper's article appeared. A fleet of 17 warships with 60 vessels loaded with supplies and what has been estimated at from 12,000 to 20,000 troops sailed from Hampton Roads for Beaufort, where a fine harbor offered the facilities the Atlantic Blockading Squadron needed. Hatteras was only an inlet through desolate sandbars, but Port Royal Sound could be made into an important naval base. The United States Marine Corps now has its training camp at Parris Island there.

The Confederates learned about the expedition and immediately sent word to the area, but little could be done to resist such a massive attack. The entrance to the harbor was protected by Forts Walker and Beauregard with 43 guns including those in their outworks. There was also a tiny Confederate fleet of four small ships. The poverty of Confederate resources compared with the Union's is nowhere better seen than here.

The invasion fleet was under the command of Samuel Francis DuPont, president of the Board of Experts. A member of the influential Delaware family, he had had a long and notable career in the United States Navy. The troops cooperating with the fleet were commanded by General Thomas West Sherman, a regular Army officer with a reputation for driving his men. The fleet, which was the largest up to that time ever assembled under the American flag, carried with it everything needed to put the projected base into immediate operation. Twenty-five of the 77 vessels went ahead with coal; horses, mules, and material for both naval and military use traveled with the fleet.

The ships, however, were not to have an easy time getting to their destination. The weather off Cape Hatteras, which seemed to come consistently to the aid of the embattled Confederacy, was so bad that several ships were lost. Actual casualties, however, were few because there were always other vessels near to take men off the foundering transports. The storm-battered fleet arrived off Port Royal on November 4. The Confederates had removed the channel markers, so soundings had to be made to indicate where deep water lay. New buoys, brought along for the purpose, were put down.

While this was going on, three of the four Confederate ships under the command of Flag Officer Josiah Tattnall (who was to be the second commander of the famous *Merrimack-Virginia*) boldly came out in defiance of the great Federal fleet. A contemporary observer on board the flagship CSS *Savannah* described what happened:

"He instantly . . . attacked them at a distance of but a mile and a half, and after a cannonading of forty minutes, during which he succeeded in entrapping three of the enemy . . . under the fire of our batteries, finding that he had to encounter English rifled guns, he retired inside the harbor.

"The day after [Tuesday] he again engaged the enemy at long shots for upward of an hour, apparently with some effect, the flagship *Savannah* receiving no further injury . . . than a temporary one to her upper works, and the remaining vessels of the squadron receiving no hurt whatever. . . . The American fleet did not attempt an entrance, and morning showed it to be in the position of the day previous. Another 24 hours passed, only to reveal the same mysterious inaction on the part of the enemy. Thursday morning, however . . . their fleet was seen to get underway. . . . At 9 o'clock, having got within range, they opened quite a heavy fire upon the batteries, which was returned by them with spirit.

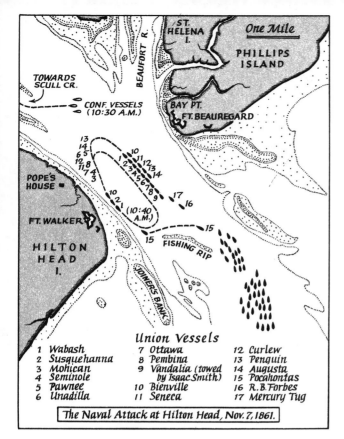

Union Vessels		
1 Wabash	7 Ottawa	12 Curlew
2 Susquehanna	8 Pembina	13 Penguin
3 Mohican	9 Vandalia (towed	14 Augusta
4 Seminole	by Isaac Smith)	15 Pocahontas
5 Pawnee	10 Bienville	16 R.B.Forbes
6 Unadilla	11 Seneca	17 Mercury Tug

The Naval Attack at Hilton Head, Nov. 7, 1861.

The Federal plan of attack "was to pass midway between Forts Walker and Beauregard, receiving and returning the fire of both, to about two and one-half miles north of the forts, then to turn toward and close in with Fort Walker, encountering it on its weakest flank, and at the same time enfilading its two water faces. . . . These evolutions were [then] to be repeated."

"Flag Officer Tattnall ordered the anchor of the *Savannah* hove up when the enemy had advanced to within a mile and a half of him, and, steaming up toward Hilton Head battery, took a raking position upon the bow of the largest American frigate, then hotly engaging it, and opened fire with his 32's upon her, to which, however, she did not deign immediately to reply.

"Our distance was too great (being that of a mile) and our guns were of too light a caliber to enable us to do her much, if any, injury. . . . All this time the enemy's frigate was gradually nearing us for the double purpose of enfilading the battery and returning the respects of our little vessel; but the Commodore, disliking to run unless under a fire, and that a hot one, only gave the order to retreat, when the frigate, rounding to, discharged her first gun at us, and the *Susquehanna* commenced a pursuit.

"We soon found the frigate to be rapidly gaining upon us, and that if we were not in the meantime blown out of the water, Skull Creek was our only haven of refuge from a prison. . . . The *Minnesota*, evidently disposed to return our attentions of the last two days once and forever, discharged, at a distance of 800 yards, three broadsides in quick succession against our miserable little cockleshell, but thanks to her poor gunnery and our luck, we were only hit once by an 11-inch shell that entered our port wheelhouse, carrying away bulkheads and stanchions, though hurting no one, from the fact that it did not explode. . . . At this juncture we were so close to the enemy's ships that their crews could . . . be distinctly seen ramming home the guns, and Flag Officer Tattnall, regretting his inability to return the high-flown compliments of Flag Officer DuPont in a more satisfactory manner, ordered his blue flag to be dipped three times to him in token of his acknowledgments of the same.

"We reached Skull Creek in safety about 11 o'clock . . . when the flag officer instantly dispatched our marines . . . to render assistance to the fatigued garrison of the battery."

The Confederate marines, however, never got to the fort. The intensive fire from Federal guns had made Fort Walker untenable before they arrived. For nearly five hours the Union fleet had circled around, firing first at one fort as they ran past it, reloading as they swung around, and then firing at the other fort when they came in range of it. Shells threw up tall columns of dust when they landed, and there were so many rising columns that it was said that they looked like a grove of poplars. Fort Walker, as the more powerful of the two forts, got most of the shelling.

The two forts returned the fire, smashing into hulls, carrying away rigging, killing eight Union seamen, and wounding 23 others. But no ships were put out of commission. They continued to steam inexorably around their course, hurling shot and shell into the forts to shatter guns and knock them off their carriages. Fifty-nine Confederates were reported killed or wounded by the time it was decided to withdraw the garrisons from the forts and march the men inland. By nightfall Federal forces had possession of Port Royal Sound. Two days later they were in Beaufort. The Union had established a permanent foothold in South Carolina.

One of the rifled guns found in Fort Beauregard after the battle was over.

THE *NASHVILLE* GOES TO SEA

The *Nashville* was a side-wheel merchant steamer which had been seized at Charleston at the beginning of the war. Plans were made to fit her with heavy guns, but it was found that her decks would not support them without extensive alterations. Her captain, Robert B. Pegram, obtained two small 6-pounders, which were her only armament.

She was supposed to take the new Confederate Commissioners Mason and Slidell to Europe. When they decided to use a smaller steamer, Pegram ran the *Nashville* through the blocking fleet on October 26 to go to England. She stopped in Bermuda and had the good fortune to meet Bulloch there when he arrived in the *Fingal* (SEE PAGE 38).

The *Nashville* had a stormy passage the rest of the way and suffered some damage from the heavy seas. On November 19 she spotted a Yankee clipper, the *Harvey Birch,* bound for Le Havre in ballast. Pegram hoisted the Confederate flag, demanded the ship's surrender, and got it without argument. He brought the captain and 31 members of the crew on board and then set fire to the $125,000 ship. When the *Nashville* left the flaming wreck, only the hull remained.

When Pegram arrived in Southampton two days later, he let the officers and crew of his prize go ashore.

But he believed that there were traitors on his own ship, because an attempt was made to burn her one night; then several desertions took place.

The *Nashville* had arrived in England while British opinion about the war in America was still unformed, but it was rapidly to change. The *Florida* and the *Alabama* were then still being built. The advisability of letting a Confederate cruiser put to sea from an English port had not yet arisen. The Admiralty's agent at Southampton agreed to permit Pegram to have his ship placed in the same condition as she was when she left Charleston. This meant that storm damage could be repaired, but she could not be altered or strengthened or take any arms and ammunition. Since the *Nashville* was owned by the Confederacy, Pegram felt that he could not break or circumvent the law.

Six days after the *Nashville* arrived in Southampton, news of the *Trent* case reached England. Public opinion immediately went strongly in favor of the South. On December 5, Pegram put his ship in dry dock and confidently waited for her to be repaired and released. On that same day, a Federal warship named the *Tuscarora* was being commissioned in the Philadelphia Navy Yard. A month later the two ships were destined to tangle (SEE PAGE 72).

The *Nashville* burns the *Harvey Birch* at sea.

JAMES M. MASON

JOHN SLIDELL

THE *TRENT* CASE:

The Union Nearly Blunders into War with England

The Yancey-Mann-Rost mission to Europe had accomplished nothing in the seven months it had been there, so two other Commissioners, James M. Mason and John Slidell, were instructed to go abroad to replace the first group.

Mason was a sixty-three-year-old Virginian who had been chairman of the Senate's Foreign Relations Committee for ten years and was therefore familiar with European affairs. He was to go to London. Slidell, five years Mason's senior, was from New York but had lived in Louisiana since 1819. He, too, had been in the Senate. His knowledge of the French language, law, and customs was responsible for his being appointed to the Paris post.

When tides, weather, and the increasing strength of the Federal blockading fleet delayed the *Nashville's* departure, the Commissioners persuaded the Confederate Government to charter the *Gordon*—a shallow-draft, very fast steamer that could elude the watchful Union blockaders. The little ship's name was changed to *Theodora,* and the two Commissioners and their secretaries left Charleston in her at 1 A.M., October 12. Two days later they were in Nassau; they then went to Cuba, where the British mail steamer *Trent* was scheduled to leave Havana on November 7.

While the Commissioners waited for the *Trent* to arrive, an American consul told Captain Charles Wilkes of the USS *San Jacinto* about their plans. Knowing that the *Trent* would have to pass through the Old Bahama Channel on its way to St. Thomas, Wilkes lay in wait at a place where the channel was at its narrowest.

When the *Trent* appeared on schedule at 11:40 A.M. on November 8, Wilkes fired two shots across the British ship's bows to make her stop. Then he ordered young Lieutenant D. M. Fairfax to have an armed boarding party seize the Commissioners and their secretaries and bring their baggage and dispatches to the *San Jacinto*. He was also to take possession of the *Trent* as a prize of war.

Fairfax got an angry reception on the *Trent*. The ship's captain and passengers, unable to resist because the powerful *San Jacinto* had its guns trained on them, seethed with helpless fury while Fairfax rounded up his four prisoners. He had to make a formal demonstration of force by having several of his officers lay

The revolver that Raphael Semmes gave to Mason.

The USS *San Jacinto* stops the British steamer *Trent*.

hands on the Confederates' coat collars as a gesture. While the Commissioners were getting their effects, Slidell's young daughter protested vehemently to Fairfax. A roll of the ship threw her against the Lieutenant, giving rise to a story, made much of later, that she had slapped him.

While all this was happening, the Commissioners' important dispatches were unobtrusively handed over to a Charleston civilian, who took them to England. Fairfax brought his prisoners to the *San Jacinto*, where they were well treated and given comfortable quarters. But the lieutenant did not attempt to take the *Trent* as a prize. He persuaded Wilkes that to do so would leave them shorthanded because they would have to put some of their own men aboard her. He also said that "the capture would seriously inconvenience innocent persons." As later events—and the interpretation of international law—were later to show, not taking the *Trent* into port as a prize of war was a serious error.

The *San Jacinto* arrived at Hampton Roads on November 15. Word was telegraphed to Washington; from there it spread rapidly across the nation and went by ship to England. Wilkes was ordered to take his noted prisoners to Fort Warren in Boston Harbor. Nine days later, when he arrived there, he found himself a national hero. He was given a banquet, thanked by Congress, congratulated by the Secretary of the Navy, and greeted everywhere as a man who had done something great. The North, suffering from a long series of military defeats at this time, was hungry for a hero. And Wilkes was glad to be in the limelight again; he had tasted fame in 1842 when he returned from a four-year exploring expedition in the Pacific and the Antarctic.

News about the *Trent* affair reached London November 27. The jubilation of the North was matched in intensity by the violent antagonism of the British press, which termed the seizure of the four Confederate passengers an outrage to the British flag. Preparations for war began. Eight thousand troops were embarked for Canada; munitions were taken out of storage to go with them; factories were ordered to make more guns and ammunition; the Atlantic fleet was alerted; and an embargo was placed on the export of arms.

Yancey, Mann, and Rost, who were still carrying on in Europe until the new Commissioners could arrive, promptly wrote to Lord John Russell, protesting Mason and Slidell's removal from a British ship. They called attention to the fact that "the only proper course was a seizure of the *Trent*, with her cargo and passengers, and a submission of the whole matter to a judicial tribunal."

Then, after he had had a chance to observe the British reaction, Mann wrote exultantly to Richmond on December 2 that "Great Britain is in downright earnestness in her purpose to humiliate by disgraceful concessions or to punish severely by force the so-called United States for the flagrant violation of the integrity of her flag upon the high seas." He also said that he had advised the British to send their new and seemingly invincible ironclad warship *Warrior* to Chesapeake Bay with a special minister to Washington to demand the liberation of the Commissioners. The British did not take Mann's advice; instead they prepared a dispatch to Lord Lyons, the British Minister in Washington, insisting that the Commissioners be released and that an apology be made. The dispatch, as originally drafted, was peremptory in tone. When it was shown to Queen Victoria for her approval, her husband, Prince Albert, who was then mortally ill with typhoid fever, persuaded her to let him tone down the language. The rewritten—and much milder—dispatch was sent to Washington, where Lyons was instructed to allow Seward just seven days for a favorable reply. If such a reply was not forthcoming, Lyons was

The Confederate Commissioners are taken off the *Trent*.

ordered to close the British Legation and return to London with his staff. This, of course, would be the first step toward war with the United States.

Since all this took time, with several weeks required for the sending of messengers back and forth across the Atlantic, war fever on both sides of the ocean began to cool off, particularly since it was now generally known that Wilkes had acted without official instructions from his Government. The British dispatch arrived in Washington on December 18; Lyons called on Seward the next day. He did not present the dispatch but gave the American Secretary of State an idea of its contents so he could think the matter over and consult his Government. Then, on December 23, Lyons officially read the dispatch to Seward and gave him a copy of it. A Cabinet meeting was held on Christmas Day to consider the matter.

Seward was already convinced that the United States would have to surrender the Commissioners. After much discussion, President Lincoln and the Cabinet were finally persuaded to agree. On December 26, Seward wrote a long letter to Lyons, reviewing the case and analyzing the difficult problems of international law involved in it. He said that Wilkes had been wrong in not bringing the *Trent* to an American port so the case could be tried by a prize court, but he quoted Wilkes's reasons for not seizing the ship, showing that some of them were based upon humane considerations. He made no apology, but ended his letter by saying: "The four persons in question are now held in military custody at Fort Warren. . . . They will be cheerfully liberated."

This answer was acceptable to the British authorities, and on January 1, 1862, the four men were sent to Provincetown Harbor, where they were taken on board the British warship *Rinaldo*. Their voyage to England, however, was not to be an easy one. The *Rinaldo* headed for Halifax but immediately ran into

MISS SLIDELL ON THE RAM-PAGE.

Commander Williams of the British Navy embroidered the case by saying that Slidell's daughter slapped the U.S. boarding officer.

The *Trent* case is discussed in American barrooms.

Captain Charles Wilkes

a heavy Arctic gale in which the ship's rigging and superstructure were solidly covered with ice. The Captain turned around and went to Bermuda. There the Commissioners were entertained at a dinner given by Admiral Alexander Milne, commander of the British West Indies and North American fleet. They were then taken by the *Rinaldo* to St. Thomas, the *Trent's* original destination. Another ship carried them from there to Southampton, where they arrived on January 29.

It is generally agreed that slow communications helped to prevent the two nations from going to war in this crisis. A transatlantic cable had been laid in 1858, but after carrying a few messages it went out of commission because of defective insulation. Communication was not re-established until 1866, when the war was over. Had the cable been working at the time of the *Trent* case, quick, angry words might have aroused more anger. As it was, the long delays between dispatches gave both sides time for thought. So the Confederacy lost its chance for European intervention over the *Trent* case and was never again to come so near to having a powerful country like England act openly in her behalf.

The career of Captain Charles Wilkes, the man who caused all the fury, went rapidly downhill after his short-lived fame in the *Trent* case. Called "troublesome, unpopular, ambitious, conceited, and self-willed" by the Secretary of the Navy and known by his fellow officers as a martinet and rigid disciplinarian who did not always obey orders himself, Wilkes later ran into grief in the West Indies—a fatal area for him. There he again almost brought on war with England. After being court-martialed in 1864 on five charges and found guilty of all of them, he was put on the retired list for the rest of the war.

Lord Lyons, the British Minister, briefs Secretary of State Seward about the British dispatch.

Irate Britain starts shipping munitions from the Tower of London to Canada.

British troops to reinforce Canada embark on the huge *Great Eastern*. This ship alone carried more than 2000 soldiers and their families from Liverpool to Quebec in the spring of 1861.

THE BLOCKADE
AND THE BLOCKADE-RUNNERS

Blockade-running is popularly thought of as the most romantic aspect of the Civil War. But the daring adventurers who ran swift, shallow-draft steamers through the watchful Federal blockading fleet for fabulous profits did not make their appearance on the scene until later in the war. There was no need for them early in 1861, for the few Union ships that were available could not hope to patrol 3549 miles of Confederate coasts with 189 inlets, bays, and rivers.

When Lincoln used the word "blockade" in his proclamations of April 19 and 27 he made a serious error, for a nation may *close its own ports* but it *blockades an enemy's*. Lincoln thus paved the way for foreign nations to recognize the Confederate States of America as a belligerent. He was evidently influenced by Secretary of State Seward, who, although an attorney, knew very little about international law. Gideon Welles, Secretary of the Navy, and Attorney General Edward Bates advised against using the word.

But if the Union blockade was to have any meaning, it had to be made effective. It was not enough simply to advise other nations—and the shipping interests of one's own—that certain Southern ports were to be considered blockaded. Federal vessels had to lie outside those ports day and night to enforce the blockade. The Yancey-Mann-Rost Commission presented Earl Russell with "a list of vessels which had arrived at or departed from various ports of the Confederate States since the proclamation of a blockade . . . up to the 20th of August [1861]." More than 400 ships had come and gone in that early period. Russell, however, took no action but continued to play his "wait and see" policy.

It was not that the Federal blockaders weren't trying to make the blockade effective. They were, but there just weren't enough of them. But they did make captures only a short time after they received orders to do so. The *Brooklyn* and the *Powhatan* began stopping suspected vessels (not necessarily actual blockade-runners) near Pensacola on May 7; the *Niagara* seized the *General Parkhill* off the coast of Charleston on May 12; while the *Cumberland,* based at Fortress Monroe, actually started seizing ships on April 24.

And Secretary Welles worked hard to enforce the blockade. He was one of the few men in the North who realized that cutting the Confederacy off from communication with the outside world must eventually bring her to terms. Other officials in both the North and the South concentrated their attention on the armies and ignored the potentiality of the navies. By the end of 1861 Welles had built the Federal blockading fleet from three ships to about 160. This was increased each year until there were 471 ships with 2245 guns in the blockade service in January 1865.

The Mexican border was an annoying problem which the Union Navy could never solve. The port of Matamoras, opposite Brownsville, Texas, and 40 miles up the Rio Grande, was an ideal place for the legal export of Confederate products. Lighters brought goods from foreign ships to Matamoras; they were then taken across the river to Texas; the same lighters carried cotton back to the ships. When several foreign vessels were seized and made test cases, American courts ruled that a neutral port could not be blockaded. After that, the Union could not legally interfere. Only the fact that Brownsville was remote from the rest of the Confederacy and had no railroad connection with it, prevented the border town from becoming a great port, at least for the duration of the war.

But the blockade brought sudden profits to other places, too, particularly Bermuda and Nassau. Bermuda was only 674 miles from Wilmington, North Carolina, while Nassau was only 500 miles from Charleston. Blockade-runners from Europe would clear for one of these neutral ports and then perhaps go on from there to the Confederacy. Better still, but somewhat less profitable, they could transfer their cargoes to a smaller vessel carrying a pilot thoroughly experienced in slipping through the Federal fleet.

It was, of course, the possibility of truly enormous profits that attracted men from all over the world to the risky trade of running manufactured goods into the Confederacy and then taking out cotton or naval stores. The luxuries brought in were auctioned off at high prices. As the Federal blockade got tighter, the profits rose. Companies organized to buy and operate blockade-runners paid 500- to 1000-per cent dividends. It was a golden bonanza which became so fantastically lucrative that the Confederate Government finally had to take steps to control it or go into the business itself.

Many blockade-runners were captured. The exact number will never be known, but it may have been as high as 1500. Some ships were reported by their captors only as "schooner, sloop, brig, or bark." And occasionally blockade-runners were lost at sea, and went down unreported, unseen, and forever unaccounted for. Their undelivered cargoes, their crews, and the ships themselves were part of the cost of the war covered by the high-premium insurance carried by their foresighted owners who were playing the game so as not to lose.

But the blockade-runners should not be judged by their failures but by their successes. And they were successful, for they kept the Confederacy going by bringing in the manufactured goods it could not make at home. They also acted as carriers of mail, of vitally important official dispatches, and they sometimes took Confederate agents overseas.

In order to elude the ever vigilant Federal fleet, new types of blockade-runners had to be designed and built for this highly specialized work. Cost did not matter; speed, shallow draft, together with seaworthiness and a silhouette that would be difficult to see were what counted. Some of the best British naval architects went to work on the problem. The ships they created were destined to have short lives, but while they lasted they were things of beauty. Their long slender hulls often had rounded forecastle decks so they could toss a breaking sea aside. Their masts were mere poles, for they depended more upon steam than wind. When the crucial time came for them to make the run through the fleet, they used anthracite coal which made little smoke, while steam was blown off under water so it could not be heard. Then telescoping funnels were lowered in order to make the silhouette as low as possible. The ships were painted a leaden gray (a forerunner of camouflage) so they would blend into fog, mist, and cloud-darkened skies. And they sometimes used smoke screens. Thus prepared, and with a good pilot to guide the ship and an experienced man to heave the lead, they were ready to make their dramatic run past the blockading vessels.

As time went on, they learned many tricks. One of the most successful was to carry signal rockets exactly like those used by the Federal fleet. At just the right time, they would fire one or more of these rockets into the air. The signal would send a Union ship off on another course, while the blockade-runner ran swiftly into port or out to sea.

Departure times were carefully calculated, with the dark of the moon favored as the best time to get through without being seen. Fog, rain, snow, and wind were the blockade-runner's delight. On fair days or bright nights he stayed in port or marked time standing out to sea. And tides, too, had to be taken into account, for the entrances to some Southern ports were so shallow that a ship could risk crossing the bar only at high water.

Because every cubic inch of space was valuable, the ships were loaded by expert stevedores who could pack the cargo together so tightly that it was said that a mouse would have no room to hide itself between the bales. The decks were loaded with cargo, and on incoming voyages the officers' cabins were crammed with the luxury goods that brought the best prices of all.

On outgoing voyages, the captain made a little extra money by accepting letters to be mailed in Europe with foreign stamps. This enabled the mail to reach destinations abroad without being intercepted by servants, postal employees, or others in the pay of Yankee spies who were naturally curious about any envelope that bore a Confederate stamp or postmark.

All kinds of things, many of them exceedingly valuable, were entrusted to the blockade. They did not always get through. Sometimes they were jettisoned if the ship was in danger of being captured. Sometimes they went down with a ship in mid-ocean or were lost when a reef or a shoal abruptly halted the daring journey. Then the waves took their toll and broke up the wreck until ship and cargo were engulfed in the devouring waters of the sea.

In this way gold bullion, plates for printing Confederate money, bonds, and postage stamps, and machinery were lost. So too were newspaper correspondents' descriptions of battles, drawings made at the front, important official letters, jewels, laces, scientific instruments, tools, weapons, and ammunition of all sorts. The sea took a rich harvest during the war years. One of the many objects it claimed was a jeweled presentation sword being sent to General Robert E. Lee by his English admirers.

PROFITS A BLOCKADE-RUNNER COULD MAKE IN ONE MONTH

DISBURSEMENTS

Wages for officers and crew	$18,840
Food for passengers and crew	5,700
Coal, oil, etc.	5,800
Insurance, pilotage, and misc.	12,625
Risks	37,500
TOTAL	$80,465

EARNINGS, OUT AND HOME

800 bales of cotton for government	$40,000
800 bales of cotton for owners	40,000
Return freight for owners	40,000
Return freight for government	40,000
Passengers' fares	12,000
TOTAL	$172,000

LEAVING A MONTHLY PROFIT OF	$91,535

CIVIL WAR NAVAL GUNS

The use of cannon (which, like gunpowder, probably originated in the Orient) can be traced in Europe as far back as the beginning of the fourteenth century. The first crude examples were intended for use only on land, but it was not long before ships carried guns. By the middle of the sixteenth century a typical naval gun consisted of a heavy metal barrel mounted on a massive wood carriage. The piece was depressed or elevated by quoins—wooden wedges—thrust under the breech, and it was fired by lighting the gunpowder through a vent in the rear of the barrel. From well before the Spanish Armada to long after Trafalgar, this simple but lethal weapon ruled the oceans of the world.

Naval guns were borne into battle on decks ranked two or even three high. The sailing ships, built of heavy timber, were slow, cumbersome, and hard to manage. They moved in until they were very close to their enemy, fired a broadside of solid shot, and then tried to put a boarding party on his deck, while men posted in the rigging with hand weapons poured in a hail of bullets. It was close-quarters combat of the bloodiest kind. Casualties were high, but ships were captured more often than they were sunk.

The wars of the American Revolution and 1812 were fought with ships and guns like these. Then, during the generation before the Civil War, both the ships and their guns improved with amazing speed. Steam, the screw propeller, and armor made men-of-war faster, more maneuverable, and far safer. Guns that could fire explosive shells to blast wooden ships apart made armor necessary. And rifled guns that could fire accurately for great distances made close-quarter fighting almost obsolete, although it still continued during the Civil War on the interior waters, where narrow channels limited the movement of vessels.

American guns had changed before the war began. The famous, widely used smooth-bore Columbiads had been invented in 1811; a heavier and improved version designed by Thomas Jackson Rodman was cast around a cooled core to enable the barrel to withstand greater internal pressure. This gun also was developed before the war. So were the powerful Dahlgren smooth-bore shell guns which were cast solid and then bored out. The much used Parrott rifle, which had a heavy wrought-iron hoop shrunk on the breech to strengthen it, was patented in October 1861, but work on it had been going on long before that.

John M. Brooke, who helped design the *Virginia,* developed the rifled gun which bore his name. It was a modification of the Parrott rifle, but its breech was strengthened by a series of narrow bands shrunk in place one after the other, whereas the Parrott breech band was put on in one solid piece.

The Confederate Navy obtained most of its cannon when it took over Federal navy yards and arsenals. It also brought many English guns through the blockade. This was particularly true of the very large coast defense guns which the South was not equipped to make. Giant British coastal cannon manufactured by Armstrong or Blakely defended Charleston and Fort Fisher, while British naval guns armed the Confederate cruisers.

Although British gunmakers, especially Armstrong, were producing large breech-loading cannon at this time, they were not used on Civil War ships (except the 300-pounder Armstrong rifle mounted in the bows of the *Stonewall,* which was never fired in battle). The long-dependable muzzle-loader was still supreme. Even the British Armstrongs, introduced into the Royal Navy in 1860, proved to be so dangerous to their crews that they were discarded in 1864.

To operate a muzzle-loader, the barrel had to be swabbed out with a damp sponge after each shot to prevent fouling and also to make sure no burning fragments were still inside to set off the next charge prematurely. (As an additional precaution, the gun captain placed his thumb over the vent to stop any air from entering the breech after the cartridge bag full of powder was rammed home because an overheated gun barrel could explode the powder if oxygen reached it.) After the cartridge bag came a wad; then the projectile, which could be a solid shot, a spherical shell, grape, canister, or case shot for a smooth bore or a conical projectile for a rifled gun. Round solid shot could be put into a gun two at a time for destructive action at close range, but two shells could not, for one might crack the other, ignite its charge, and blow up the gun.

A sharp-pointed metal pick was then thrust down the vent to clear it and penetrate the cartridge bag to expose some loose powder for igniting. A percussion primer—or a friction primer—was inserted into the vent, and a lanyard (usually a 12-foot piece of cod line) was attached to it. The gun was run forward on its wheels, pointed to the right or left by moving it with handspikes, and given the proper elevation by placing wedge-shaped quoins under the breech or by turning an elevating screw. Sights were used to aim the gun; reasonably accurate ones had only recently been invented.

To fire the gun at its target was no problem in calm water, but when the ship was rolling or pitching, only an experienced gunner could determine the exact moment to discharge the piece. Since too low a shot would plunge into the water and be wasted, gunners were instructed to aim high, for it was better to hit the target ship's rigging than to lose the shot by having it sink without doing any damage.

When a gun on a rolling deck came to the precise point above the horizon which long practice had taught the gunner was the correct place to fire, he ordered the lanyard pulled. The primer detonated the charge instantaneously; it went off loudly, sending the projectile toward the enemy ship. The gun slammed back on its recoil run as smoke billowed out. If the piece was mounted on a truck carriage (with four wheels) or on a Marsilly carriage (with two wheels in front and skids in the rear), a breeching rope, strung through or twisted around the cascabel (a pro-

jection on the breech), and fastened forward to the bulwarks on either side of the port, limited the violent backward movement.

The recoil mechanism used on a pivot gun was a vast improvement over the primitive breeching rope which had been in use for centuries. The carriage for such a gun was mounted so it could be swung in a wide horizontal arc centering on a pivot. Wheels running on sections of circular tracks made it easy to move the gun sideways to fire out of any one of two or three ports when it was inside a casemate or to almost any desired position when it was mounted on an open deck. Recoil was limited by having the gun run back on metal slides on which compressor screws on either side of the carriage could be turned down to press steel-shod blocks tightly against the slides. Friction between blocks and slides then retarded the recoil action. After being discharged, the gun was reloaded and was run forward by jacking it up on its wheels. When it came to the firing position, the gun was dropped down, and the compressors were again screwed down. The gun was then ready to be fired.

The commonest mounting of the period. Note quoin under the breech to adjust elevation. Breech ring opens so breeching rope can quickly be inserted or removed. The heavy wooden carriage is strengthened by long metal bolts run from top to bottom. Gun moves forward or back on wheels, is swung sideways by pushing it with handspikes.

NAVAL TRUCK CARRIAGE

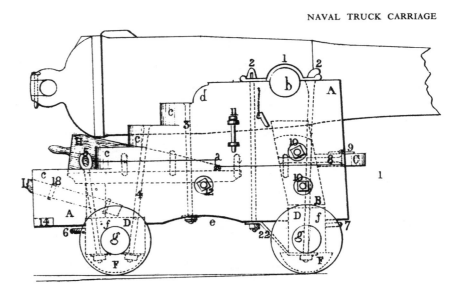

This vastly improved mounting permits gun to turn in a wide arc from its pivot (here at rear; sometimes in front). Note compressor screw at side; another on opposite side. When wound down, this forces steel-shod wooden block tight against iron slides on carriage. When recoil slams gun back, friction between compressor screw and slides slows it.

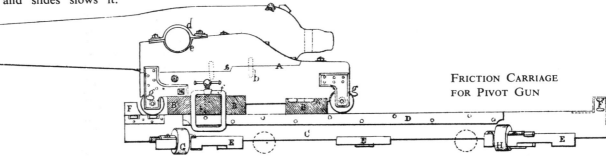

FRICTION CARRIAGE
FOR PIVOT GUN

The C.S. ironclad *Virginia* rams the *Cumberland*.

The year 1862 began well for the Confederates. The Union had had to let Mason and Slidell proceed to England, where the Florida and the Alabama were being made ready to sail. In Norfolk, men were working day and night to finish the great ironclad Virginia, which was being built on the burned hull of the former Merrimack.

The North, however, was also busy. A Federal fleet was getting ready to attack Roanoke Island. Plans were being made to capture Forts Henry and Donelson and even New Orleans. And in New York, the Monitor, the Union's reply to the Virginia, was being rushed to completion.

1862.

JANUARY								JULY						
Sun.	M.	T.	W.	T.	F.	Sat.		Sun.	M.	T.	W.	T.	F.	Sat.
..	..	..	1	2	3	4		..	..	1	2	3	4	5
5	6	7	8	9	10	11		6	7	8	9	10	11	12
12	13	14	15	16	17	18		13	14	15	16	17	18	19
19	20	21	22	23	24	25		20	21	22	23	24	25	26
26	27	28	29	30	31	..		27	28	29	30	31	..	..

FEBRUARY								AUGUST						
..	..	..	..	..	..	1		..	..	..	..	..	1	2
2	3	4	5	6	7	8		3	4	5	6	7	8	9
9	10	11	12	13	14	15		10	11	12	13	14	15	16
16	17	18	19	20	21	22		17	18	19	20	21	22	23
23	24	25	26	27	28	..		24	25	26	27	28	29	30
..	..	..	..	..	..	..		31	..	..	..	..	..	..

MARCH								SEPTEMBER						
..	..	..	..	..	..	1		..	1	2	3	4	5	6
2	3	4	5	6	7	8		7	8	9	10	11	12	13
9	10	11	12	13	14	15		14	15	16	17	18	19	20
16	17	18	19	20	21	22		21	22	23	24	25	26	27
23	24	25	26	27	28	29		28	29	30	..	..	..	..
30	31	..	..	..	..	..		..	..	..	..	..	..	..

APRIL								OCTOBER						
..	..	1	2	3	4	5		..	..	..	1	2	3	4
6	7	8	9	10	11	12		5	6	7	8	9	10	11
13	14	15	16	17	18	19		12	13	14	15	16	17	18
20	21	22	23	24	25	26		19	20	21	22	23	24	25
27	28	29	30	..	..	..		26	27	28	29	30	31	..

MAY								NOVEMBER						
..	..	..	..	1	2	3		..	..	..	..	..	..	1
4	5	6	7	8	9	10		2	3	4	5	6	7	8
11	12	13	14	15	16	17		9	10	11	12	13	14	15
18	19	20	21	22	23	24		16	17	18	19	20	21	22
25	26	27	28	29	30	31		23	24	25	26	27	28	29
..	..	..	..	..	..	..		30	..	..	..	..	..	..

JUNE								DECEMBER						
1	2	3	4	5	6	7		..	1	2	3	4	5	6
8	9	10	11	12	13	14		7	8	9	10	11	12	13
15	16	17	18	19	20	21		14	15	16	17	18	19	20
22	23	24	25	26	27	28		21	22	23	24	25	26	27
29	30	..	..	..	..	..		28	29	30	31	..	..	..

The Union fleet tries to get through rough water to reach Hatteras Inlet.

INVADING NORTH CAROLINA'S COASTAL SOUNDS

After Federal forces had consolidated their positions on Hatteras Island in October 1861 (SEE PAGE 53) they had to protect themselves from the Confederates in the forts on Roanoke Island and in other places on Pamlico and Albemarle sounds. On November 11, 1861, Flag Officer L. M. Goldsborough suggested to Gideon Welles that a combined attack be made on Roanoke Island, which commanded both sounds. And north of that island were waterways leading to Norfolk and Richmond.

Union Army and Navy agents were sent out to buy all kinds of existing ships. Since the Army had little experience in such dealings, it acquired some odd-looking vessels. When the big flotilla was finally assembled in Hampton Roads early in January 1862, the Army transports, which were to carry troops under the command of General Ambrose E. Burnside (who was destined to come to grief at Fredericksburg in December), were looked at with much foreboding by sea-knowledgeable Navy officers.

The Burnside Expedition sailed south on January 12 with 120 ships of which 17 were gunboats mounting 43 guns. The weather off Hatteras again came to the aid of the Confederacy. A great Atlantic storm scattered the Federal fleet, delaying it, and doing much damage to its vessels. At Hatteras Inlet some of the ships—especially the Army transports—had so much trouble getting over the bar that it took more than three

weeks to bring the entire fleet through the dangerous, shallow entrance. Continuing bad weather also hampered the operation. On February 5 the invading fleet finally sailed north to Roanoke Island.

The Confederates, as usual, had been kept well informed of the plans and movements of the Federal fleet, and had sent two ships down to Hatteras on January 20 to make observations. What they saw was disheartening, for they knew that they did not have enough trained men to handle the few guns on Roanoke Island. And the three forts there were poorly designed and badly built.

General Henry A. Wise had recently arrived with 800 troops to add to the garrison already on hand. He had done his best to strengthen the earthworks and drive piles into the bottom of the sound to stop the Federal fleet. But he became ill and had to direct defense operations from his bed when the menacing shapes of the invading vessels loomed up through the rain on February 6. The weather was so thick that the invaders had to delay their attack.

W. F. Lynch, who had already seen action on the Potomac and at Hatteras, was in command of the tiny Confederate fleet of two old side-wheelers, six screw-steamers, and a schooner—all of which carried a total of only nine guns. Army officers contemptuously dubbed this sorry lot of vessels "the Mosquito Fleet," and Wise, who was highly critical of Lynch, reported

Some of the men from the Federal invading fleet are drowned at sea near Cape Hatteras.

that "the enemy did not take time to brush it away."

The invaders hardly needed to, for the Federal fleet and the Army transports so far outnumbered the Confederates that the outcome of the attack was easily foreseen. On February 7 some 4000 troops were quickly put ashore while the guns of the Federal fleet hammered away at the forts. Before the next day dawned 10,000 men had been landed, and steam launches had brought in naval howitzers for them.

The Union ships could not get close to the Confederate fleet because the pilings in the bay barred their way, but the little defense fleet ran down several times in order to draw fire away from the forts. As a result, one Confederate ship, the *Forrest,* was disabled, and another, the *Curlew,* was sunk. The Confederate vessels were soon out of ammunition. It was then decided to take them to Elizabeth City, where there was a fort guarding the southern terminus of the Dismal Swamp Canal. After informing the commandant on the island of their decision to attempt to save the ships, what was left of the fleet was sailed across Albemarle Sound during the night.

The men in the forts had been under attack all day in a dismal downpour of rain. They had no chance against repeated assaults by the well-prepared, well-armed, and much larger Union land forces. One after another the three forts fell, and nearly all the troops which had defended them were taken prisoner—about 3000 men according to Federal reports. Casualties were remarkably light on both sides, especially on the ships.

Fourteen ships of the Federal fleet went to Elizabeth City, where they found six Confederate vessels near a small fort with four guns which had been deserted by its garrison. The Union ships came on at full speed, ramming and sinking the *Seabird* and capturing the *Ellis.* The schooner *Black Warrior* was set on fire by its crew, while the tugboat *Fanny,* which had been taken from the Federals on October 1 (SEE PAGE 52), had to be run ashore and blown up. The *Appomattox* tried to get to the Dismal Swamp Canal, but was too wide to enter it and had to be destroyed. Only the *Beaufort* got away to Norfolk. Confederates, who had been sent into the fort from the ships, spiked its guns, and retreated under fire through a woods, passing near Elizabeth City on their way. They found it already occupied by Union forces.

Most of the officers and crews finally reached the Norfolk Navy Yard, where the Confederate ironclad

NAVAL AND AMPHIBIOUS OPERATIONS IN NORTH CAROLINA

Virginia was being built on the hull of the former USS *Merrimack;* some of them were to see service on her.

After capturing Roanoke Island and destroying nearly all the Confederate naval vessels in North Carolina waters, the Federal invading forces turned their attention to the southern end of Pamlico Sound. On March 12, 1862, a few days after the Confederate ironclad *Virginia* had made world history at Hampton Roads, a Federal fleet appeared in the Neuse River below New Bern, and the next morning began an amphibious attack on that city. The Confederates had no armed vessels left, so the invading fleet was able to proceed upstream with only the shore batteries, the obstructions sunk in the river, and about 30 under-

Blowing up the obstructions placed in the Pamlico River to stop the Union fleet.

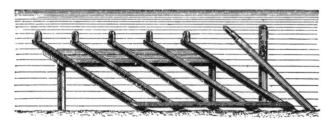

ABOVE: A timberwork frame supported on piles and carrying a row of underwater torpedoes. RIGHT: A photograph of a pile torpedo now in the Smithsonian Institution. This would be exploded by coming in contact with the bottom of a passing ship. Pile torpedoes were only one of many various types developed by the Confederate Navy.

water torpedoes to oppose their progress. The Union ships shelled the shores, but most of the fighting was done by troops which had been landed in an effort to capture the forts and batteries from the rear. Heavy rain and fog hampered them, but the superior strength of the Union invaders again prevailed. The forts along the river and New Bern itself were captured in a two-day action, and were occupied for the rest of the war by Federal forces.

Although the Confederates had used torpedoes (now called mines) against shipping in the Potomac River as early as July 1861, they were only now beginning to realize how effective these new weapons could be. In the Neuse River, however, Union ships did not come near enough to the 30 torpedoes for them to be detonated. They were formidable ones, each containing 200 pounds of powder. The Confederates had also built another system of underwater defense. This was a row of piles driven into the bottom, inclined at an angle and capped by sharp iron points to tear open the bottom of a ship. Three Union vessels were damaged by them.

As the Federal amphibious forces extended their efforts to gain control of the waters of the North Carolina sounds and their tributary streams, they ran into more torpedoes. In order to deal with them, they had to develop new techniques and train special crews to destroy them. In this way the wartime cycle of having the effectiveness of novel offensive weapons countered by increasing knowledge of defensive methods began its customary course. This time, however, the Confederates were far ahead. They were more ingenious in devising new types of torpedoes than their opponents were in avoiding them.

South of the Neuse River, Fort Macon dominated an inlet from the sea leading to Beaufort and Morehead City. This was the Union's next target. Three batteries had to be built on the shores to shell the casemated fort. Since it took time to bring in guns and mortars for these batteries, it was April 25 before they were ready to fire. Ships from the Federal fleet then came in to help. They steamed around in a circle about a mile and a quarter from the fort, firing as they came in and reloading as they moved away. Rough water made the gunners' aim uncertain, but acting in concert with the Union shore batteries they dropped so many shells into the fort that its garrison had to run up a flag of truce before nightfall. It was from this area that the CSS *Nashville* had already got away on March 17 (SEE PAGE 73).

Later in 1862 the Federal Navy made a number of forays up the rivers of North Carolina. An expedition was sent against Hamilton on the Roanoke River in July and again in October; in October, against Franklin on the Blackwater River; and in November, against Washington on the Pamlico River.

On November 23 the steamer *Ellis,* which had been captured from the Confederates at Elizabeth City after the battle of Roanoke Island, entered the New River about 40 miles west of Beaufort. She soon encountered a Confederate ship coming downstream loaded with cotton and turpentine. Rather than be taken, the Confederates set the inflammable cargo on fire and destroyed their ship.

The *Ellis* continued her raid up the river, attacked the town of Jacksonville, and captured two schooners. She then started downstream with her prizes in tow. The long run could not be made in the darkness, so the ship had to anchor for the night. When morning came, two Confederate artillery pieces had been placed on shore to command the narrowest part of the river. Ship and guns fought back and forth for an hour, then the *Ellis* made a run for it and went hard aground. Her commander brought one of his prize schooners alongside during the following night, lightened the *Ellis* by putting everything on the schooner except the pivot gun, some ammunition, two tons of coal, and a few hand weapons. He then called for six volunteers to stay with him to man the gun, and sent the rest of the crew down the river on the schooner, telling them to run to sea if the *Ellis* was destroyed.

The Confederates had brought up four heavy rifled guns during the night. At dawn they directed a deadly cross fire from these at the stranded ship. Shells smashed into the *Ellis,* disabling the engine and tearing up the ship. Faced with the alternative of surrendering or trying to row for a mile and a half in a small boat under fire, the young lieutenant set his ship on fire, left the gun loaded so it would shoot its last shot when the flames reached it, piled his six men into the boat, and ordered them to row down the river to the schooner. He reached it successfully and then had to sail through surf breaking on the bar. He got to the ocean just as several companies of Confederate cavalry came dashing along the shore to fire at the schooner. On the way to Beaufort his men heard the *Ellis* blow up when flames reached her magazines.

This daring young Union lieutenant, who was learning his way around the waters of North Carolina, was to be heard from later in 1864 in connection with a commando raid on the Confederate ironclad *Albemarle* (SEE PAGE 220). His name was William B. Cushing. When his former instructor at the Naval Academy heard of his exploit on the *Ellis,* the officer, then in the Confederate Navy, said of his pupil: "Knowing him to be at that time but nineteen years old, I comprehended his heroic qualities and was not at all surprised to hear more of him."

The Union fleet fires at Fort Thompson on the Neuse River during the Battle of New Bern.

General Burnside visits a Confederate battery which had been protected by cotton bales.

The *Ellis,* sketched when she fought for the Confederates, before being made into a Union gunboat.

The *Nashville* (flying the Confederate flag) in Southampton
while the USS *Tuscarora* lies in wait for her (right rear).

THE *NASHVILLE* ESCAPES

The *Nashville*, which had gone into dry dock at Southampton on December 5 (SEE PAGE 56), was almost ready to sail when the new Federal warship *Tuscarora*, Captain T. A. Craven commanding, entered that port on January 8. The British notified Craven that international law required "that 24 hours should elapse before the departure of one belligerent ship in pursuit of the other." A cat-and-mouse game then went on for nearly a month. It was made difficult for Craven because there are two exits from Southampton, and one ship could not watch both. On February 3 the *Nashville* got safely away and went to Bermuda, where she obtained Confederate pilots to take her into Beaufort, North Carolina. After making one capture at sea, she arrived off Beaufort on February 28 and had to evade a Federal blockader to enter the inlet.

By this time, ships and men from the Burnside expedition were spreading through the North Carolina sounds. The *Nashville* had to be taken away to avoid being captured. She was again run through the now well-patrolled inlet on March 17 and was brought into Georgetown, South Carolina. Then she became a

The *Nashville* escapes from Beaufort. First reports in the North said the Confederates blew up Fort Macon at this time. Actually it held out for more than a month.

blockade-runner under the name *Thomas L. Wragg* for a while. Later the protean ship was made into a cruiser again and rechristened the *Rattlesnake*. She was never able to get to sea again and was destroyed in the Ogeechee River by the monitor *Montauk* on February 28, 1863.

Northern people were angry at the ease with which the *Nashville* had run in and out of Beaufort and called for the removal of Secretary Welles. Here Currier and Ives poke fun at the Union ships that missed the elusive Confederate vessel.

Currier and Ives celebrate the fall of Fort Pulaski by publishing this print to be sold in the North.

FORT PULASKI

Rifled Guns Prove to Be Stronger Than Brick Walls

The interior of Fort Pulaski, showing the effect of rifled guns on its solid brickwork.

In order to extend its control of the Confederacy's Atlantic Coast, the Federal Navy's next move was an attempt to cut Savannah off from the sea. Tybee Island at the mouth of the Savannah River had been briefly visited by Federal forces on November 24, 1861, two weeks after they took Port Royal. And in December they had tried to block the mouth of the river by sinking stone-laden vessels in the channel. This seemingly simple scheme, like similar attempts at Hatteras and Charleston, was a failure because the restless waters quickly cut new channels.

But Tybee Island was only a mile from important Fort Pulaski, a large brick casemated structure on Cockspur Island, which had been built at great expense by the Federal Government. Robert E. Lee's first assignment as an Army Engineer after graduating from West Point in 1829 was at this fort, where construction work was then just beginning. He was sent to the area again on November 10 and 11, 1861, and went to Fort Pulaski to advise about strengthening its defenses. Early in December, Federal forces took over Tybee Island without opposition and began building eleven batteries there and on nearby marshy islands.

At that time half a mile was about as far as smoothbore cannon could be effective against a well-built brick fort. But the Federals brought in 10-inch Columbiads and heavy rifled guns to breach the walls, while 13-inch mortars were to drop huge explosive shells inside the fort.

Pulaski's massive walls stood 25 feet above the water and were seven and a half feet thick. The fort, pentagonal like Fort Sumter, also like Sumter did not yet have all its guns. Only 48 of the full complement of 140 were in place. But the Confederates believed that the seemingly impregnable defenses of the big fort could withstand any kind of bombardment. Others outside the Confederacy agreed with them. When Washington asked General J. G. Totten, Chief Engineer of the United States Army, for his opinion of the projected attack, he said that Fort Pulaski "could not be reduced in a month's firing with any number of guns of manageable calibers."

He was wrong. And so were the Confederates. When the eleven Union batteries opened fire on April 10, it took them just 30 hours (during which they fired 5275 shots) to breach the walls and compel the garrison to surrender. The white flag was run up at 2 P.M., April 11.

The Savannah *Republican* described the condition of the shattered fort: "At the close of the fight all the parapet guns were dismounted except three. . . . Every casemate gun in the southeast section of the fort . . . including all that could be brought to bear upon the enemy's batteries except one, were dismounted, and the casemate walls breached in almost every instance to the top of the arch—say between five and six feet in width. The moat outside was so filled with brick and mortar that one could have passed over dry-shod. The officers' quarters were torn to pieces, the bombproof timbers scattered in every direction over the yard, and the gates to the entrance knocked off. The parapet walls on the Tybee side were all gone, in many places down to the level of the earth on the casemates. The protection to the magazine in the northwest angle of the fort had all been shot away; the entire corner of the magazine next to the passageway was shot off, and the powder exposed, while three shots had actually penetrated the chamber. . . . Such was the condition of affairs when Colonel Olmstead called a council of officers in a casemate; and without a dissenting voice they acquiesced in the necessity of a capitulation in order to save the garrison from utter destruction by an explosion, which was momentarily threatened."

The Union hauls in big guns on sling carts to arm their batteries. A mortar is shown here.

The projectiles from the rifled guns "bored into the brickwork like a drill." Then the impact of the heavy solid shot from the 10-inch Columbiads loosened the bricks and finally brought them tumbling down. The mortar shells were surprisingly ineffective, so casualties were light. But the fall of Fort Pulaski showed that the day of elaborate—and expensive—stone or brick forts was over. Earthworks, quickly thrown up by inexperienced labor working only with picks and shovels, proved to be much better defensive works than hard walls. They were more effective at stopping shells and could quickly be repaired when damaged. Fort Pulaski fell hardly more than a month after the encounter between the two ironclads, the *Virginia* and the *Monitor,* showed that wooden ships were also obsolete. The double lesson was a hard one for the brass of the world to learn.

While the batteries to reduce Fort Pulaski were being laboriously built on nearby swampy islands, the Federal fleet had gone farther south to invade the east coast of Florida. Beginning on March 2, when nearly 30 ships sailed into Cumberland Sound to take Fort Clinch and Fernandina, town after town in Florida was occupied. St. Augustine was taken on March 11, and Jacksonville on March 12. These were small places then (the entire white population of Florida in 1860 was only 78,000), but they were situated on useful inlets from the sea and had more strategic importance than their size indicated.

The 13-inch mortars in Union Battery Stanton. The man at the right is filling a shell with powder.

Federal gunboats attack Fort Henry. The three wooden ones have paddle-wheel housings.

THE WAR ON WESTERN WATERS

Very different from the naval fighting on the high seas and in saltwater inlets or harbors was the war of attrition that went on between the Union and Confederate navies—and armies—on the rivers of the West. The geography of the enormous Mississippi Valley river system determined the nature of naval combat there. The rivers are shallow and winding (Cairo, Illinois, for instance, is only 480 miles from the Gulf as the crow flies, but it is 1097 miles by boat on the tortuous courses of the Mississippi). The narrowness of navigable channels made it impossible to use sailing ships—unless they were towed as floating batteries. It also meant that the historic method of broadside fighting developed on open water was less feasible than a head-on encounter. As a result, river gunboats sometimes carried as many as four guns in the bow and two in the stern. Since they could be built much wider than seagoing vessels, there was room on their broad-beamed flat hulls to mount this many guns fore and aft. And they were often armored only in front.

The screw propeller, which was so useful at sea, gave way to paddle wheels in the shallow rivers. These were placed one on each side—as on passenger steamers—or, more advantageously for positioning the guns, at the stern or near the stern, where they could be covered for protection from shellfire.

The seagoing ships of the Civil War, clumsy and makeshift as some of them had to be, were streamlined beauties compared to the strange-looking fighting craft developed for use on the rivers. They were big, squat, and ugly. They often resembled an unwieldy barn perched on a giant raft. But they did their work, and

their heavy guns could be used with devastating effect. So could their rams, which were sometimes made of wood instead of iron.

Most of the river navies' boats and ironclads were built or converted from existing vessels in local yards. The Confederates had only three yards of any importance—at Memphis, at New Orleans, and, later, at Yazoo City, Mississippi.

The Confederate Navy built or started to build more than 30 ironclads—five or more of them in Europe. One of the great mysteries of Confederate naval history is the unnamed monster ironclad ram —310 feet long and 70 feet beam—which was under construction at Yazoo City but which had to be destroyed when Union forces came there in 1863. This giant vessel was to have 4½-inch armor, six engines, four side wheels, and two propellers. Her planned armament is not known, but she could have carried the largest battery of heavy guns ever put on a riverboat. Information about her—particularly from Confederate sources—is unfortunately scant.

The Union, with its greater resources, was naturally able to move more quickly than the Confederacy in placing a large number of gunboats on the Western rivers. James B. Eads of St. Louis wrote to Secretary Welles on April 29, 1861, outlining a detailed plan for blockading Confederate commerce on the Mississippi. Eads had been a steamboat salvager and had studied the great river that was the chief transportation system of the West. He suggested that Cairo be used as the main base of operation and that the powerful twin-hulled boats used for pulling out snags be made into floating batteries with bales of cotton used to protect them from gunfire.

Welles referred the letter to the War Department, which promptly passed it on to General George B. McClellan, who was then in charge of that area. Welles also ordered Commander John Rodgers to go to Cincinnati to assist McClellan. By June 8, Rodgers had negotiated contracts to buy three wooden vessels to be converted into gunboats. They were the *A. O. Tyler,* the *Lexington,* and the *Conestoga,* side-wheel steamers that had to be strengthened to bear the weight of heavy guns. Oak planking five inches thick was installed as bulwarks to stop rifle bullets. Otherwise, the three gunboats were not armored. They were to be under the jurisdiction of the Union Army, as Welles was careful to point out to Rodgers when he wanted to purchase them for the Navy. They were ready for service late in July, but did not reach Cairo until the end of August because the river was low. But they were in action before the Confederates had anything with which to oppose them, except batteries and riflemen along the shores.

Meanwhile, Eads had been in Washington where he established a reputation for himself as an expert on the Western rivers. In July, when the Army advertised for bids for building seven ironclad gunboats, Eads received the contract for all of them. He agreed to finish them in 65 days and launched the first one, the *St. Louis* (later *Baron de Kalb*) in 45 days. The *Carondelet, Cincinnati, Louisville, Mound City, Cairo,* and *Pittsburgh* were completed soon afterward. He also converted a snag boat into the heavily armed *Benton.* In addition to these, the former *New Era* was hastily made into the ironclad *Essex.*

Before the new armored fleet was ready, Rodgers was replaced by Captain A. H. Foote. Then Rodgers' superior, Commander Henry Walke, was also sent to the area. Rodgers had made himself unpopular by driving too hard, by not bothering to send official reports, and by taking on more personal responsibility than Washington thought advisable. He was given the choice of staying in the West or of returning to the East. He promptly requested sea duty, writing aggrievedly to Welles that "when the plant thus watered and cultivated gives its first prematurely ripe fruit, the crop is turned over to another with cold words."

The three wooden gunboats cooperated in several actions—notably at Belmont, Missouri, on November 7—with an Army officer who was beginning to make a reputation for himself in the West. His name was Ulysses S. Grant.

When the first four ironclads, *Essex, Carondelet, St. Louis,* and *Cincinnati,* were ready, Foote proposed to Grant that a combined attack be made on the important Confederate stronghold Fort Henry on the Tennessee River. The roads were so bad in February 1862 that the troops had to be transported to the area on the riverboats. The three wooden gunboats also accompanied the expedition.

Fort Henry had been placed at what its commander, General Lloyd Tilghman, called "a wretched military position." He said: "I should explain fully the unfortunate location of Fort Henry in reference to resistance by a small force against an attack by land cooperating with the gunboats, as well as its disadvantages in even an engagement with boats alone. The entire fort . . . is enfiladed from three or four points on the opposite shore. . . . The history of military engineering records no parallel to this case. Points within a few miles of it, possessing great advantages and few disadvantages, were totally neglected, and a location fixed upon without one redeeming feature or filling one of the many requirements of a site for a work such as Fort Henry. . . . An enemy had but to use their common sense in obtaining the advantage of high water . . . to have complete and entire control of the position."

The high water which aided the gunboats came near flooding the magazines in the fort and rose to within a few feet of swamping its guns. On February 6, 1862, the four ironclads went ahead while the more vulnerable wooden gunboats remained farther away to fire shells at long range. The Confederates in the fort replied with a lively and accurate fire that did serious damage to the inadequately armored ironclads. But there were 75 guns on the river fleet, and only 11 of the 17 in the fort were placed to repel an attack by water. And the two largest had no projectiles.

A rifled gun in Fort Henry bursts and kills its crew. Although Leslie's *Weekly,* which first printed this engraving, described the gun as a 42-pounder, contemporary Confederate reports call it a 24-pounder and also a 32-pounder. Since only one 24-pounder rifled gun was listed in the fort's armament, it seems likely that this is what it

I.   THE WAR ON WESTERN WATERS

Forts Henry and Donelson

Not only poor location but bad luck dogged the 2610 Confederates in Fort Henry. About 15,000 Federal troops had been landed on both sides of the river, and Tilghman, knowing that he was hopelessly outnumbered, ordered everyone not needed for manning the big guns to march overland to Fort Donelson, a more defensible position on the Cumberland River. Donelson was only 10 miles away, but the troops had to march 22 miles through the woods to get there.

The Union fleet began firing at 11:45 A.M. and came on inexorably, throwing shells ahead as the gunboats approached. At 12:35, a Confederate rifled gun blew up, horribly injuring and killing its crew. Nevertheless, the grimly fighting Confederates damaged the *Essex,* which went out of control and drifted downstream. Then a 10-inch Columbiad in the fort was rendered useless when a venthole clogged. Another accident disabled a third gun, and a shell from the fleet struck the muzzle of a fourth.

Urged to surrender by his officers, Tilghman waved a flag of truce from the parapet at 1:50 P.M. It was not seen because of the heavy gun smoke. Five minutes later the Confederate flag on the shell-damaged main staff was hauled down, and the unequal battle was over. Only 94 men were captured with the fort.

The three wooden gunboats then went on a raid up the Tennessee River during which they destroyed bridges, transport and supply vessels, and torpedoes, and captured two small steamers and the 280-foot *Eastport,* which was being converted into an ironclad gunboat.

The *Tyler* and the *Conestoga* returned in time to join four ironclads in the attack on Fort Donelson. All the boats had to make a long run down the Tennessee River, go east along the Ohio, and then south up the Cumberland River to reach the scene of action. When they arrived at Fort Donelson, they found that Grant had already invested their objective on the land side.

The officers and crews on the gunboats made the

was. There were no projectiles in the fort to fit the two 42-pounders so it is unlikely that a gun crew would be serving guns that could not be used.

mistake of thinking that they could repeat their easy victory at Fort Henry. But the Confederate defense there had been only a holding action by very few men. Donelson was very different. There were 18,000 men in the much stronger and better located fort, and they were determined not to be beaten by gunboats. The overconfident Federal ironclads then made another mistake by steaming in quickly to the fort when they might better have subjected it to long-distance fire.

After a preliminary bombardment from the *Carondelet,* the main naval attack began at 3 P.M. on February 14 in bitter cold weather. The Federal ironclads threw everything they had at the fort, but the naval bombardment lasted just seventy-five minutes. Accurate fire from the Confederate guns in Donelson shot away the steering mechanism of two ironclads and so badly damaged the other two that three of the four went drifting downstream. The vulnerable wooden gunboats, of course, could not be brought in close. In the action, Foote was injured by a shell that killed the pilot standing next to him.

Encouraged by the repulse of the Federal fleet, the Confederates attempted the next day to break out of the iron grip Grant had on the fort. When the desperate—and almost successful—effort to cut through the encircling Union lines was finally stopped, Grant's officers noticed that Confederates who had not been captured or killed were carrying knapsacks filled with food—a sure sign that they meant to keep on going. Grant then urged the battered Federal gunboats to return for the effect they would have on morale. The *St. Louis* and the *Louisville* reappeared to fire a few shells as a demonstration, but their help was not needed. By this time the Confederate garrison knew it could not hold out any longer. During the night a message asking for terms was sent to Grant. To this he made his famous demand for "unconditional and immediate surrender." General Simon Bolivar Buckner, a former friend of Grant's, replied with a note in which he said that he would "accept the ungenerous and unchivalrous terms."

Generals John B. Floyd and Gideon Pillow loaded some of their troops on transports and escaped on them while Bedford Forrest boldly led his cavalrymen through the swamps near the fort. The remainder of the garrison then surrendered to Grant.

The water battery on the Cumberland River at Fort Donelson.

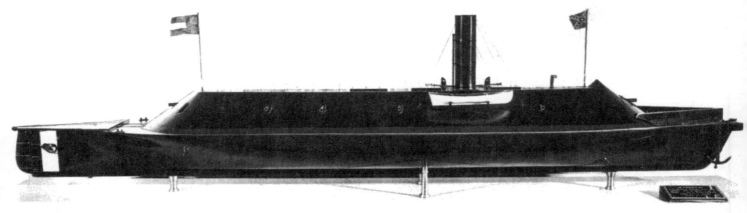

A scale model of the CSS *Virginia*.

CSS *VIRGINIA*

Back in Norfolk, the burned-out hull and saltwater-soaked engines of the *Merrimack* were being converted into the fighting ironclad *Virginia*. The Confederacy was poorly equipped for doing such a job, because it had few trained engineers, skilled mechanics, shipwrights, and sources for material. The final product was clumsy and slow, but it was a brilliant improvisation that made use of whatever was available. Mallory said that at least 1500 men worked to bring the great ironclad to completion.

The work was done hastily, since there was urgent need for a ship that could win a victory in the spring of 1862. After the loss of Forts Henry and Donelson in Tennessee and Roanoke Island in North Carolina, Virginia was now under the threat of invasion by the huge army McClellan was training near Washington. A naval victory at this time might bring much hoped-for recognition and perhaps actual assistance from England and France.

Some Confederates had naïve ideas of the *Virginia's* ability to go up shallow rivers or even venture out on the ocean. On February 28, D. F. Forrest, son of the commander of the Norfolk Navy Yard, wrote to Secretary Mallory to suggest that the new ironclad be sent up the Potomac to attack Washington, destroy the Navy Yard and arsenal there, bombard the White House, and sink the shipping in the river. Mallory already had the same idea; he expanded it further on March 7, the day before the *Virginia's* first battle, when he wrote to her commander, Franklin Buchanan, asking him whether he thought the huge ironclad could "steam to New York . . . to shell and burn the city and the shipping." If so, then he thought that "peace would inevitably follow. Bankers would draw their capital from the city. The Brooklyn Navy Yard and its magazines and all the lower part of the city would be destroyed."

Both men should have known better, although important officials in the North were soon to indulge in such fancies and translate them into hysterical fears. But the deep-hulled *Virginia,* even at high water, could not get past the Kettle Bottom Shoals that barred her way up the Potomac, nor was she built to navigate the high seas.

The last-minute efforts to speed up the completion of the *Virginia* were truly heroic. Nearly a hundred blacksmiths, helpers, and finishers volunteered to work overtime without pay to get the ship into action as

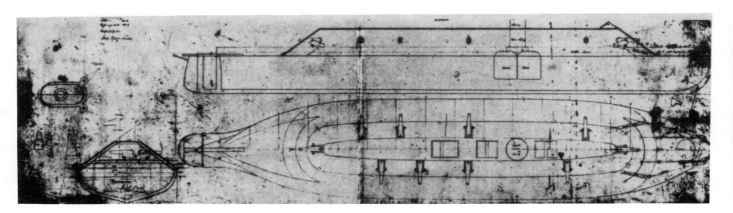

Profile and deck plan of the *Virginia* as drawn by John L. Porter in 1861.

The hull of the *Merrimack* being converted to the armored ram *Virginia* in the Norfolk Navy Yard, 1861–1862.

soon as possible. Southerners knew that the Union's first ironclad was completed; some even believed rumors that the *Monitor* had already arrived in Chesapeake Bay.

The prewar Federal Navy had had many Southern officers but almost no Southern sailors. It was therefore necessary to raise a crew for the *Virginia* by calling for volunteers from the Confederate Army, which was in no position to spare them just then. But some soldiers did volunteer, and they, with a few trained seamen, gunners, and 45 Marines, made up the big ironclad's crew of more than 300 men. They were ready to go on board on February 17.

Then, at the last minute, powder proved to be so scarce that every possible source had to be scoured for it. Mallory instructed Buchanan to depend upon the *Virginia's* ram as much as he could in order to save ammunition.

There was neither time nor powder enough to make adequate tests of the guns that had just been installed. Nor could a real trial run be made to show just how the new warship would behave when her engines moved her through the water. The Confederates wanted to get their ironclad to Hampton Roads to at-

tack the wooden ships there before the mysterious Ericsson "steel-clad battery" could arrive.

SPECIFICATIONS FOR CSS *VIRGINIA*

LENGTH: 263 feet
BEAM: 51 feet
DRAFT: 19 to 22 feet depending on load
TONNAGE: 3200
SPEED: rated—9 knots; actual—4 to 5 knots
ENGINES: 2 horizontal, back acting; 2 cylinders, 72 inches in diameter, 3-foot stroke
BOILERS: 5 tubular; 4 main, 1 auxiliary, Martin type
HORSEPOWER: 1294
COAL CONSUMPTION: 3400 pounds of anthracite per hour
PROPELLER: 2-blade Griffiths, diameter 17 feet 4 inches
BATTERY: eight 9-inch rifled Dahlgren shell guns in broadside; two 7-inch Dahlgren pivot guns, bow and stern, each firing through 3 available ports
RAM: 1500 pounds, cast iron, 2 feet long
ANCHORS: two at the bow

These specifications were compiled from original plans and data at The Mariners Museum, Newport News, Virginia. They represent the ship as she was at the time of her first battle on March 8, 1862. Some alterations were made immediately after that.

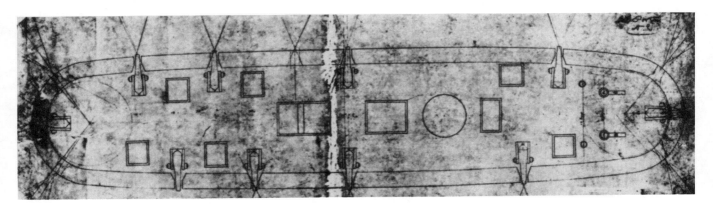

Gun-deck arrangement of the *Virginia* as drawn by John L. Porter in 1861.

The *Virginia* and her two escorts pass
a Confederate battery on Craney Island.

The VIRGINIA Goes into Action

Late in the morning of March 8, 1862, the hardly
finished *Virginia* cast off her moorings to steam down
the narrow channel of the Elizabeth River against a
rising tide. The weather was cool and windy with occasional clouds obscuring the sun. As the big Confederate ironclad moved majestically along, admiring
spectators lined the banks of the river and came out
in small boats to watch her pass. With her went two
small Confederate ships, the *Beaufort* and the *Raleigh,*
each carrying a single deck gun.

Hampton Roads, the Union Navy's jealously guarded

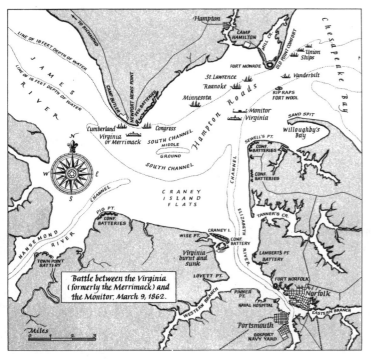

Battle between the *Virginia*
(formerly the *Merrimack*) and
the *Monitor,* March 9, 1862.

HAMPTON ROADS

domain, lay just ahead. But Federal forces did not have
that wide expanse of water all to themselves; Confederate batteries lined the eastern and southern shores,
and the James River was in Confederate hands.

When the *Virginia* entered the deep channels in
Hampton Roads, her lookouts could see a number of
Union warships to the north, lying under the protec-
tion of Fort Monroe's heavy guns. To the west, the
Congress, a 50-gun frigate with a temporary crew on
board, and the *Cumberland,* a 24-gun sloop of war,
swung at anchor. Sailors' laundry was hanging from
the rigging, a sure sign that no attack was expected.
The ponderous ironclad headed for the *Cumberland.*
Over the water came the sudden staccato sounds of
Union drums beating somnolent crews to quarters. The
laundry was frantically hauled down.

The *Virginia* lumbered through the water. Three
Union warships hurriedly got under way to come
down from Fort Monroe, but, one after another, they
grounded on the mud flats. Soon after action started,
three Confederate gunboats sailed out of the James
to help.

As the *Virginia* pushed toward the *Cumberland,*
the *Beaufort,* one of the small gunboats accompanying
her, fired the first shot. The *Virginia* passed the *Congress,* receiving and returning a broadside as she went
by. When she drew near the *Cumberland,* her bow
gun, the only one she could bring to bear while moving forward, fired a shot that tore a big hole in the
Cumberland's hull. The gun crews of the Union ship,
other Federal naval vessels, and shore batteries all
kept up a steady fire on the oncoming ironclad. When
the projectiles struck, they exploded harmlessly, rolled
down her iron sides, or went ricocheting away. Tal-
low had been spread over her armor to make shots
that struck her at an angle glance off. There was no
stopping the inexorable monster, although the *Cumberland* succeeded in damaging two of the *Virginia's*
guns.

The big ironclad closed the gap between her and
the *Cumberland.* She traveled slowly, but she carried
the enormous moving force of 3200 tons. Buchanan,
obeying instructions, was conserving ammunition and
was getting ready to use his iron ram. Guns from the
Cumberland kept firing down at the *Virginia* as she
approached. Then, with a mighty crunch, she drove
her 1500-pound underwater ram into the wooden side
of her opponent.

When the ram struck, men in the *Virginia's* engine
room were hurled to the floor by the shock. Engineers jumped up and ran around examining boilers
and engines to make sure nothing had been torn loose.
Then the ship was thrown into reverse; her propeller
churned madly and pulled her away with a jerk that

A shell explodes in the sick bay of the *Cumberland*.

left her iron ram embedded in the hull of the *Cumberland*.

The wooden ship rapidly began to sink. Her crew kept firing their guns as long as they were above water. Then, as she listed steeply to port, a pivot gun broke loose and rolled madly down the slanting deck, crushing and mangling one man. The ship settled slowly until she reached bottom. Only her three masts, still flying flags and pointing toward the sky at a 45-degree angle, remained above the surface. Around the wreck drifted the flotsam of battle—clothing, shattered spars, wood splinters, and the limp bodies of the dead.

While the *Cumberland* was sinking, the *Congress* had retreated to shallower water, where she ran aground. The *Virginia* came after her, dragging her keel in the mud as she tried to get closer. After much maneuvering, she stopped warily about two hundred yards away in a position where she could use her broadside guns. The smaller Confederate ships had already begun firing at the stranded *Congress*. All the attacking ships worked together to pour a terrible fire into the motionless frigate, knocking out her guns one after the other until only the two at the stern could be used. Then one of these was blown off its carriage, and the other had its muzzle smashed off. At that point white flags were run up to signify surrender. When the firing ceased, a boat was sent from the *Beaufort* to take possession of the defeated ship, let the crew go ashore, and make the officers prisoners.

While this was going on, the shore batteries began to shoot again, and Union riflemen attempted to pick off men on the Confederate ships. Several men on the decks were killed or wounded. Buchanan, incensed by this seeming violation of a truce, called his men back from the *Congress*. Solid shot were heated to a red glow in the furnaces of the *Virginia* and fired into the wooden ship, which soon started to burn. One of the bullets from shore struck Buchanan, wounding him in the thigh. After he was taken below, command devolved upon Lieutenant Catesby ap R. Jones.

The crew of the *Congress* swim away from the doomed ship.

The *Congress* blows up.

This contemporary engraving from *Le Monde Illustré* shows the interior of the *Virginia* as a French artist imagined it. It looks very real, but almost everything about it from the sailors' berets to the breech-loading guns firing through wide ports is wrong. The small American engraving at the left, although also imaginary, is far more correct.

The grounded *Minnesota* was a tempting target, but night was coming on, and the tide was falling. Jones fired a few shots at the *Minnesota* and then reluctantly gave orders to take the ship back. As she steamed away, the darkening surface of the bay was stained a lurid red by flames from the burning *Congress*. She kept blazing until the fire reached her magazines shortly after midnight. Then she blew up with a tremendous roar, scattering timbers over the black water.

Word of what the new Confederate ironclad had done was flashed everywhere by telegraph. There was much jubilation over the victory in the South; reaction in the North was violent and fearful. In Washington, Gideon Welles described how Secretary of War Stanton behaved when the disastrous news reached the White House: "Stanton . . . ran from room to room, sat down and jumped up . . . swung his arms, scolded, and raved." According to Welles, Stanton said that the ironclad might "come up the Potomac

and disperse Congress, destroy the Capitol and public buildings; or she might go to New York and Boston and destroy those cities, or levy from them contributions to carry on the war." Welles also told how President Lincoln and Stanton "went repeatedly to the window and looked down the Potomac . . . to see if the *Merrimac* [*Virginia*] was not coming to Washington." Stanton ordered a number of barges to be loaded with stone to be sunk at Kettle Bottom Shoals to make the Potomac impassable. Then he "telegraphed to the governors of the Northern states and mayors of some of the cities . . . advising . . . that obstructions should be placed at the mouths of the harbors."

But the *Virginia,* far from having any such intentions, had anchored off Sewell's Point for the night, expecting to finish off the *Minnesota* in the morning. Her new commander reported that the *Virginia's* loss was two men killed and eight wounded. The prow was

FRANKLIN BUCHANAN, first Commander of the *Virginia*.

twisted from ramming the *Cumberland* and had to be repaired during the night to prevent water from coming in. "The armor was somewhat damaged; the anchors and all flagstaffs shot away and smokestack and steampipe were riddled." But Jones was ready to take his ship into battle at dawn.

The commander of the French warship *Gassendi,* who had seen the combat, said that "the terrible engine of war, so often announced, had at length appeared, and . . . had destroyed two of the strongest ships of the Union, silenced two powerful land batteries, and seen the rest of the naval force, which the day before blockaded the two rivers, retreat before her. Several vessels changed their anchorage, and all held themselves in readiness to stand out to sea at the first movement of the enemy. Everything was in confusion at Fort Monroe; ferryboats, gunboats, and tugboats were coming and going in all directions; drums and bugles beat and sounded with unusual spirit. Fort Monroe and the battery of the Rip Raps exchanged night signals without intermission. In spite of the assistance of half a dozen steamers, the *Minnesota* could not succeed in getting afloat again, and I learned even that a council of war . . . entertained . . . the thought of burning her."

Welles and the Union Navy came in for a great deal of criticism in the Northern press. And tribute was paid to Confederate ingenuity for converting the *Merrimack* into the fighting ironclad *Virginia*. The New York *Herald* said: "The rebel ironclad . . . by many thought to be a failure as a war machine, has proved not only a success, but one of the most formidable engines of destruction, as events . . . have shown." When casualty figures were released, they showed that the fighting that day had killed or wounded nearly 300 men in the Federal fleet, while Confederate casualties were only 31.

JACK: "Mr. Secretary! Mr. Secretary! Wake up! Here's the *Merrimac* got out and sunk the *Cumberland* and taken the *Congress!*"
MR. SECRETARY [Welles]: "Ah! (*yawns*) you don't say so? I must get Morgan to buy some more boats then!"

"Sinbad Lincoln and the Old Man of the Sea," a contemporary cartoon criticizing Gideon Welles for inadequate preparation against the *Merrimack* [*Virginia*] and for letting the Confederate raider *Nashville* escape.

The World's First Battle Between Ironclads

The men on the *Monitor* had had a bad time of it while their ship was being towed from New York to Hampton Roads, where they arrived while the *Congress* was still burning. There had been no sleeping because of rough seas, and after the new ironclad had been anchored protectively near the grounded *Minnesota,* the tired crew had to get up in the middle of the night to move their ship away from the big warship, which was mistakenly thought to be working loose from the mud. Early in the morning the low, shedlike shape of the *Virginia* was seen coming from Sewell's Point. She ran east and then swung around to head for the *Minnesota,* hurling a 150-pound shot at her as she approached. An officer on the Confederate gunboat *Patrick Henry* described what he then saw alongside the *Minnesota:* "There lay such a craft as the eyes of a seaman never looked upon before—an immense shingle floating on the water, with a gigantic cheese box rising from its center; no sails, no wheels, no smokestack, no guns. . . . Some thought it a wa-

ter tank sent to supply the *Minnesota* . . . others . . . that it was a floating magazine replenishing her . . . ammunition; a few visionary characters feebly intimated that it might be the *Monitor.* . . ."

The Union ironclad with her 20-foot-wide turret looked very small beside the long bulk of the *Virginia.* The *Monitor* fired one gun, and the 170-pound solid iron shot hit her opponent's armor a tremendous blow, cracking the iron but not breaking through. Then the second gun was run out and fired with no better result. The *Virginia* replied with the enormous power of her four broadside guns. One of her rifled shells hit the *Monitor's* turret, making a big dent in it. The men inside were almost deafened by the impact, but they recovered quickly, relieved to find that the direct hit had not driven off the boltheads that fastened the armor.

Now the two ships, evenly matched, moved around each other in slow and stately circles like prizefighters seeking an opening. Neither was able to gain an advantage. The guns kept firing at regular intervals, but the armor on both ships was strong enough to withstand the hammering of the guns. Then the *Monitor* tried to cripple the *Virginia's* propeller by running into it, but missed. At one time the *Virginia* ran

A contemporary British artist's idea of the battle between the *Virginia* and the *Monitor*. He evidently had seen the *Scientific American's* early picture of the *Virginia* (SEE PAGE 48).

aground. While motionless, she threw shells into the *Minnesota,* one of which smashed four staterooms into one, while another blew up the boiler of the tug *Dragon,* which was standing by. The explosion killed or wounded most of the tugboat's crew.

The *Virginia* finally got out of the mud. Her commander then tried to ram the *Monitor.* But her bow, with its iron prow gone, could do no damage, except to reopen its own seams and let water in.

When the *Monitor* got away she sought refuge in shallow water, for ammunition in the turret was running low, and more could be passed up only by lining up a scuttle in the turret's floor with an opening in the deck below. When she returned to battle, the *Virginia* concentrated her fire on the *Monitor's* pilothouse. One shell exploded squarely over the eyehole, temporarily blinding her commander, Lt. John L. Worden. With no one to guide her, the *Monitor* drifted for a while across the shoals. By the time her second-in-command was able to take over, the *Virginia,* which could not follow her opponent into the shallow water, had turned away and was steaming toward Norfolk. The tide was falling, and the deep-draft ironclad had to return to port while there was still enough water in the channels to keep her afloat.

The iron monsters fight at close range. At times they almost touched each other as their big guns roared out.

Who Won the Battle?

Although thousands of people had seen the encounter between the *Virginia* and the *Monitor,* there was to be much dispute for years to come as to which ship was the victor. One thing is certain: the Federal authorities were still very much afraid of what the *Virginia* might do. The day after the battle, President Lincoln learned from the wounded commander of the *Monitor* that the little ironclad was exceedingly vulnerable if boarded by a determined crew who could drive iron wedges under the turret to prevent it from revolving and then pour in water to drown the engines. Lincoln notified Welles that Worden was "decidedly of the opinion that she should not go skylarking up to Norfolk." Welles immediately issued orders restricting the *Monitor's* movements. Fast wooden steamers were reinforced with heavy timbers over their bows and held in readiness to run into the *Virginia* in a desperate attempt to cripple her or capture her by boarding. The *Monitor* was to be kept as a final defense for the entrance to the Potomac in case the *Virginia* came out again.

Meanwhile, the *Virginia* remained in dry dock for repairs and improvements. More armor was placed below the waterline; a new and heavier ram was put on; iron shutters were installed to close the gunports when not in use; and 100 tons of ballast were put aboard. These improvements added so much weight that they increased the draft to 23 feet and slowed the speed to four knots. Because of seniority, Josiah Tattnall was given command. The refurbished *Virginia* steamed boldly into Hampton Roads on April 11 accompanied by six Confederate gunboats. As Worden had predicted, they had plans for boarding and capturing the *Monitor* by wedging the turret, throwing hand grenades into the ship, and covering all openings to cut off the air.

But their intended prey, after getting up steam and slipping her anchor, remained under the guns of the batteries, immobilized by orders. Nor did the wooden steamers which were supposed to run down the *Virginia* make a move. It was an ignominious day for the Federal Navy, for its ships had to stand by and watch a Confederate gunboat coolly capture three sailing vessels, hoist their American flags upside down as a taunt, and tow away the easily taken prizes. Northern newspapers were caustically critical of the Federal fleet's inaction, but this was at the time when McClellan was at Yorktown, getting ready to launch his campaign up the Peninsula, and the Northern authorities did not want to endanger their transports and supply vessels.

But the cranky engines on the Confederate ironclad broke down again, and she had to return to dry dock. While she was under repair a private citizen wrote to Secretary Welles offering to destroy the *Virginia* in 20 days by means of torpedoes and "four submarine armors" for $500,000. Welles was evidently receptive to the scheme (with $100,000 as compensation, however), but the swift march of events made it unnecessary.

On May 3 the Confederates left Yorktown to defend Richmond. On that day Mallory gave instructions to abandon Norfolk. Ships and essential supplies in the Navy Yard were to be sent to Richmond; everything else was to be destroyed. While these preparations were going on, the *Virginia* went to Hampton Roads and stayed in its vicinity for several days, guarding the vital entrance to the James. The *Monitor* and the wooden steamers that had been refitted to attack her remained cautiously in the shelter of the Federal forts.

The President of the United States then took direct action. Annoyed by McClellan's long delay on the Peninsula, Lincoln went to Fort Monroe on May 6, and after sizing up the situation, urged that Federal troops be landed north of Norfolk to capture that city. On May 8, Union ships (including the *Monitor*) began bombarding the batteries on Sewell's Point to prepare for the landing. The *Virginia* came out, and at the sight of her the Union ships, according to Tattnall, "retired with all speed under the protection of the guns of the fortress." The *Virginia* remained there until morning when it was seen that the Confederate batteries had been evacuated.

Her presence along the shore prevented Federal troops from landing at Sewell's Point. They went instead to Ocean View, where it was too shallow for the *Virginia* to follow. As they marched toward Norfolk they met with little resistance. They occupied the abandoned city and took over what was left of the burning Navy Yard.

Tattnall made a desperate effort to save the *Virginia* by lightening her draft in order to take her up the James. But as the ship rose out of the water, part of her vulnerable wooden hull was exposed. And the pilots suddenly became apprehensive about getting across the Jamestown Flats and advised against trying it.

The historic vessel was run ashore at Craney Island and was set on fire at 3 A.M., May 11. Two hours later she blew up when the flames touched off the powder in her magazines. And so ended the brief career of the pioneer ironclad that had caused a revolution in the building of the navies of the world.

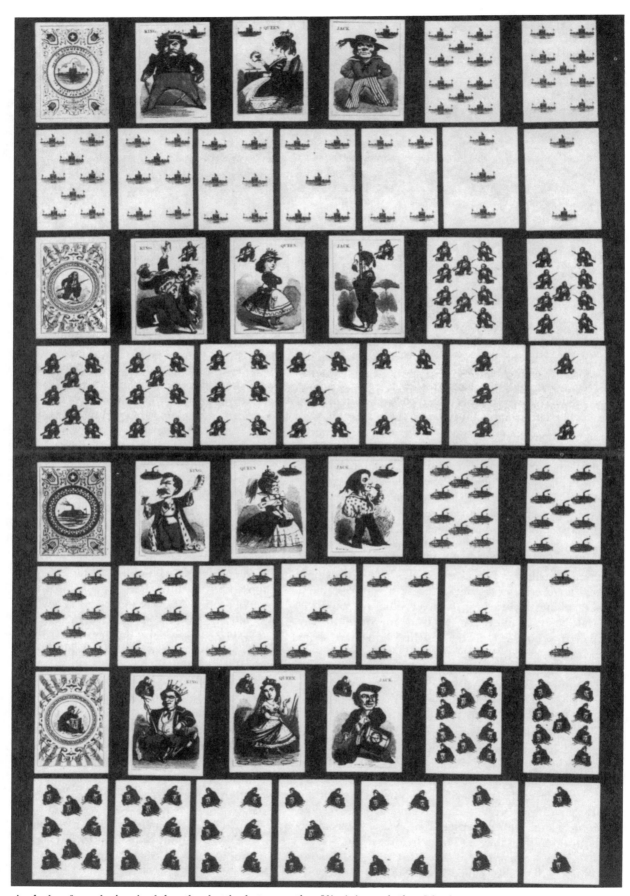

A deck of cards inspired by the battle between the *Virginia* and the *Monitor*.

The Confederate fort on Drewry's Bluff and the obstructions in the river.

The Union Navy Tries to Take Richmond

As soon as the *Virginia* was out of the way, the long-restrained *Monitor* was ordered to accompany a small fleet that was to run up the James River to Richmond and "shell the place into a surrender." Union intelligence knew that obstructions had been placed in the river to prevent such an attempt, but it was hopefully believed that a passageway could be cleared. The naval operation was to be coordinated with McClellan's drive up the Peninsula.

The fleet set out, preceded by the armored *Galena*, and in command of John Rodgers, who had organized the first Union attempts to create a navy on Western waters. The ships met with no serious opposition until they were about eight miles below Richmond, where further progress was barred by the obstructions which were more elaborate than the Union commander had been led to believe. The Confederates had sunk ships, barges, huge crates of stones, and scrap iron between rows of pilings driven into the riverbed. Nor could the Federal Navy leisurely go to work to open a way through this barrier, for the heights along the shore were strongly fortified.

The Confederate battery at Drewry's Bluff—called Fort Darling in Union dispatches—had heavy guns from Jamestown. To these, several naval guns had recently been added. The fort was a formidable one, 200 feet above the water—so high that it was hard to elevate a ship's gun to reach it, although the cannon in the fort were mounted so they could fire down at the river. Some of the men manning the battery had come there from the *Virginia* or her escorting ships. Now they were facing their old enemy, the *Monitor* again, but this time they were in a much better position than they had been before.

At 7:30 A.M. on May 15, the *Monitor*, the *Galena*, the *Naugatuck* (also called the "Stevens Battery"), an armored vessel carrying one powerful long-distance gun, and two wooden ships came in sight of the fort. The *Galena* boldly ran up to inspect the obstructions, anchored, and began firing up at the battery. The men on the *Monitor* quickly discovered that at such close range they could not elevate their guns through the turret's small ports to reach the fort on the bluff. They had to drop farther down the river, where the flatter angle of fire enabled them to aim their shots higher.

The hill battery wasted only three shots on the *Monitor's* thick armor and concentrated on the more thinly plated *Galena*. The heavy shells, plunging down, broke through the iron covering and exploded inside the ship, splintering iron and wood into lethal fragments that killed 14 men and wounded ten others. It was the first test by battle of the ironclad that had been ordered by the Union Navy at the same time as the *Monitor*. As the *Galena's* commander, John Rodgers, said in quiet understatement: "We demonstrated that she is not shot proof."

The *Naugatuck* fared no better. She was not only exposed to shellfire; her single gun, one of the 100-pounder rifled Parrotts that were to give trouble, blew up, hurling part of its massive breech into the river.

Only the seemingly invulnerable *Monitor* escaped punishment. The two wooden gunboats, even though farther away, were hit several times by accurately aimed shots. After nearly four hours, the thoroughly riddled *Galena* (hit 28 times and perforated 18 times) was running out of ammunition. The five ships started down the river, plagued along the way by Minié balls fired from concealed rifle pits on the shores. When the *Galena* was examined later, she was found to be so badly shot up that her cracked armor had to be removed, and she became an ordinary wooden gunboat.

Thus ended the attempt to take Richmond by naval power. No Union ship was to get through to that stubbornly defended city until the very last days of the war.

This wood engraving of the action between a Federal fleet and the fort on Drewry's Bluff appeared in Harper's *Weekly*, May 31, 1862. The ironclads *Monitor* (right center) and *Galena* are correct, but the artist has fanci- fully added an extra wooden paddle-steamer. He also has the *Naugatuck* facing downstream with her bow gun pointing away from the fort. Richmond and Manchester (across the river from it) can be seen in the distance.

The North Calls for More Monitors

The successful design of the original Ericsson *Monitor,* with its invulnerability to cannon fire proved again at Drewry's Bluff, induced the Union Navy to go on a monitor-building spree. Even before the *Monitor* had been tested in combat, Congress had authorized the spending of $10,000,000 for more armored ships. Ericsson was awarded contracts for six monitors, all somewhat larger than the original. The new ones had the pilothouse located on top of the turret in order to give a better view and keep this vital control point out of the way of the ship's own guns. Ericsson generously gave his plans to the Navy so other firms could build monitors. Since the first one to be launched was named the *Passaic,* single-turreted monitors built to the same plan were said to be of the *Passaic* class.

The new Federal fleet of monitors grew so fast that some were sent south early in 1863 to go into action there. The monitor *Montauk* destroyed the Con-federate commerce-raider *Nashville* on February 28 when that ship was lying under the protection of the guns of Fort McAllister in Georgia's Ogeechee River. And then in June, the Federal monitors attacked and captured the redoubtable Confederate ironclad ram *Atlanta* (SEE PAGE 138). Monitors were used at Charleston in 1863; the well-defended waters there turned out to be a proving ground for their effectiveness in combat.

Ericsson also designed two very large monitors, the *Puritan* and the *Dictator,* of which only the latter got into service during the war. Not all monitors were of Ericsson design. Four huge double-turreted ones with 15-inch guns were not his, nor were four others built locally for use on the western waters. Nor was Ericsson responsible for the unlucky *Keokuk,* a round-backed armored "turtle" with alternate strips of iron and wood covered by thin iron plating. She was riddled by Confederate shots at Charleston in 1863 and sank the next morning. Nor did the Swedish inventor have anything to do with the plan to convert the *Roanoke,* a wooden frigate similar to but even bigger than the old *Merrimack,* into a triple-turreted monitor with an

Some of the monitors, ironclads, and wooden ships of the growing Federal Navy shown in Harper's *Weekly,*

underwater ram. This monster ironclad was so heavy and so badly balanced that she rolled dangerously and was considered unsafe.

But Ericsson was involved in the project for building 20 light-draft monitors, even though his connection with this unhappy scheme was remote. These special monitors, which were to draw only six feet, were intended for use in the shallow rivers of the West. Ericsson drew the general plans for them and turned over the supervision of their building to Chief Engineer A. C. Stimers, the Navy's general inspector of ironclads, who had been on the *Monitor* at Hampton Roads. Many changes were made in Ericsson's plans which increased the special monitors' weight and draft so much that the first one launched was barely able to stay afloat. The ships had to be altered, a great deal of money was wasted, and so much time was lost that the war ended before work on the modified versions was completed.

The original *Monitor* herself came to a disastrous end on the last night of the year 1862 when she foundered in a terrible winter storm while being towed past Cape Hatteras.

GRAND MARCH,

Monitor mania seized the Northern public after Hampton Roads. This is a song commemorating the battle.

The big monitors built by the Union during the war proved to be more successful as oceangoing ships. One of them, the *Monadnock,* went under escort around Cape Horn to San Francisco in 1865–66. And another, the *Miantonomoh* (also under escort and towed part of the way) crossed the Atlantic in 1866 to visit England and Russia, where this example of American inventive ingenuity was examined with admiring curiosity by thousands of Europeans.

September 13, 1862, although many of the ships illustrated were not yet launched.

II. THE WAR ON WESTERN WATERS

Island No. 10 and Fort Pillow

After the Federals took Forts Henry and Donelson (SEE PAGE 78), they turned their attention to a key area on the Mississippi River which the Confederates had strongly fortified. This was the section where the Kentucky-Tennessee border ends at the eastern shore of the river, while Missouri is on the western side. There New Madrid was the objective of the Union Army which forced the Confederates to evacuate the town on March 15, 1862. Island No. 10 was in a huge bend of the river southeast of the town. The Confederates had made this island a stronghold and had placed field batteries on the hills around it.

A combined operation was planned against this strategically located island which enabled the Confederates to control the river. The entire Union fleet and most of the Federal troops belonging to General John Pope's army were still upstream. To get the men down to New Madrid, a channel six miles long and 50 feet wide was laboriously cut north of the bend. This was accomplished in 19 days by Union engineers who constructed floating platforms from which men could work long flexible saws. With these they cut down trees four feet below the surface of the water so shallow-draft troop transports could be floated through.

After Pope's reinforcements arrived in New Madrid

by this route, the ironclads still had to be brought down the river because they drew too much water to use the man-made channel. In those early days of the war it was believed almost impossible for a ship to run past heavily armed shore batteries, but Henry Walke, commander of the *Carondelet,* was willing to try. His imperfectly armored ship was given extra protection for the dangerous trip by putting thick planks on deck, by coiling an 11-inch hawser around the pilothouse, and by placing cordwood over the boilers. As an added precaution, a barge loaded with coal and bales of hay was tied fast to the side which would face the shore batteries.

At 10 P.M. on April 4 the *Carondelet* started down the river in the midst of a heavy thunderstorm. All lights on the boat had been put out, but the brilliant electrical display illuminated the river with occasional flashes. The hurrying ironclad got past the first battery without being noticed, but soot in her funnels caught on fire and alerted the lookouts in the forts farther down the river. Guns on the Kentucky shore and on the island spat vivid tongues of fire into the night. Shells fell all around the *Carondelet,* but she kept going. Finally she passed all the guns that lined the shores and came in sight of New Madrid without hav-

The Federal fleet of river ironclads bombarding Island No. 10 in March 1862. New Madrid is in the bend of the river at the far right (north). Seven Union mortar boats are shown firing close to shore beyond the fleet.

The naval battle at Fort Pillow on May 10. Confederate ships *General Van Dorn* and *McRae* are in the center; the Federal ironclad *Carondelet* is at the far right; next to it is USS *Cincinnati;* USS *Benton* is at the far left.

ing been struck by a single shot although the protecting barge was hit several times.

Two nights later, encouraged by the *Carondelet's* example, the *Pittsburgh* made the same run. With these two ships available, Pope was able to take his men across the river to attack Island No. 10 from the rear. With the field batteries on the hills silenced by heavy fire from the two Union ships, the island, with its guns mounted to repel an attack by water, could not be defended. Some of the Confederates tried to get away, but they found it almost impossible to escape from a place which had been chosen because of its inaccessibility. About 7000 men surrendered at 3:25 A.M. on April 7. Huge supplies of arms, ammunition, and supplies were captured with them.

The Federals now had possession of the upper Mississippi. But their plan to strangle the Confederacy required that they gain control of the entire river. While preparations were being made to seize New Orleans, the Union fleet moved down from Island No. 10 to Fort Pillow.

At this point there were eight Confederate converted gunboats with rams and makeshift armor consisting of 1-inch iron plates up forward while cotton bales and lumber protected their engines and boilers. Every day the Federals sent down a mortar boat to hurl 13-inch shells at the little fleet hoping to put some of the gunboats out of commission before the attack was made on the fort.

In an effort to stop this irritating fire, the Confederate ships steamed up the river on May 10 to fight what has been called the first fleet engagement of the Civil War. Oddly enough, both fleets were under Army orders although the boats were manned by Navy men. The Confederates did somewhat better in the brief naval battle, but afterward it was decided that Fort Pillow should be abandoned, and on June 4, boats and troops moved down to Memphis.

Taking the U.S. transport *Terry* through the newly cut channel in back of Island No. 10.

95

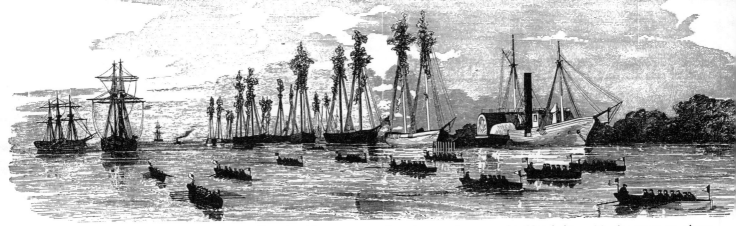

Porter's mortar boats camouflaged with evergreen boughs so they would blend in with the trees on shore.

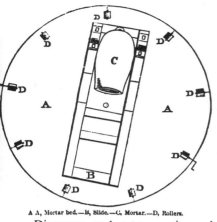

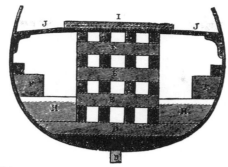

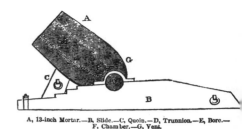

A, 13-inch Mortar.—B, Slide.—C, Quoin.—D, Trunnion.—E, Bore.—
F, Chamber.—G, Vent.

A A, Mortar bed.—B, Slide.—C, Mortar.—D, Rollers.

A, Keelson.—B, Keel.—C, Oak filling.—D, Oak floor timbers.—E. Pine cross-timbers.—
F, Lockers.—G, Hummock lockers.—H, Water tanks.—I, Mortar bed.—J, Main deck.

Diagrams and cross sections showing how the mortar boats were built and rein- forced with heavy timbers.

The Battle for New Orleans

The most important loss for the Confederacy in the early part of the war was undoubtedly the capture of the thriving Mississippi River port, New Orleans, the South's largest city. Yet the city was so poorly defended in 1861 that it could have been seized at any time that year. By the spring of 1862, the two forts guarding the river 90 miles below New Orleans had been strengthened and were now considered impregnable. Fort St. Philip had held off the British fleet in 1815; newer Fort Jackson was named for the man who had won the battle against the invaders.

A protective boom made of old hulks and massive timbers chained together had been placed across the Mississippi below the forts. And the forts themselves had 126 guns. To pass such formidable barriers seemed out of the question. But the Union Naval Planning Board had put New Orleans high on its list of Confederate ports to be captured. And in November 1861, Assistant Secretary Gustavus V. Fox proposed a plan for taking the city. Gideon Welles, General McClellan, and President Lincoln took part in the early discussion. So did David D. Porter, who was later to claim the plan as his own.

A sixty-year-old Tennessean, Captain David Glasgow Farragut, was selected as a possible commander. Porter was sent to New York to sound out the semi-retired officer. Farragut agreed that New Orleans could be taken by a naval attack and gladly consented to assume command. Porter wanted the expedition to use a fleet of mortar vessels in addition to the regular fleet,

FARRAGUT'S FLEET PASSING THE FORTS
Fort Jackson is at bottom; Fort St. Philip at top. The river flows from left to right. This wood engraving from *Le Monde Illustré* shows the fleet after it had passed through the obstructions. The French artist had a good sense of the dramatic, and his picture gives an excellent bird's-eye view of the scene, but its details are not accurate; also, the battle took place at night.

and Farragut also agreed to this. Ship Island in the Gulf of Mexico was to be the base of operations. Farragut arrived there on February 20, 1862, in his flagship, the *Hartford*. Soon after him came the Army chief in charge of 18,000 troops, General Benjamin F. Butler, who was destined to have his name forever linked with New Orleans—but in a way that would not enhance his reputation.

In the Confederate fleet of fewer than 20 ships was the historic little *Manassas*, the first ironclad ever to go into action (SEE PAGE 44). There were also three naval vessels, six river defense boats, two gunboats belonging to the Louisiana State Navy, various tugs and launches, and a big, unfinished ironclad named the *Louisiana*. This still-embryonic ship had to be towed into place at the last minute to be used as a floating battery because her inadequate engines were not powerful enough to move her. Mechanics were still working on her as she came down the river.

The Union fleet which took part in the battle consisted of 17 warships and six gunboats which were to tow 19 mortar schooners into position. The big *Colorado* had to be left in the Gulf because she drew too much water to get over the bar. Many days were lost while other deep-draft ships were dragged into the river by brute force by the steamers attached to the mortar flotilla.

The Union ships were then stripped for action, and heavy anchor chains were draped along their wooden sides to protect their engines, boilers, and magazines. This was a trick that was later to stand the USS *Kearsarge* in good stead when she met the CSS *Alabama* off the coast of France in June 1864. The mortar boats were sent up the river to bombard the forts, and their stubby, 13-inch, 25,000-pound mortars began firing at 10 A.M. on April 18. They concentrated on Fort Jackson and dropped so many shells into the big walled structure that everything there that would burn was soon in flames. The 19 mortar boats kept sending up shells at the rate of one every minute. One of them was sunk the next morning by a lucky Confederate shot, but the firing from the 18 others continued hour after hour, day and night.

On April 20 an effort was made to cut a passage through the great boom stretched across the river. Men who were landed at night on one of the hulks to blow it up found that the chains holding the obstructions together could be slipped loose. Then the gunboat *Itasca* went upstream through the narrow opening, turned around and dashed under full steam downriver with the current to smash more chains and widen the gap. Soon after this, the Confederates began to set adrift the first of several flaming rafts in an attempt to set some of the Union ships on fire.

The men in the forts and in the Confederate fleet expected Farragut to start up the river soon after the obstructions were cut. But firing from the mortar boats was continued for three more days in an effort to reduce the forts. When Farragut was finally convinced that the mortars alone could not put the forts out of commission, he gave orders for the Union fleet to move up on the night of April 23–24.

It was too early in the war for the Confederates to hamper the Union fleet's progress with torpedoes as they were to do two years later at Mobile.

The night was cool and clear with the stars shining brightly when two red lights were displayed on the flagship at 2 A.M. to give the signal to start. After an hour and a half the fleet drew near the forts. The Confederates there saw the dark shapes moving on the water and immediately began to fire at them. The Federal fleet replied, and the mortar boats downstream quickened their rate of firing. Confederate ships pulled away from shore as the Union fleet started to pass through the opening in the obstructions. Huge piles of wood along the shore were ignited to illuminate the scene and enable the gunners in the forts to see their targets. Fire rafts were hurriedly let loose to drift down the river and tangle with the invaders.

Everyone testified to the grandeur of the spectacle as hundreds of guns and mortars roared out and licking flames leaped up into the darkness. Farragut said that it was "as if the artillery of heaven were playing on the earth." A Confederate captain in Fort Jackson agreed with his foe about the splendor of the scene but complained that the shimmering illumination made it difficult for his gunners to calculate the correct distance when they fired at the moving targets.

Things happened so fast on that eventful night that the records of the great battle are a confused series of

The C.S. ram *Manassas* is attacked by the USS *Mississippi* which tries to run down the thin-shelled ironclad.

Grapeshot from Fort Jackson kills eight men and wounds seven when it hits a gun crew on the USS *Iroquois*.

recollections which sometimes contradict each other. Only the casualties in men and ships are reasonably certain.

One of the first Confederate vessels to go into action was the thinly armored *Manassas* defiantly brandishing her single gun. Heading into the stream, she rammed a side-wheel steamer, escaped its broadside because her deck was so low, and then found herself drifting under the fire from her own forts. Turning upstream, she rammed a ship-rigged vessel and disabled her only gun by the collision. After more brief encounters, the *Manassas* saw the CSS *McRae* fighting four Union gunboats and went to her assistance. Two of the Union gunboats soon forced her ashore, a shell-riddled wreck. Her men and officers escaped into a swamp under a hail of grapeshot while the cigar-shaped hull of the primitive ironclad filled with water and slid down into the depths of the river.

Farragut's flagship had a narrow escape when a blazing fire raft was pushed up to her by the daring little Confederate tug *Mosher*. The *Brooklyn* came to the *Hartford's* aid and stood between the burning ship and the forts to ward off their shots. The *Hartford* finally wrenched free from the raft and blasted the *Mosher* with her big guns. The tug sank with all on board.

The *Governor Moore* of the Louisiana State Navy, after being heavily shelled at the beginning of the battle, dashed upstream in pursuit of the USS *Varunna*, which was the fastest of all the Federal ships. When the *Moore* overtook her and came alongside, she was so close that her big bow gun could not be pointed at the *Varunna*. The gun was depressed and deliberately fired through the *Moore's* bow to send a shell into her adversary's hull.

Fighting along the river went on until dawn when the sun that rose above the marshy banks of the Mississippi saw the Confederate fleet almost entirely destroyed. The unfinished ram *Louisiana* survived the battle; around her were clustered the *McRae*, the *Resolute*, and two small tenders. The *McRae* had fought bravely. After her commander, Lieutenant Thomas B. Huger, had been mortally wounded during the night, a young lieutenant from Mississippi, Charles ("Savey") W. Read, who was to establish an outstand-

The *Governor Moore*, too near the USS *Varunna* to use bow gun in any other way, fires through her own hull.

ing reputation for courage, took over. When he saw the *Resolute* put up a white flag he sent an officer with ten men to board her with orders to haul down the flag and keep her guns ready for firing.

The next day, the commander of the *Louisiana* ordered Read to take the wounded from the Confederate ships to New Orleans for hospitalization. Read put the disabled men ashore there and found that his ship was leaking so badly that there was no hope of saving her. After she sank, he heard that the forts had been surrendered, so he left New Orleans and later served on the *Florida*.

On the morning of April 25 the Union fleet reached the river batteries at Chalmette, where Jackson had won his victory over the British in 1815. The batteries

there tried to halt the progress of the fleet but were quickly silenced by the superior firepower of the Federal guns. From Chalmette to the city was less than four miles. During it, many cargo ships which had been set on fire by the Confederates were seen drifting down the river.

Shortly after noon, when the Federal fleet reached the city, the entire dockfront area was burning briskly. Warehouses, nearly 30,000 bales of cotton, and ships tied up to the levee were ablaze. And the unfinished ironclad *Mississippi,* which was even larger than the *Louisiana,* had been put to the flames and turned adrift.

The city of nearly 170,000 inhabitants was not easy to subdue even though it lay under the guns of the

UNION NAVAL OFFICERS DEMAND THE SURRENDER OF NEW ORLEANS. After the Federal fleet arrived at the city on April 25, Captain Theodorus Bailey and Lieutenant George H. Perkins were rowed to the landing where steamboats ordinarily left to go to Memphis. They were received by a defiant crowd which jeered threateningly at them as they made their way through the streets to

City Hall. There, neither the mayor nor the commanding general felt that he had the authority to surrender the city, so the two officers returned to the fleet. The next day two other officers who went ashore with a marine guard met with an even harder time. Not until April 29, when Farragut sent an armed expedition into the city, did the Federals gain possession of it.

When the Federal fleet approached New Orleans, alarm bells were tolled, and people ran down to the levee where men had been at work all night to bring cotton to the wharves to burn it so it would not fall into the hands of the invaders. And ships loaded with cotton were set on fire and cast loose to drift down the river.

Federal fleet. Its people were resentful and unruly, and they yielded only when they were convinced that they had no choice in the matter.

The forts held out until April 28, when some of the men in Fort Jackson, believing that an attack was to be made on them by land as well as by water, refused to serve any longer. They seized guard posts, spiked guns, and even fired on their officers. In the morning, loyal troops set the *Louisiana* on fire and blew her up to prevent her capture. The forts surrendered at 2:54 P.M. when the Confederate flags were hauled down.

The fall of New Orleans, then complete, was a major disaster for the Confederacy. J. T. Scharf said candidly that "there is nothing about the naval defense of New Orleans to which a Confederate can look back without a feeling of disappointment, except the magnificent courage and seamanship displayed by Kennon in the *Moore,* Huger and Read in the *McRae,* by Warley in the *Manassas,* and by Mitchell in the immovable *Louisiana.*"

On May 1, General Butler moved into the rebellious city with 2500 troops. The day after he arrived, a Union battery clattered down St. Charles Street at full speed with bugles sounding the charge to demonstrate that the army of occupation meant business. Butler proclaimed martial law, hanged a man who had torn down an American flag, and on May 15 issued his famous General Order No. 28 which declared that "when any female shall . . . insult or show contempt for any officer or soldier of the United States, she shall be regarded and held liable to be treated as a woman of the town plying her avocation." The "Woman Order" had worldwide repercussions and was denounced by Lord Palmerston in the House of Commons.

With the loss of New Orleans the Confederates had now been driven from both ends of the great river that ran through much of their territory. But so long as they held the middle portions of the Mississippi, Yankee traffic could not get through.

A drawing of the *Louisiana* showing her as she was to look when completed. She had two covered paddle wheels plus two propellers to help with the steering.

This fine impressionistic drawing of the *Louisiana* being blown up by her own crew was made on the spot by William Waud for Leslie's *Weekly.*

101

The Battle of Memphis

Since the North was much more highly industrialized than the South, it was fortunate in having the services of a number of talented engineers, some of whom, like John Ericsson and James Eads, used their specialized knowledge to develop new ideas for naval warfare. Another Northern engineer, Charles Ellet, Jr., had built a number of railroad bridges and was so interested in the Mississippi Valley that he wrote two books about its physical geography. Ellet had been an observer in the Crimean War and had proposed that "ram-boats" be used then. During the early part of the Civil War he offered his services to the Federal Government but was rebuffed until the CSS *Virginia* terrified Washington in March 1862. Ellet was immediately commissioned a colonel and sent to the Ohio River to prepare a fleet of wooden steam rams which were to be under Army command. His basic idea was simple, cheap, fast, and relatively easy to put into effect. He proposed using the powerful steam engines of existing riverboats to drive rams made of sharp-pointed heavy timbers. Whenever possible, his boats were to run down with the current to add its force to their engines.

He purchased nine river steamers and quickly converted them. His little fleet arrived at Fort Pillow just after the Confederates evacuated it on June 4. Ellet kept going until he was about 25 miles north of Memphis. There his wooden rams were prepared for battle. Since they were relying on their hammering power rather than on guns, they were soon ready. Early on June 6 they went down to join the Union fleet anchored a mile above Memphis. They had hardly got there when firing was heard from Confederate gunboats coming up to meet them. Ellet led the attack in the *Queen of the West,* a steamer that was to make history in the fighting on the rivers. He headed her straight for the *General Lovell,* which turned slightly as the ram approached. The massive bow of the *Queen* plunged into the Confederate gunboat with such force that the *Lovell* was nearly cut in two and sank immediately. Meanwhile, the USS *Monarch* smashed into the *General Price,* knocking off the starboard paddle wheel and making the vessel unmanageable.

The CSS *Beauregard* and the *Sumter* (not to be confused with Semmes's raider) concentrated their fire on the *Queen.* In the conflict that followed, one of the *Queen's* paddle wheels was put out of commission, and her commander received a bullet in the knee. When she was run ashore near the *General Price,* a board-

THE BATTLE OF MEMPHIS. Ellet's wooden rams tangle

ing party was sent to the *Price* to make prisoners of her crew. The *Monarch* crashed into the *Beauregard,* forced her to surrender, and then went on to drive another Confederate steamer ashore.

Most of this decisive battle took place in full view of the city of Memphis, where tens of thousands of people had gathered on the bluffs to watch the spectacle. As the Confederates saw vessel after vessel in their fleet sunk, disabled, or captured, "many gazed through their flowing tears upon the struggle until the last hope gave way, and then the lamentations of the bereaved burst upon the ear in deep, heart-rending cries of anguish."

The Confederate spectators had good reason to grieve. A running battle down the river carried the fighting fleets out of sight, but when the day was over seven out of eight Confederate riverboats had been lost. Only the *General Earl Van Dorn* got away.

Colonel Ellet sent his son on shore with three men under a flag of truce to demand the surrender of Memphis. They met with a reception like that which had greeted the similar surrender party at New Orleans, but they finally reached the post office where they hauled down the Confederate flag and replaced it with the Union colors. The formal surrender of the city,

with the Confederate River Defense Fleet while the people of Memphis watch.

however, took place later when Federal troops arrived.

Ellet's leg wound at first did not seem to be serious, but like many apparently minor wounds in that day of inadequate medical knowledge, it brought on his death on June 21 while he was being taken up the river to Cairo. Strangely enough, he was the only casualty in the Union's wooden ram fleet. Confederate losses are not known because the gunboats were so widely scattered that it was impossible to determine how many men were killed or wounded. Many escaped by getting safely ashore.

A few days after the fall of Memphis, four Union gunboats and several troop transports went on a minor expedition that would probably have been forgotten if one of the most dreadful accidents in Civil War naval history had not made it memorable. The tiny fleet was on its way up the White River in Arkansas on June 17 when Confederate pickets opened fire on the gunboats. Troops were put ashore to drive back the pickets while the fleet proceeded, firing as it went. It soon came to a place where the river had been obstructed by sinking three boats in the channel. Commanding this was a battery on a bluff where the guns were hidden by a heavy growth of trees. The gunboats and the battery rapidly exchanged shots. Then the *Mound*

City steamed up to within 600 yards of the battery. As it approached, a shell from a gun on the bluff went through the port casemate, killing three men as it went on to blow up the steam drum. The interior of the gunboat was instantly filled with a roaring cloud of scalding steam. A few men jumped overboard, but most of the crew were terribly burned. Out of 175 men and officers more than a hundred died, and only 26 escaped injury.

When a new commander came on board to replace the badly scalded senior officer, he found that some of the survivors had ransacked the liquor stores and were so drunk that they were on a wild rampage. According to him, they robbed dying men, broke into officers' quarters to steal and wantonly smash everything in sight. The gunboat, oddly enough, was not seriously damaged and was soon back in service.

The Confederate battery on the bluff was charged by the infantry who captured it without difficulty. But the men in the fleet who witnessed the suffering of the injured on the *Mound City* never forgot what they saw that day. One of them wrote in an official report, "to endeavor to describe the howling of the wounded and the moaning of the dying is beyond the power of my feeble pen."

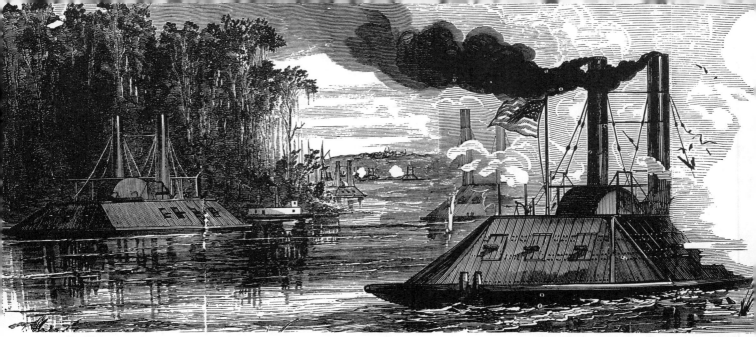

Leslie's *Weekly* again prints a highly inaccurate picture of the fight between the *Arkansas* and the *Carondelet*.

"*The ARKANSAS Is Coming!*"

Some warships, like the *Constitution* and Nelson's *Victory,* last for more than a century to become revered relics. Others, like the CS ram *Arkansas,* are used up quickly. This famous Confederate fighting ironclad's meteoric career lasted just 21 days—from July 15 to August 6—but in that short time she made naval history.

Her construction was begun in October 1861 in Memphis alongside the *Tennessee* (not to be confused with the ironclad that fought at Mobile in 1864), but the companion vessel had to be destroyed on June 5, 1862, when Ellet's wooden rams threatened the city. Before that time, the *Arkansas* had been removed in an unfinished state to the Yazoo River for completion. Work on her dragged until a new commander, Isaac N. Brown, arrived on May 29. He got rid of the previous commander although he said that he nearly had to shoot him to make him leave. Brown pushed construction and in a few weeks had the ironclad so far along that on June 24, General Earl Van Dorn suggested that the *Arkansas* come out of the Yazoo to run past the Union fleet in the Mississippi to inflict as much damage as possible. Then, much to Brown's disgust, the only Confederate vessels able to support him, the *General Earl Van Dorn, Polk,* and *Livingston* were burned to avoid capture when two Union rams came up the Yazoo on June 27.

But Brown went on with his plans for the *Arkansas.* The hurriedly built vessel was covered with railroad iron for armor; since there was no time to bend the metal, boiler plate was tacked over the curves "for appearance's sake." With ten guns, a crew of nearly 200, and with the ever present Lieutenant Charles W. Read as one of her officers, the *Arkansas* was ready to descend the Yazoo on July 12. Her engines gave trouble from the start. Steam leaked into the forward magazine and soaked the powder there. The ironclad stopped at a deserted sawmill where the wet powder was spread out on tarpaulins to dry in the sun. After three hours' sleep for the crew that night, the *Arkansas* was approaching the Mississippi at dawn. Read described her as she was made ready for battle: "The morning was warm and perfectly calm; the funnel rose high above the trees, and we knew that the enemy would soon be on the lookout for us. Pretty soon we discovered smoke above the trees. . . . The men of the *Arkansas* were now all at their stations, the guns were loaded and cast loose, their tackles in the hands of willing seamen ready to train; primers in the vents; locks thrown back and the lanyards in the hands of the gun captains; the decks sprinkled with sand and tourniquets and bandages at hand; t·ıbs filled with fresh water were between the guns, and down in the berth deck were the surgeons with their bright instruments, stimulants and lint, while along the passageways stood rows of men to pass powder, shell, and shot, and all was quiet save the dull thump, thump, of the propellers."

Soon a Union tug, which had been sent up the river to watch, dashed back to the Federal fleet with the

Actually it took place far from the Union fleet.

terrifying words: "The *Arkansas* is coming!"

The ironclad *Carondelet,* the *Tyler,* and the *Queen of the West* steamed up to meet the crude-looking monster which they described as "chocolate colored" because the *Arkansas'* iron was still covered with rust.

The *Tyler* was in the lead. She fired and then backed down the river in order to keep her powerful bow guns in action. The *Arkansas* ran down with the current and plunged into the *Carondelet,* forcing her aground. She then went for the *Tyler,* which turned and fled downstream with her less well-protected stern receiving the fire of the rapidly moving ironclad. Gwin, commander of the *Tyler,* shouted to Hunter of the *Queen* to ram the *Arkansas,* but Hunter scurried away to seek the shelter of the main fleet, using the excuse that he had been ordered to return and report if he saw the dreaded Confederate ironclad.

With no one to oppose her now, the *Arkansas* chased the *Tyler* into the Mississippi and advanced steadily toward the Union fleet which was lying above Vicksburg. There were 33 vessels in it—sloops of war, ironclads, wooden rams and gunboats, transports, mortar boats, and tugs, which presented, as Brown termed it, a forest of masts and smokestacks. The *Arkansas* headed for the long line of vessels, running in close so they could not get under way.

The *Lancaster* was one of her first victims. As the *Arkansas* went past, she fired more than 80 shots into the luckless gunboat, killing, scalding, and wounding many of her crew. Then on she ran with shot and shell from the outraged fleet bouncing off her iron sides. When she came in sight of the USS *Kineo,* a

fellow lieutenant sent for Read. He knew that Read felt that this gunboat was responsible for the death of Huger, the commander of the *McRae,* at New Orleans. The lieutenant said that Read came forward "leisurely and carelessly, swinging a primer lanyard. . . . I have never looked at a person displaying such coolness and self-possession." Read, who was in command of the two stern rifles, returned to them like a man entranced. When the *Arkansas* passed the *Kineo,* one of her bow guns put a shell through her, the port broadside roared out, and then Read had the last chance at her with his two 6-inch rifles.

The speeding ram, running downstream with the current, sent hasty shots at Farragut's *Hartford,* the *Richmond,* the *Benton,* and other big Union ships. But the firing from the massed guns of the Federal fleet riddled the *Arkansas'* tall smokestack, smashed her port shutters, while shrapnel and Minié balls penetrated the interior. Down below, in the inadequately ventilated engine room, the firemen were sweating in a temperature of 120°.

Vicksburg finally came in sight. People were crowding the shores there to greet the battered ironclad that had defied the entire Union fleet. But when some of the civilians saw what was in the gun deck, they hastily turned away. The *Arkansas* had had to pay dearly for her success. Acting Master's Mate J. A. Wilson said that "blood and brains bespattered everything, whilst arms, legs, and several headless trunks were strewn about." Besides injuries to some of the officers, 12 men had been killed and 18 were wounded. Union casualties were well over a hundred.

The *Arkansas* had already fought two battles that day, but she had to fight a third before midnight. At 9 P.M., 14 Union ships came down the river to attack her as she lay in the shadow of the high bluff at Vicksburg. Before she could get under way, a 160-pound bolt crashed through her makeshift armor and entered the engine room, killing and wounding more men. But the ram kept firing at the moving Union vessels as they passed. When they were gone, another burial party had to be sent ashore to inter 8 more men, while 11 wounded had to be cared for.

The Union naval commanders on the Mississippi had good reason to fear the *Arkansas.* It seemed as though the Confederates had at last built an ironclad that was fast, well-armored, and able to make good use of her heavy guns. They were afraid that so formidable a vessel might run down to New Orleans and spearhead a drive to recapture that important city. But the Union officers did not know that the *Arkansas'* engines were cranky and undependable.

Day after day, Federal mortar boats lobbed 13-inch

The *Arkansas* was particularly vulnerable from the rear, for she had no stern armor. When she ran into mechanical trouble near Baton Rouge and the *Essex* came after her, her engines worked just long enough to take her about 300 yards when the starboard one abruptly stopped. The ironclad was then steered into the riverbank, and her crew had a chance to escape the fire of the *Essex* by going ashore over the bows. The *Arkansas* was set on fire and turned adrift. Blazing brightly, she went down the river until she blew up. Lieutenant Read remained at the stern rifles firing at the advancing *Essex* until the *Arkansas* was in flames. He was one of the last to leave the doomed vessel.

shells in the general direction of the Vicksburg waterfront in an effort to hit the *Arkansas*. If one of them could be dropped to explode squarely on top of the ironclad it would surely wreck her, for she had no roof armor. The big shells fell all around her, but they did not make a direct hit.

Just before dawn on July 22 the Union fleet dropped down the river and for half an hour bombarded Vicksburg and its waterfront. Then the ironclad ram *Essex* emerged from the smoke and headed at full speed for the *Arkansas*.

The Confederate ram was in no condition to meet her adversary. Most of her crew were in hospitals, and she had trouble getting up enough steam to be maneuverable. One of her officers describes the engagement: "On she came like a mad bull, nothing daunted or overawed. As soon as Capt. Brown got a fair view of her . . . he divined her intent, and seeing that she was as square across the bow as a flat boat or scow, and we were as sharp as a wedge, he determined at once to foil her tactics. Slacking off the hawser which held our head to the bank, he went ahead on the starboard screw, and thus our sharp prow was turned directly to her to hit against. This disconcerted the enemy and destroyed his plan. A collision would surely cut him down and leave us uninjured. All this time we had not been idle spectators. The two Columbiads had been ringing on his front and piercing him every shot; to which he did not reply until he found that the shoving game was out of the question; then, and when not more than fifty yards distant, he triced up his three bow port shutters and poured out his fire. A nine-inch shot struck our armor a few inches forward of the unlucky forward port, and crawling along the side entered. Seven men were killed outright and six wounded. Splinters flew in all directions. In an in-

stant the enemy was alongside, and his momentum was so great that he ran aground a short distance astern of us. As he passed, we poured out our port broadside, and as soon as the stern rifles could be cleared . . . we went ahead on our port screw and turned our stern guns on him, every man—we had but seventeen left—and officer went to them. As he passed he did not fire; nor did he whilst we were riddling him close aboard. His only effort was to get away from us. . . . But *our* troubles were not over. We had scarcely shook this fellow off before we were called to the other end of the ship—we ran from one gun to another to get ready for a second attack. The *Queen* [*of the West*] was now close to us, evidently determined to ram us. The guns had been fired and were now empty and inboard. *Somehow* we got them loaded and run out, and by the time she commenced to round to . . . we struck her with the Columbiads as she came down. . . . Capt. Brown adopted the plan of turning his head to her also, and thus received her blow glancing. She came into us going at . . . fifteen miles an hour. . . . His blow, though glancing, was a heavy one. His prow . . . made a hole through our side and caused the ship to career and roll heavily; but we all knew in an instant that no serious damage had been done. . . . He ran into the bank astern of us and got the contents of the stern battery; but . . . was soon off into deep water. . . . Beating off these two vessels, under the circumstances, was the best achievement of the *Arkansas*."

General Van Dorn then ordered the *Arkansas* to go to Baton Rouge to support an army attack there. The Confederate ironclad got to within a few miles of the city when her starboard engine gave out. Her nemesis, the *Essex,* appeared in the morning and began firing. In order to avoid capture, the *Arkansas* was destroyed.

THE TORPEDO THAT SANK THE *CAIRO*

Captain I. N. Brown, who had been in command of the historic *Arkansas* when she ran the Union fleet, was left to guard the Yazoo River after his ironclad was blown up. He made this crude torpedo from 5-gallon glass demijohns filled with gunpowder borrowed from the Army. The *Cairo* hit two of these glass containers supported by wooden floats and connected by a wire. She drew them against her sides as she went forward and pulled the friction primers which fired both torpedoes with fatal effect. RIGHT: A photograph of the *Cairo*.

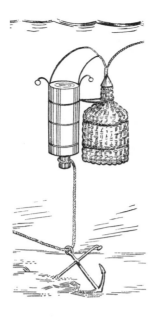

A Torpedo Sinks the USS CAIRO

Naval history was made on December 12, 1862, when a Confederate torpedo blew up the USS *Cairo*, for that was the first time an underwater mine ever successfully sank a ship of war. The *Cairo* was one of the Eads ironclads which had just been made shot-proof by placing railroad iron over her most vulnerable spots.

She was sent up the Yazoo River on a reconnaissance in company with three gunboats and the ever active *Queen of the West*. It was known that the Yazoo was heavily mined at this time, but so many of the early torpedoes had proved to be harmless that, as Admiral Porter wrote to Gideon Welles, "officers have not felt that respect for them to which they are entitled." Porter thought that the one which destroyed the *Cairo* must have been fired by a galvanic battery, but it was not. It was one of the common, homemade variety shown above.

When sharpshooters on one of the gunboats leading the way up the river began firing at a block of wood floating in the water, Lieutenant Selfridge, who was in command of the *Cairo,* ordered the ironclad to go ahead so he could see what was happening.

Two boats were lowered and sent out with men who were told to examine the buoy. One man found a line running from the shore into the river. When he cut this with his sword, a large object rose out of the water. He pulled this toward him and saw that it was a torpedo. He was ordered to destroy the strange device.

When the cumbersome riverboats got under way again, there was some difficulty about which one was to go first. While this was being straightened out, Lieutenant Selfridge reported that "two sudden explosions in quick succession occurred, one close to my port quarter, the other under my port bow—the latter so severe as to raise the guns . . . some distance from the deck. . . . [The *Cairo*] commenced to fill so rapidly that in two or three minutes the water was over her forecastle. . . . Her whole frame was so completely shattered that I found immediately that nothing more could be effected than to move the sick and the arms. . . . The *Cairo* sank in about 12 minutes after the explosion, going totally out of sight, except the top of her chimneys, in about six fathoms of water. I am happy to say that though some half a dozen men were injured, no lives were lost."

The other boats quickly destroyed everything that remained above water so the Confederates could not salvage metal and guns from the *Cairo*. She remained on the bottom of the Yazoo River for nearly a century.

In the autumn of 1956, Edwin C. Bearss, Research Historian of the National Park Service at Vicksburg, went exploring the river with a geologist friend in an effort to find the wreck of the *Cairo*. By using a compass dip, they were finally able to locate the huge mass of sunken metal. They then ran long probes into the muddy bed of the Yazoo to trace the outlines of the long-submerged hulk. Skin divers went down to examine the wreck. They found it half silted over but in surprisingly good condition. After long preparation, a boat-crane was brought up, and on September 14, 1960, the pilothouse of the *Cairo* was hauled from the water. (SEE PAGE 254 for a naval gun which was recovered at the same time.) There are plans to raise the entire ironclad and restore it to the way it looked during the Civil War.

The pilothouse of the *Cairo* is raised in 1960.

The *Teaser's* 32-pounder. Note compressor slide screw.

THE CAPTURE OF THE CSS *TEASER*

On July 4, 1862, the USS *Maratzana,* a new double-ender side-wheel steamer, went up the James River accompanied by the *Monitor* to investigate some Confederate gunboats said to be lying near Turkey Bend. Late in the afternoon the two ships caught sight of the CSS *Teaser,* a former tug armed with a 32-pounder and a 12-pounder. The *Teaser* had met the *Monitor* when she accompanied the *Virginia* in the historic battle of the ironclads at Hampton Roads.

Some say that the *Teaser* was aground; others that the nature of her work (laying torpedoes) made it impossible for her to get away. So she stood her ground and fired defiantly at the two much more powerful vessels that were rapidly bearing down on her.

The *Maratzana* fired back, sending two shots in rapid succession across the water. Confederate officers and crew hastily piled into small boats to row ashore, for they knew they had no chance in the uneven encounter. They had hardly pulled away from the *Teaser* when a shell from the *Maratzana* struck the abandoned tug amidships and blew up her boiler. The *Maratzana* then hauled the captured gunboat down the river to be repaired and turned over to the Union Navy.

On the face of it, the incident seems so trivial that it would ordinarily not be worth reporting. The little *Teaser* wasn't worth much, and she was badly damaged. But worth far more than the tiny gunboat was the vital information she carried. On her were found the following ultrasecret papers:

1. A map showing the positions of 19 large torpedoes in the James River that could be detonated electrically from the shore.

The shattered deck of the *Teaser*.

The *Teaser's* 12-pounder.

2. A long letter to Secretary Mallory from the Confederate scientist Matthew Fontaine Maury (SEE PAGE 120) describing the torpedoes and explaining how they worked.

3. A letter from Mallory to Lieutenant Hunter Davidson dated June 20, 1862, ordering him to relieve Maury of the torpedo work on the river. Davidson had been in command of the *Teaser* and had safely escaped, but he had not had time to take or destroy these papers. He also had had to abandon what the Union report described as "a Confederate balloon, a quantity of submarine telegraphic wire, and other appliances for submarine batteries."

In addition to all this booty, the luckless *Teaser* yielded an even more important find. This was detailed information about the ironclad *Richmond* (sometimes called the *Virginia* No. 2), which was then under construction at the capital city of the Confederacy. Federal authorities had known about this ship from the moment of her inception, for a notice appealing to the public to donate money to build her had appeared in the Richmond *Dispatch* on March 17, 1862. Citizens of Virginia eagerly contributed cash, and the women of the state organized a Ladies Defense Association to solicit jewelry, silver, and other valuable objects to help finance the undertaking. Iron railings were pulled down from houses, and scrap from farms, homes, and factories was gathered to furnish raw material so the furnaces of the Tredegar Ironworks could make armor for the ship.

Construction work had gone forward on the *Richmond* day and night with Mallory calling for extra hands to be brought into the city to expedite the already stepped-up schedule. She was to be ready for action a few weeks after the detailed plans on the *Teaser* were captured. Harper's *Weekly* published them on July 26. She appears there to be a much more formidable vessel than she actually was, for she carried only four guns, not nine as the Harper's sketches indicate.

Even so, she was formidable enough to give good cause for worry to the Federal Navy. All sorts of strange plans were made to destroy her. Perhaps the strangest of all was one that called for lashing two gunboats together with a pair of giant spring tongs held between them. With this device they were to seize the *Richmond* and push her ashore. Needless to say, the plan was never put into effect.

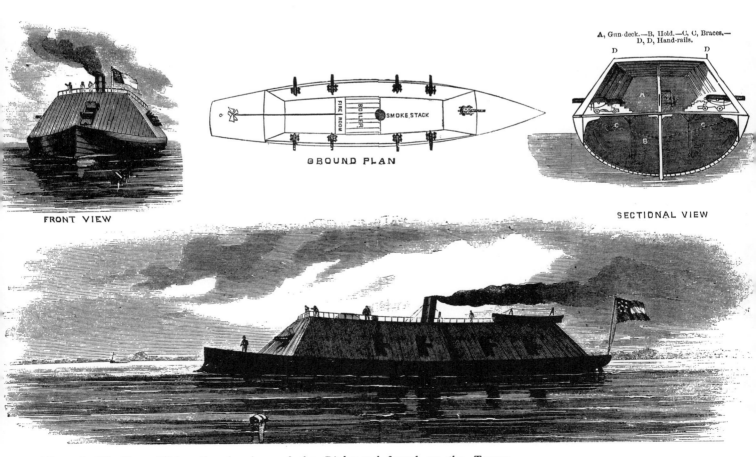

FRONT VIEW

GROUND PLAN

A, Gun-deck.—B, Hold.—C, C, Braces,—D, D, Hand-rails.

SECTIONAL VIEW

Harper's *Weekly* publishes the drawings of the *Richmond* found on the *Teaser*.

CAPTURES AND RECAPTURES

In January 1961 the world was startled when a group of Portuguese insurgents, disguised as passengers, seized the Portuguese cruise ship *Santa Maria* at sea. International law is so hazy on such an infrequent occurrence that highly placed governmental officials in several neutral countries called the seizure piracy. They soon changed their minds or at least became silent. The ship went to a Brazilian port where the passengers and crew were put ashore, and the insurgents were allowed to go free. The *Santa Maria* was returned to Portugal.

The point at issue, of course, was whether the men who seized the ship did so for personal gain or for political purposes. Had they done so for personal gain their act might have been declared piracy—i.e., robbery on the high seas. Similar legal difficulties arose during the Civil War when bands of Confederates dis-

guised as passengers took over Northern vessels at the point of a gun. At first the Union attempted to charge the men with piracy, but when the Confederacy threatened to retaliate—as it did in the case of captured privateersmen—the charges were modified.

An early instance of a seizure of a ship during the Civil War was Zarvona's capture of the *St. Nicholas,* already mentioned on page 39. Other seizures and counterseizures, under widely varying circumstances, soon took place. One of the most unusual was the case of the sailing ship *Emily St. Pierre* which was captured off Charleston on March 18, 1862, by the USS *James Adger.* The *Emily St. Pierre* had British papers and had come from Calcutta with a cargo of 2173 bales of gunny cloth. But she was on the Union blockade list of suspected vessels because she had formerly been of Charleston ownership. Acting Master Josiah Stone and a small prize crew were put on board her with orders to deliver her to the U. S. District Attorney in Philadelphia for adjudication.

Three days later, when the ship was sailing in good weather about 30 miles off Cape Hatteras, the British captain, William Wilson, asked the Acting Master in a pleasant voice to be good enough to go to the cabin and show him the ship's position on the chart. Stone agreed to do so. He describes what happened then: "While in the cabin, Captain Wilson grabbed me by my collar and drew a belaying pin from under his vest; at the same time the cook and steward sprang out of a room, put two revolvers at my head, threatened my life, put me in irons, put me in a small room, and locked me in and then told me that he had taken Mr. Hornsby, the master's mate, and Mr. John S. Smith the same way. He went into these officers' rooms while they were asleep, put them in irons, and put gags in their mouths; after this he went on deck. Six of the men being asleep in the forecastle he locked them in. He then got three of the men that were on deck to go down aft in a scuttle and pass up a coil of rigging; told the men that I wanted it. When the men were down he put the hatches on and thus had all the crew fastened up except three. He then got some of the crew to help him work the ship. . . . He shot one man at the time, but did not kill him; he is getting well, and one man on the passage fell from the foreyard on deck and died the next day, of which I was not told. . . . Myself and master's mate were kept confined all the passage, 31 days."

When Williams brought his recaptured ship into Liverpool on April 21, the British greeted him as a

CAPTAIN WILLIAM WILSON of the *Emily St. Pierre.*

hero for outwitting the Yankees. The ship's owner awarded him £2000, and at a testimonial dinner he was presented with "a magnificent service of plate" and a gold chronometer watch. When his officers and crew arrived from America they gave him a fine sextant. (Oddly enough, this sextant was found among the navigational instruments on an American merchant ship at Norfolk after the Second World War and was deposited in the Mariners Museum at Newport News in 1948.)

Another ship capture that attracted a great deal of attention was that of the Charleston gunboat *Planter*, formerly a wood-burning cotton boat. This small steamer had white officers and a Negro crew of eight. Headed by Robert Smalls, a slave, the crew plotted to run off with the boat, and at 3 A.M., May 3, 1862, when the officers were asleep on shore, the Negroes brought their families on board and steamed out into the harbor flying the Confederate flag. When they approached Fort Sumter, they gave the usual signal on the steam whistle and were allowed to pass unchallenged by the unsuspecting sentinel there. They headed toward the Federal blockading fleet, hoisted a white flag, and turned the vessel over to the nearest ship.

Since the *Planter* was not only armed with a 32-pounder and a 24-pounder howitzer but also had on board five large unmounted guns which were to be taken to a new battery that day, Smalls and his crew were given an enthusiastic welcome. The Northern press made much of the story, and Congress passed a special act awarding Smalls and his men half the appraised value of the *Planter* and the guns, a sum which amounted to $4584 as a reward.

Smalls may have been encouraged to capture the *Planter* by two even bolder deeds committed by Negroes the year before. Shortly after the *Enchantress* had been seized by the Confederate privateer *Jefferson Davis* on July 6, 1861, and was being sent to Charleston as a prize, she was stopped at sea by the USS *Albatross* for questioning. While the interrogation was going on, the Negro cook, who had been captured with the vessel, jumped overboard and swam to the *Albatross* to tell her captain the true state of affairs. The suspected ship was then seized by the *Albatross*.

Far more violent was the affair of the schooner *S. J. Waring*, which was captured by the *Jefferson Davis* the day after it took the *Enchantress*. Again a colored cook was left on board to serve the prize crew. When the ship was nearing Charleston, the cook crept into the cabin during the night and killed the captain and the two mates. He then brought the ship into New York where he was received as a hero, employed as an attraction by Barnum's Museum, and awarded $7000 as prize money.

ROBERT SMALLS

The sextant presented to Captain Wilson.

The *Planter* running past Fort Sumter.

COLUMBIA   PETREL   MEMPHIS   ELIZABETH   ELLA WARLY   PATRAS   ALLIANCE   ANN STETTIN

Captured British blockade-runners lying at anchor in New York Harbor.

BLOCKADE-RUNNING IN 1862

This picture of captured blockade-runners, published in Harper's *Weekly* on October 18, 1862, a year and a half after the beginning of the war, is evidence that the Federal blockade was tightening. By this time the Federal Navy had 256 ships for blockade duty and was constantly adding to them. Even Earl Russell had reluctantly admitted early in 1862 that the blockade was effective because it was becoming dangerous for a ship to try to enter a Southern port. He still felt, however, that America was large enough to support two republics and that the war would end with Southern independence successfully established.

In 1861, after the blockade had been proclaimed, some 500 or 600 ships entered and left Southern ports. Only one out of ten was captured. In 1862 the story was changing. The ratio of successful voyages fell to eight in one. It was to fall still further in the years to come.

Most of the ships engaged in blockade-running were of British registry. And some of their captains were British Navy officers temporarily retired from service who sailed under assumed names. Prominent among them was Hugh Burgoyne who went down with the ill-fated *Captain* on a trial run with her designer, Cowper Coles of ironclad-turret fame, when she capsized in a gale in September 1870 and sank with nearly 500 men. Another was W. N. W. Hewett who became a vice-admiral in 1884 after a long and eventful career in Her Majesty's Navy. An officer known during the Civil War years only as "Murray" later became Admiral Murray-Aynsley. Most remarkable of all, however, was the adventurous captain who called himself Roberts. Actually he was the third son of the sixth Earl of Buckinghamshire and was christened Augustus Charles Hobart-Hampden. He was a successful blockade-runner, making eighteen successful voyages, but he achieved even greater fame afterward as commander of the Turkish fleet. In 1869 the Sultan awarded him the title of Pasha, and as Hobart Pasha he became one of the most glamorous of British naval heroes.

When ships like those shown in the illustration were captured they were usually put into blockade service, so there are many instances of former blockade-runners being used against ships that were trying to bring in arms and supplies for the South. And the capture of Confederate ports on the Atlantic and Gulf coasts cut down the number of places to which a blockade-runner could go. Nevertheless, the highly profitable trade continued almost unabated even though it became more and more difficult for a ship to get through.

CIRCASSIAN   *TUBAL*   *CAIN*

CONFEDERATE RAIDERS

The FLORIDA

The blockade-runners were glamour ships that brought rich rewards to their owners and the men who sailed them, but the sea raiders had a thankless and unpleasant job to do. Destroying enemy commerce was necessary in an all-out war, but no one liked having to do it. Bulloch, who was in charge of building the sea raiders in Europe, candidly admitted his distaste for their work: "There can be no doubt that the destruction of unarmed and peaceful merchant ships, while quietly pursuing their voyages on the high seas, is a practice not defensible upon the principles of the moral law; and it does not in these modern times harmonize with the general sentiments of commercial nations. . . . The feeling everywhere in Europe is strongly against the destruction of private property at sea, which cannot always be identified as that of your enemy. . . . The individual members of the Government at Richmond no doubt held opinions on the above subject which were in harmony with the common sentiment of Europe; and if in matters of state policy, and under pressure of great political convulsions, the application of the moral law could be regulated upon the principles which should be paramount in the personal relations among men, they would have been happy to spare the commerce of the United States, and the peaceful trader would have been left to pursue his commercial voyages without fear or molestation. But no one will pretend that Cabinets and Ministers in their collective capacities can act under the same restraints of conscience or of law as control the conduct of individuals in their personal intercourse with each other; and when two nations unhappily fall out and go to war, the government of each does its best to inflict the greatest possible amount of injury upon the other on the principle that the more burdensome and afflicting the state of war can be made to the opposing party, the more quickly will he consent to terms of peace."

The two sea raiders which Bulloch was having built on the Mersey were now nearing completion. The first to sail was the *Oreto* (later the *Manassas* and then the *Florida*) which departed from Liverpool on March 22, 1862. She left England without arms and went to the Bahamas to pick up her Confederate commander, Captain John Newland Maffitt, who had entered the United States Navy as a midshipman when he was thirteen years old. After a long and varied career he resigned on April 28, 1861, to become a lieutenant in the Confederate States Navy. He served on the gunboat *Savannah* and was in command of her during the battle of Port Royal on November 7, 1861. When Bulloch brought the *Fingal* through the blockade a few days later, and his heavily laden ship grounded in the Savannah River, Maffitt was on hand to pull him free. The two men first met then. Bulloch was so impressed with the obviously capable and experienced officer that he recommended him to Richmond as a commander for one of the raiders under construction in England.

When the *Oreto* left Liverpool, a ship named the *Bahama* sailed from Scotland with the guns and ammunition which British law would not permit the intended sea raider to take on board. The *Oreto* arrived in Nassau first. She was promptly seized upon

JOHN NEWLAND MAFFITT

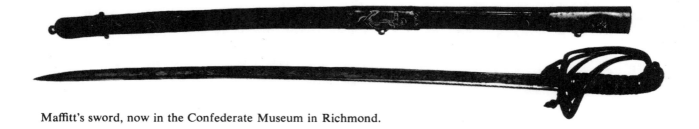

Maffitt's sword, now in the Confederate Museum in Richmond.

A painting of the *Florida* believed to have been made while she was in the Bahamas.

complaint of the American consul there, but after court action was finally let go. Meanwhile Maffitt had lost his crew and had to sail with 20 hastily hired local men instead of the 130 the ship needed for cruising and going into action. With her went a small schooner with the guns and ammunition brought from England in the *Bahama*. The two ships anchored near Green Key, a small coral island about 75 miles south of Nassau.

Transhipping then began. It was August, the sun was hot, there weren't enough men to do the work; and, worst of all, yellow fever, already encountered in Nassau, struck the crew. One man died, and several others were stricken, but the work of loading had to go on. On the morning of August 17, 1862, the ship at last got under way, flying a Confederate flag for the first time, and bearing her new name *Florida*.

She carried the terrible scourge of yellow fever with her. Two days later she had to put into Cardenas, Cuba, for medical aid. By this time the ship had become a floating hospital. Maffitt himself was struck by the disease. The week from August 22 to 29 was a total blank to him. When he became aware of what

was going on around him he found that his stepson, who had sailed with him, was dying. Four others died at the same time.

Maffitt insisted on going on to Havana as soon as they had buried their dead. They picked up a pilot there who knew the entrance to the nearest Confederate port—Mobile—and Maffitt resolved to keep going, for the Yankee fleet was looking for him. He avoided it by sailing close inshore while he ran along the coast of Cuba at night. Then, still ill, and with some of the crew afflicted with fever, he headed northwest across the open waters of the Gulf toward Mobile.

His pilot had told him that only one Federal blockader was guarding the port, but as often happened in wartime, this information was out of date. Three Union ships were waiting off Fort Morgan at the entrance to Mobile Bay when Maffitt arrived there on September 4. The nightmare voyage was now climaxed by a misfortune that rendered them helpless when they had to face the enemy's armed ships. Through some oversight, or perhaps from too great haste in loading, equipment needed to operate the *Florida's* guns had not been put on board. The defenseless ship would have to run through devastating fire without being able to reply.

Maffitt was so weakened by fever that he had to be carried on deck to command the *Florida* when she ran the gauntlet. He ordered the British flag to be displayed, hoping that the ruse would make the Federal officers hesitate to fire on what was obviously a British-built ship. Then he steamed full speed ahead, straight at the flagship *Oneida*. Maffitt describes what happened: "When quite near the *Oneida* I was hailed and ordered to heave to immediately. . . . A shot was fired across my bow previously to the hail. I declined . . . to obey the order, and immediately received a broadside, the effect of which was to carry away all my hammock nettings and much of my standing and running rigging. The superior speed of the *Florida* enabled me to pass the *Oneida*. She continued her bombardment. One 11-inch shell passed through the coal bunkers on the port side, struck the port forward boiler, took off one man's head as it passed on the berth deck, wounding nine men. If it had exploded, which it failed to do, I no doubt would have lost every man in the vessel except the two men at the helm, as I had ordered all the crew below. Immediately after this a shot from the *Winona* entered the cabin and passed through the pantry; an 11-inch shell from the *Oneida* exploded close to the port gangway and seriously wounded the vessel. The fire from . . . the *Oneida*, increased in warmth and destruction, carrying away all the standing and most of the running rigging of my vessel. I endeavored to make sail and succeeded so far only as letting fall the topsails. Several men were wounded in the rigging, the sheets and tyes shot away, so that I was not enabled to set the sails properly. At this moment I hauled down the English flag, under which I was sailing as a *ruse de guerre,* and gave the order to one of the helmsmen to hoist the Confederate flag. At that moment he . . . lost his forefinger with a shrapnel shot, so that my order in regard to the flag could not be complied with. During all this time shell and shrapnel were bursting over us and around us, the shrapnel striking the hull and the spars at almost every discharge. We made no effort at resistance, for though armed, we were not at all equipped, having neither rammers nor sponges, sights, quoins, nor elevating screws. . . . When we anchored under the guns of Fort Morgan shortly after sundown, the *Florida* was a perfect wreck, and only succeeded in escaping by the smoothness of the sea and her superior speed. The 11-inch shell which came in and passed along the berth deck entered three inches above the waterline, and if there had been any sea on our bilge pumps would not have saved the vessel from sinking. An idea of the damage done to the *Florida* may be comprehended by the fact that it took three months and a half to repair her."

Again the *Florida* buried her dead, and more were to die of yellow fever on shore. But Maffitt had brought his ship in, damaged but still afloat.

During the long months while the *Florida* was under repair, Maffitt slowly got a crew together. Since it was considered an honor to serve under so daring a captain, he had his pick of the best young officers in the Confederate Navy. At least one of them was to distinguish himself the next summer by a series of independent raids along the Atlantic Coast. This was Lieutenant Charles W. Read, who had already made a reputation for himself as a fearless fighter at the battle of New Orleans when he had taken over the *McRae* after her commander was mortally wounded. And then he had been on the ram *Arkansas* while she fought Federal gunboats up and down the Mississippi River. Maffitt had asked for this remarkable young man's services and was glad to have him on board.

A painting showing the *Florida* running into Mobile Bay.

The *Alabama* stops a merchant ship at sea.

The ALABAMA

The other Confederate sea raider building on the Mersey was also nearing completion in the spring of 1862. Known only by her shipyard number, 290, the new raider was christened the *Henrica* when she was launched on May 15. Now that they had seen how easily the *Florida* had escaped, American diplomatic and consular officials in England kept close watch on the building of the 290 and brought pressure to bear on the British not to let her go to sea.

She made a successful trial trip on June 14. Bulloch had made the same kind of plans to arm her outside England as he had done with the *Florida*. This time, however, he chose an isolated bay on the island of Terceira in the Azores as a rendezvous. (This was the place he had noted when the *Fingal* put in there the year before.) A bark named the *Agrippina* was to sail from London with the arms, ammunition, and coal to meet her there.

Bulloch had expected to be given command of the new raider and was looking forward to being in active service again. But Semmes's cruise in the *Sumter* had come to an end in Gibraltar in April when his ship, with her engines played out, had been blockaded in that port by Federal men of war. Word came from

Richmond for Semmes to take command of the new raider while Bulloch was to concentrate on trying to obtain ironclads for the Confederacy.

On July 26, Bulloch was privately informed that he had better get his ship out of the Mersey in less than 48 hours in order to save her from being impounded by the British. He told the Lairds that he wanted to take the ship for another trial run. He then put his British captain and a skeleton crew on board, invited guests to watch the test of speed, dressed the ship with flags as if for a gala excursion, and took her down the river accompanied by a steam tug. When he reached open water he told his guests that he wanted to keep the ship out all night and politely requested them to return to Liverpool with him on the tug. The next morning he had the same tug take him and the rest of the crew to the waiting ship. When he left the landing stage, a telegram was handed to him, telling him that the USS *Tuscarora* had sailed from Southampton and would be searching for him.

On August 1, when the ship was near the Giant's Causeway on the coast of Ireland, Bulloch went ashore in a fishing boat and returned to Liverpool, where he telegraphed to London to send the *Agrippina* to the rendezvous off Terceira.

Semmes came to England, and Bulloch went with

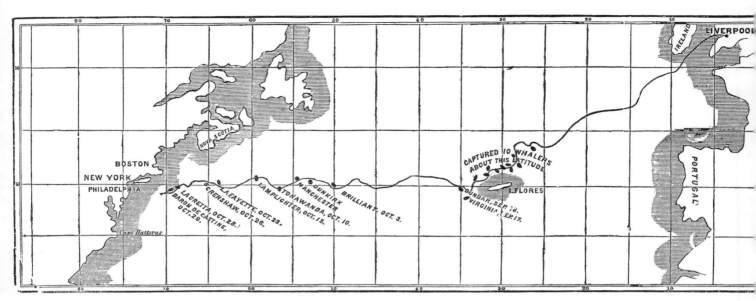

Harper's *Weekly* prints a chart showing the probable course of the *Alabama.*

The *Alabama* in a hurricane on October 16, 1862.

him to Terceira, where they arrived on August 20. They had everything quickly transferred to the new raider which then received the name *Alabama.* On the twenty-fourth the new raider displayed the Confederate flag for the first time and began her operations as a commerce destroyer.

During his seven months' cruise on the *Sumter,* Semmes had stopped about 70 ships at sea. Most of them had been let go as neutrals, but he had captured 18, of which he burned seven. This was just a prelude to his exploits in the *Alabama.* In her he was to carry

the Confederate flag to the far corners of the world and practically drive all Yankee shipping off the oceans.

Semmes described with expert accuracy the new ship he was proudly taking to sea: "She was of about 900 tons burden, 230 feet in length, 32 feet in breadth, 20 feet in depth, and drew, when provisioned and coaled for a cruise, 15 feet of water. Her model was of the most perfect symmetry, and she sat upon the water with the lightness and grace of a swan. She was barkentine-rigged, with long lower masts, which enabled her to carry large fore-and-aft sails, as jibs and try-sails, which are of so much importance to a steamer in so many emergencies. Her sticks were of the best yellow pine that would bend in a gale like a willow wand without breaking, and her rigging was of the best of Swedish iron wire. The scantling of the vessel was light, compared with vessels of her class in the Federal Navy, but this was scarcely a disadvantage as she was designed as a scourge of the enemy's commerce rather than for battle. She was to defend herself simply if defence should become necessary. Her engine was of three hundred horsepower, and she had attached an apparatus for condensing from the vapor of seawater all the fresh water that her crew might require. She was a perfect steamer and a perfect sailing ship at the same time, neither of her two modes of locomotion being at all dependent upon the other. . . . The *Alabama* was so constructed that in fifteen minutes her propeller could be detached from the shaft and lifted (in a well contrived for the purpose) sufficiently high out of the water not to be an impediment to her speed. When this was done, and her sails spread, she was to all intents and purposes a sailing ship. On the other hand, when I desired to use her as a steamer, I had only to start the fires, lower the propeller, and if the wind was adverse, brace her yards to the wind, and the conversion was complete. The speed of the *Alabama* was always greatly overrated by the enemy. She was ordinarily about a tenknot ship. She was said to have made eleven knots and a half on her trial trip, but we never afterward got it out of her. Under steam and sail both, we logged on one occasion thirteen knots and a quarter, which was her utmost speed.

"Her armament consisted of eight guns; six 32-pounders, in broadside, and two pivot guns amidships; one on the forecastle, and the other abaft the mainmast—the former a 100-pounder rifled Blakeley, and the latter a smooth-bore eight-inch. The Blakeley gun was so deficient in metal compared with the weight of shot it threw that after the first few discharges, when it became a little heated, it was of comparatively small use to us, to such an extent were we obliged to reduce the charge of powder on account of the recoil. The average crew of the *Alabama* before the mast was about 120 men and 24 officers, as follows: A captain, four lieutenants, surgeon, paymaster, master, marine officer, four engineers, two midshipmen, and four master's mates, a captain's clerk, boatswain, gunner, sailmaker, and carpenter. The cost of the ship, with everything complete, was $250,000."

Yankee whalers were finishing their season near the Azores late in August, for their quarry moves to other feeding grounds as the year wanes. Semmes thus had to hurry. On September 5 he saw the *Ocmulgee* of Edgartown, Massachusetts, lying to with a huge whale alongside, which the crew were stripping of blubber. The ship was an easy capture. Semmes took her crew of 37 and some stores to feed them while they lived on the *Alabama* and then burned the ship the next morning. The oil-soaked timbers burned fiercely and sent up a great cloud of smoke. Semmes carried his prisoners to one of the nearby islands and sent them ashore in their own whaleboats.

Since the whaling season in the Azores was ending, and since he had already destroyed a good part of the Yankee whaling fleet there, Semmes decided to sail west along the sea-lane where American ships bound for Europe laden with newly harvested grain would pass.

He burned a number of ships along this route and was interrupted only by a violent hurricane that came roaring up from the south. It reached its height on October 16 when the *Alabama* passed through its center, but, despite much buffeting, managed to survive. Semmes continued his work of destruction for the next month; then he ran into Fort de France Bay on the western side of Martinique to meet his tender, the *Agrippina,* which was waiting there for him with a much-needed supply of coal. Knowing that he could not load it in the harbor, he sent the tender to the island of Blanquilla off the coast of Venezuela. It was lucky he did so, for he immediately ran into trouble.

Bumboats which came out to the ship to sell fruit and tobacco to the sailors also sold them hard liquor. Many of the crew got drunk and became riotous; some of them even threatened mutiny. Semmes had the worst offenders arrested and then doused with buckets of seawater until they were not only sober but sorry. It was the only mutiny on the *Alabama*.

This was minor trouble, but real disaster loomed the next morning when a large ship entered the harbor and hoisted the American flag. It was the *San Jacinto* of *Trent* and Mason and Slidell fame. Since the man-of-war was far more heavily armed than the much smaller *Alabama,* Semmes knew he could not stand up against her in battle, but he also knew that his ship was much faster. All day the men on the *Alabama* watched the sailors on the Federal warship prepare her for action. But when night came on and rain set in, Semmes headed his ship out of the harbor with all lights out and every gun manned. He ran out, avoiding notice in the darkness, and went to Blanquilla to meet the *Agrippina*. Then he prepared to go on to Galveston, Texas, where northern newspapers taken from ships captured at sea had told him that a Federal expedition was expected to attack that port early in January.

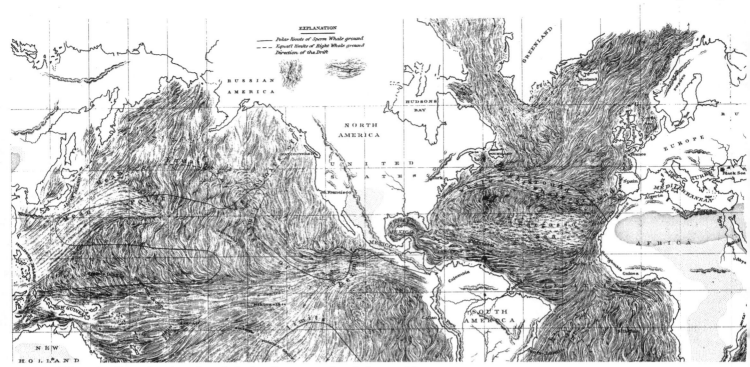

Maury's chart showing the whale-hunting grounds of the world.

CONFEDERATE SCIENTIST—

Matthew Fontaine Maury

Just as the South had acquired the services of the country's best practical shipping man when James Dunwoody Bulloch joined its cause, so did it obtain the services of the nation's outstanding oceanographer when Virginia-born Matthew Fontaine Maury threw in his lot with the Confederacy as soon as his native state seceded. Maury had begun his career in the United States Navy in 1825 as a midshipman and had many years of practical experience at sea. In 1834 he brought out a useful book entitled *A New Theoretical and Practical Treatise on Navigation.* In 1842 he was appointed superintendent of the Depot of Charts and Instruments, which later became the United States Naval Observatory and Hydrographical Office.

Using old logbooks and reports as the basis for information, Maury issued in 1847 his famous *Wind and Current Charts of the North Atlantic,* which he later amplified by using data sent to him by ship captains all over the world. His charts and sailing directions made it possible to save many days on long sea voyages. His *Physical Geography of the Sea,* published in 1855, was translated into many languages, bringing its author international fame. He played an important role in planning the first transatlantic cable, and also

mapped two ocean lanes across the Atlantic to prevent collisions between ships bound on opposing courses.

When it became known that Maury had joined the Confederate Navy, Grand Duke Constantine invited him to come to Russia where he would be free to continue his scientific researches. Soon afterward he received a similar invitation from Napoleon III to settle in France. He refused both offers and concentrated all his efforts to help the Confederacy.

At first he was put in charge of fortifying Jamestown Island and Gloucester Point, but he soon began to make plans for defending the waters of the Confederacy by using torpedoes. His first idea was to tie them together in pairs to float downstream and catch on the bows of a ship. One or both of the torpedoes would then be brought to the side of the ship by the current and explode on contact. The plan seemed fine on paper, but it worked out poorly in practice (SEE PAGE 182).

Maury promptly turned his inventive ability to torpedoes to be exploded by electricity. This had been tried years before by Robert Fulton and also by Samuel Colt, but since the time of their experiments insulation for underwater cables had been greatly improved; so had electric batteries. It was now possible to send enough current to a distant underwater torpedo to explode it. Maury conducted his first experiments on the James River. When he was able to demonstrate the effectiveness of his new weapon, some Confederate officials opposed the idea of using torpedoes because they considered them inhuman. They were overruled, and a Torpedo Bureau was organized in Richmond.

Maury also devised a scheme to attack the Federal Navy in a series of well-planned and well-coordinated raids to be made by squads of five or ten inexpensive wooden steam launches. These forerunners of the PT boats of World War II were to be 112 feet long, 21 feet in beam, and draw only 6 feet of water. Each was to carry two large guns, one forward and one aft. Maury wanted 100 of them built, but when the *Merrimack-Virginia* proved herself at Hampton Roads, Confederate Navy brass became enamored with ironclads and lost interest in Maury's launches.

He was sent to England, and after arriving there in the autumn of 1862 he continued his investigations on electric torpedoes, but spent most of his time looking for ships for the Confederate Navy. Maury was a great scientist and an experienced naval officer, but he did not have Bulloch's practical background in shipping. Also he was unfortunate in arriving late on the scene, so the ships he purchased were inferior to Bulloch's. The most successful of them was an iron screw-steamer originally named the *Japan* but renamed the *Georgia* when she was armed at sea off the coast of France in April 1863. One of the men who sailed on her said that "she was as absolutely unfitted for the work as any vessel could be. . . . Her sail power was insufficient, and . . . she was slow under either sail or steam or both together." Even more disastrous were the lignum-vitae cogs which worked on iron teeth on her propeller shaft. The wooden cogs would sometimes break and fly around the engine room like shrapnel. Still, the *Georgia* remained at sea for seven months and made eight or nine captures.

Maury did badly when he bought his first ship, but he did far worse with the second one. This was the *Victor,* a former dispatch boat condemned by the British Navy and sold as surplus. Maury hurried her away from England on November 22, 1863, and sent her to Calais as the Confederate ship *Rappahannock.* She never saw action but remained in Calais for the rest of the war. She was used as a depot where men and supplies intended for other ships could be held until needed.

Maury's stay in Europe was more successful when he turned his hand to propaganda for the Confederate

MATTHEW FONTAINE MAURY

cause. His name on a letter to an important newspaper assured its being printed, and he wrote many such letters. He was also connected with Napoleon III's scheme to put Maximilian of Austria on the throne in Mexico. This was to be tied in to an alliance with the Confederacy and possibly with the restoration of California to Mexico. Napoleon favored the plan while the Confederacy was winning victories, but by the time Maximilian was ready to go to Mexico in 1864, the Confederacy was no longer strong, and Napoleon persuaded him to ignore its emissaries.

When the war ended, Maury was on his way to America, hoping to land in Galveston with much-needed supplies for operating electrically exploded torpedoes. At St. Thomas in the Virgin Islands he learned that the Confederacy had ceased functioning as a government. He then decided to go to Mexico and try to persuade Maximilian to encourage former Confederates to settle in Mexico. The plan was accepted, and Maury was employed to carry it out. While he was on leave in England the next year, the immigration scheme was abandoned. The whole idea came to nothing, of course, in 1867 when Maximilian was court-martialed and shot.

Maury left England in 1868 to teach meteorology at the Virginia Military Institute in Lexington. He remained there until he died in 1873.

His devotion to the Confederacy had ruined his career and left him penniless. But his name was long to be remembered in scientific circles. And to this day the ocean Pilot Charts issued by the United States Government carry a notice saying that they are based on Maury's originals.

THE CONFEDERATE BATTERY
AT PORT HUDSON
FIRES DOWN AT FARRAGUT'S FLEET

One of the most spectacular battles of the Civil War took place on the night of March 14–15, 1863, when Admiral Farragut tried to run past the powerful Confederate batteries on the bluff above the Mississippi River at Port Hudson in order to reinforce the Union Army at Vicksburg. The fire directed at the slow-mov-

1863

The year 1863 began well enough for the Confederacy, but it was to be the year that marked a turn in the tide of its fortunes. After the fall of Vicksburg and Port Hudson in July, the Confederacy lost control of the vital Mississippi River. But her commerce-raiders still roamed the oceans of the world, and she still hoped to obtain more fighting ships, including ironclads, from Europe. Her torpedo warfare was becoming more deadly, and she was developing the world's first effective submarine. Along the shores of creeks and rivers and bayous, workmen were building vessels of all kinds to keep the Confederate Navy going.

ing vessels was so intense that only two got through. These were Farragut's own flagship, the *Hartford*, and its accompanying gunboat, the *Albatross*. The big side-wheeler *Mississippi* was destroyed. Its executive officer was among those who escaped. His name was George Dewey; he was later to be heard from at Manila.

1863.

JANUARY								JULY						
Sun.	M.	T.	W.	T.	F.	Sat.		Sun.	M.	T.	W.	T.	F.	Sat.
..	..	..	..	1	2	3		..	..	..	1	2	3	4
4	5	6	7	8	9	10		5	6	7	8	9	10	11
11	12	13	14	15	16	17		12	13	14	15	16	17	18
18	19	20	21	22	23	24		19	20	21	22	23	24	25
25	26	27	28	29	30	31		26	27	28	29	30	31	..

FEBRUARY								AUGUST						
1	2	3	4	5	6	7		..	..	..	..	..	..	1
8	9	10	11	12	13	14		2	3	4	5	6	7	8
15	16	17	18	19	20	21		9	10	11	12	13	14	15
22	23	24	25	26	27	28		16	17	18	19	20	21	22
..	..	..	..	..	..	..		23	24	25	26	27	28	29
..	..	..	..	..	..	..		30	31	..	..	..	..	..

MARCH								SEPTEMBER						
1	2	3	4	5	6	7		..	..	1	2	3	4	5
8	9	10	11	12	13	14		6	7	8	9	10	11	12
15	16	17	18	19	20	21		13	14	15	16	17	18	19
22	23	24	25	26	27	28		20	21	22	23	24	25	26
29	30	31	..	..	..	..		27	28	29	30	..	..	..

APRIL								OCTOBER						
..	..	..	1	2	3	4		..	..	..	..	1	2	3
5	6	7	8	9	10	11		4	5	6	7	8	9	10
12	13	14	15	16	17	18		11	12	13	14	15	16	17
19	20	21	22	23	24	25		18	19	20	21	22	23	24
26	27	28	29	30	..	..		25	26	27	28	29	30	31

MAY								NOVEMBER						
..	..	..	..	..	1	2		1	2	3	4	5	6	7
3	4	5	6	7	8	9		8	9	10	11	12	13	14
10	11	12	13	14	15	16		15	16	17	18	19	20	21
17	18	19	20	21	22	23		22	23	24	25	26	27	28
24	25	26	27	28	29	30		29	30	..	..	..	..	..
31	..	..	..	..	..	..		..	..	..	..	..	..	..

JUNE								DECEMBER						
..	1	2	3	4	5	6		..	..	1	2	3	4	5
7	8	9	10	11	12	13		6	7	8	9	10	11	12
14	15	16	17	18	19	20		13	14	15	16	17	18	19
21	22	23	24	25	26	27		20	21	22	23	24	25	26
28	29	30	..	..	..	..		27	28	29	30	31	..	..

The capture of the U.S. gunboat *Harriet Lane* and the destruction of the flagship *Westfield* in the harbor of

THE NAVAL WAR
IN TEXAS

Galveston had been captured on October 8, 1862, by a Union naval force under Commander William B. Renshaw. The Confederates, angered by the loss of this important Texas port, resolved to retake the city. They chose New Year's Day, 1863, as the time to

strike. A ground force under General John B. Magruder moved against the occupying army shortly after 2 A.M. when 14 fieldpieces, six siege guns, and an 8-inch Dahlgren mounted on a railroad car began firing at a wharf where the Federal troops were quartered.

After 4 A.M. when the moon went down, two Confederate steamers, the *Bayou City* and the *Neptune,* with their decks protected by cotton bales, accompanied by two small tenders carrying wood for fuel, and loaded with troops and spectators, moved against the Federal fleet in the harbor. The *Harriet Lane* and the *Westfield* were the most important Union vessels. The *Harriet Lane* was manned by crews who had survived the *Virginia's* attack on the *Cumberland* and the *Congress* at Hampton Roads.

The Union ships were taking part in the fighting, and Confederate cannon on shore were replying to them. Rosin was thrown into the furnaces of the *Bayou City* and the *Neptune* to make hot, quick fires and raise steam pressure. At dawn the *Bayou City* tried to come alongside the *Harriet Lane* to board her. The strong tide swung her aside, and the ships collided, tearing the planking off the *Bayou City's* port wheel-

Magruder's men take the *Harriet Lane* in one of the few instances of capture by boarding during the Civil War.

Galveston, Texas, on January 1, 1863. The *Westfield* was actually several miles away.

house. The *Neptune* then rammed the *Harriet Lane,* but was badly damaged herself by the impact and began to sink. The *Bayou City* slammed in again and ran her bow so far into the *Harriet Lane* that the two ships locked fast. The Confederates then boarded the Union vessel, driving most of her crew below deck where they quickly surrendered.

When Confederate Major Albert M. Lea went on board the captured *Harriet Lane,* he found his son Edward, second in command on the Union ship, mortally wounded. The captain, Jonathan M. Wainwright, was already dead. The bodies of the two Federal officers were later taken ashore to be buried in the same grave with full military honors. Major Lea read the funeral services.

As soon as the *Harriet Lane* was captured, a message under flag of truce was sent to Renshaw, commander of the Union fleet, demanding its surrender and giving him three hours to reply. Renshaw's ship, the *Westfield,* had run aground, and he decided to blow her up rather than let her fall into Confederate hands. Turpentine was poured on her decks, and all the officers and crew pulled away in small boats. When a torch was applied, a flash of flame ran along the

deck and evidently reached the magazine, for the *Westfield* blew up with a tremendous explosion that instantly killed everyone in the commodore's boat.

The loss of the *Harriet Lane* and the *Westfield* demoralized what was left of the Union fleet. Several ships broke the truce and hurried out of the harbor, while the Confederates captured the smaller vessels and their supplies. On January 5, General Magruder issued a proclamation announcing the raising of the blockade of Galveston.

The *Sachem* and the *Clifton,* two of the Union steamers which escaped from Galveston, were captured on September 8 at Sabine Pass, Texas. A Federal fleet of 22 vessels arrived there to attack Fort Griffin, which had only three small guns. The battle began at 3:30 P.M. and lasted until five. During the first part of it, the Confederates in the fort remained quiet and did not reply to the fire of the Union fleet. When the *Sachem* and the *Clifton* ran in close, the guns of the little fort quickly put them out of action. The Confederate gunboat *Uncle Ben* ran down to the *Sachem* and brought her in. Then the *Clifton* was taken by a boarding party. The Confederate loss was reported as "strictly and positively, nobody hurt."

125

The *Alabama* sinks the *Hatteras* off the Texas coast.

The ALABAMA
Off the Texas Coast

The *Alabama* met her coaling bark, the *Agrippina,* at the Arcas Islands off the coast of Yucatan late in December 1862. Christmas week was spent overhauling the ship and taking on coal while the crew of 110 men were given shore leave on the uninhabited coral islets. Then, on January 5, the *Alabama* headed for Galveston. Semmes, of course, did not know that the Confederates had retaken the city.

He arrived off the coast of Galveston late in the afternoon of January 11. It was clear weather, and Semmes could see the Federal fleet bombarding the city. Among the ships he recognized the *Brooklyn,* the big warship that had chased him in the *Sumter* when she sailed out of the Mississippi in 1861.

While he watched, he saw one of the steamers get up steam and sail toward him. Semmes ran slowly along the coast to draw the ship away from the protection of the fleet and to wait for nightfall. As soon as it was dark he furled the topsails, beat to quarters, and turned toward his pursuer under steam. When the Federal captain challenged him to give his ship's name, he replied: "Her Majesty's steamer *Petrel.*" He heard a voice shout that "he was the United States something or other," but he could not make out the name. He also heard that a boat was going to be sent to the *Alabama,* and although Semmes did not know it, a boat with six men was put overboard. They rowed around in the darkness, watching the battle that began. After it was over, they pulled back to the Federal fleet at Galveston to tell the captain of the *Brooklyn* what had happened.

As soon as Semmes had confirmed the fact that his dimly seen opponent was a Federal warship, he ordered his first lieutenant to call out boldly the name of the Confederate steamer *Alabama* and gave the command to fire.

The broadside guns flashed redly in the night, sending shot and shell at the dark ship only 200 yards away. The stranger immediately replied, and then ran toward the *Alabama,* stopping when she was less than 100 feet away. The men on deck exchanged musket and pistol shots while the big naval guns kept firing at close range. Shells from the *Alabama* set fire to her opponent and smashed into the engine, filling the hold with steam and cutting off the power. Whole sheets of iron were torn off the side, permitting water to rush in so rapidly that she began to sink. Her captain ordered the magazine to be flooded in order to prevent it from exploding. At the same time he had a gun fired on the far side of the ship to indicate that he was ready to surrender. The battle had lasted just 13 minutes.

An invitation for an overtaken vessel to heave to.

The *Alabama* in the harbor of Port Royal, Jamaica.

Semmes sent boats to take off the officers and crew. Ten minutes after they were safely on board the *Alabama,* the stricken ship went down. It now became known that she was the USS *Hatteras,* a 210-foot iron side-wheel steamer armed with five guns. This was the first and only time that the Confederate Navy sank a Federal warship at sea. Two men on the *Hatteras* had been killed and five wounded; while only one man on the *Alabama* was hurt. Semmes had the *Hatteras* crew of 103 men ironed on deck to prevent any possibility of an uprising. The five wounded men and the 18 officers were given the run of the ship while Semmes sailed east through several days of storm to reach Jamaica on January 20 and put his prisoners ashore at Port Royal.

The *Alabama* had been struck by five shells from the *Hatteras.* According to a British account, when repairs were being made in Jamaica, it was found that one of the Union shells which had not exploded was loaded with black sand instead of powder. This was probably the product of one of the numerous contractors who sold the Federal Government defective arms and shoddy supplies in their greedy haste to profit from the war.

Semmes encountered several English men-of-war at Port Royal. Their officers courteously called on him, and the island's British governor permitted him to take on coal. While his ship was being refitted, Semmes explored Jamaica on horseback. When he returned to his ship he found that some of his crew were on shore, blind drunk. Police assistance had to be called to round them up.

The *Alabama* left Jamaica on January 25 and captured and burned the *Golden Rule* the next day. Semmes then sailed east through the West Indies, destroying Yankee ships as he went. On February 15 he noted in his journal that this was the second anniversary of his resignation from the United States Navy and added that in the North "politicians had become political stockjobbers, and the seekers of wealth had become knaves and swindlers."

On April 10 the *Alabama* reached the island of Fernando de Noronha, an island off the coast of Brazil where the shoreline bends south. Here Semmes took on coal from a prize he had captured. But he had to wait for the *Agrippina,* which had gone on to England and was expected to meet him at the island. Ship traffic was heavy along the coast, so Semmes spent the time capturing more prizes. He then went to Bahia where he accidentally met the CSS *Georgia.*

After putting to sea, Semmes captured the bark *Conrad* on June 20; he commissioned and armed the ship as the Confederate cruiser *Tuscaloosa.* He then prepared to go to the Cape of Good Hope.

Sailors from the *Alabama* spend Christmas on Arcas Keys.

Sword practice on the deck of the *Alabama.*

The *Florida* running out of Mobile Bay through the Federal blockade.

THE *FLORIDA* ESCAPES FROM MOBILE

Maffitt had brought the *Florida* into Mobile Bay under fire on September 4, 1862. It had taken four months to repair the damage done to the ship by the enemy fleet. By the end of the year everything was in order; Maffitt had enlisted a full crew and was ready to go. But the Federal Navy, still smarting because of the way Maffitt had run the blockade in September, was determined not to let him get out of Mobile Bay. Nine warships had been sent to patrol the entrance to the bay and make sure he did not escape.

On January 13 the much-feared Confederate captain brought the *Florida* down to Fort Morgan to study his chances of running out. Word of his presence near the entrance channel spread through the Federal fleet, which promptly redoubled its vigilance. Maffitt's first trip down Mobile Bay turned out badly, for his pilot put him aground, and coal, guns, and cargo had to be taken off to get the *Florida* afloat again.

At 2 A.M. on January 16, Maffitt was awakened to be told that a chilly wind was coming from the northwest. A storm had just blown itself out. The stars could be seen, but a light mist lay over the water. Maffitt shrewdly figured that the captains of the Federal vessels had probably expected him to try to run out during the storm. Now that it was over they might relax their watch. Steam had been kept up on the *Florida,* and Maffitt gave orders to start at once.

At two-forty he passed the first Union ship; she was lying inside the bar and was very close, but her lookouts did not see him. He passed another; then, when nearing a third, the men stoking the furnaces of the *Florida* ran out of hard coal and had to put dusty soft coal on the hot fires. Red flames leaped up from the *Florida's* funnels to alert the Federal fleet. Lights on the ships waiting for him suddenly appeared as their crews were roused out to go into action.

Maffitt ordered sail made, and the chase was on. Just before dawn a big ship bowling along under top-sails was seen just ahead. Maffitt correctly took her to be his nemesis, the powerful *Brooklyn*. He quickly changed course, but had to pass so near to the towering warship that she could easily have sunk the *Florida* with her heavy guns. The men on her could not believe that the fast-moving ship they saw in the uncertain dawnlight was a Confederate vessel, so they let her go, thinking that she was one of their own fleet.

Three days later the *Florida* made her first capture, the brig *Estelle,* bound from Boston to Cuba and valued at $130,000. Maffitt ran in to Havana and Nassau for coal, then he sailed on, taking and burning many prizes. On February 12 he burned the *Jacob Bell,* a large ship in the New York-China trade, worth $2,000,000. The Federal fleet now had good reason to regret the *Florida's* escape.

On March 28, when Maffitt captured a Boston bark named the *Lapwing* he put a lieutenant with 18 men and two boat howitzers on board and commissioned her at sea to act as an independent raider as Semmes was to do in June with the *Conrad-Tuscaloosa*. The *Florida* was breeding offspring that were to be almost as dangerous as she was herself. On May 6 he captured the brig *Clarence* and put Lieutenant Charles Read in command of her. Read was to prove that the promise he had shown in Mississippi River fighting could be put to good use at sea. He headed north to run along the east coast to the United States where his exploits as a raider who changed from ship to ship baffled the Federal Navy, which sought him in vain while he took prize after prize only a few miles offshore (SEE PAGE 140).

Maffitt sailed on through the summer, working under such pressure that his health failed, and he was compelled to ask to be relieved of command. He brought the *Florida* into Brest on August 23, 1863, and turned her over to Commodore J. N. Barney a few weeks later.

The *Florida* burns the *Jacob Bell,* a New York ship in the China trade. She carried a cargo of 1380 tons of tea, 10,000 boxes of firecrackers, and other Oriental goods with a total value of about $2,000,000 in U.S. currency. This took place several hundred miles north of Puerto Rico on February 12, 1863.

The *Florida* as a French artist saw her in the harbor of Brest.

The *Palmetto State* rams the *Mercedita* while the *Chicora* (at right) attacks the *Keystone State*.

CONFEDERATE IRONCLADS TAKE THE OFFENSIVE AT CHARLESTON

Starting early in 1862, several casemated ironclads resembling the *Virginia* in general design, were built near Charleston. The first was the *Palmetto State;* the second, the *Chicora.* They were to be used against the Federal blockading fleet.

Just before these ships went into action, the Confederates made a carefully planned capture near Charleston. The Federal gunboat *Isaac P. Smith* was allowed to go up the Stono River on January 30, 1863. When it came down again, masked batteries on both shores fired at it, killing eight and wounding 16 men. A shot through the engine put the gunboat out of commission. It was then surrendered and was

made part of the Confederate Navy under the name *Stono.*

The next morning at 4:30 A.M., the two Confederate ironclads left the harbor in a thick haze which prevented the lookouts on ships in the Federal fleet from seeing the squat, bluish-gray rams until they closed in. The *Palmetto State* rammed the USS *Mercedita* and fired her bow gun into her. The ram was so much lower than the wooden steamer that the latter could not depress her guns enough to reply. Nor did she have time to, for the first shot went through one of her boilers. Her captain then had to surrender. Men and officers were quickly paroled. The *Palmetto*

State went on to chase other Union vessels, but they easily got away from the slow-moving ram.

The *Chicora* fired at a schooner which burst into flames, shelled two other vessels, and then attacked the *Keystone State,* a large armed side-wheel steamer. A shot through the hull set the ship on fire. (Federal officers said the Confederates were using a new kind of incendiary shell and sent a sample of one to Admiral DuPont.) The captain of the *Keystone State* tried to run the ram down, but a shot through both steam chests stopped her. Ten rifled shells then smashed into the stricken ship, most of them in the hull near or below the waterline. About a quarter of the crew were killed or wounded from gunfire or scalding steam. The shots from the *Keystone State* made no impression upon the armored sides of the *Chicora*. With dead and dying littering his ship, the *Keystone State's* captain ordered her colors struck. He said that the *Chicora* kept firing, so he raised his colors again and tried to move away, using one engine. But Tucker, of the *Chicora,* claimed that he fired only when he saw the steamer start to move off after having lowered her colors. The wounded steamer, with only one engine working badly, was still faster than the heavy ram, so she got away. Both captains accused each other of breaking the truce.

The Confederate rams were undamaged. They steamed slowly around, looking for an adversary, and firing at any ship that came within range. The Federal fleet cautiously withdrew from its accustomed position outside the entrance to the harbor while the rams anchored near Sullivans Island. Their draft was so great that they could cross the bar only at high water.

While the Federal fleet was eight or ten miles away, several foreign consuls went out to see for themselves that it had gone. General Beauregard, doubtless influenced by what had happened at Galveston on the first of the year (SEE PAGE 124), issued a proclamation stating that the blockade of Charleston was officially raised. But the Federal fleet soon came back, and an engineer on the *Chicora* wrote: "A good bit of glory, but not a prize or ship destroyed, and we all felt disappointed. . . . They say we raised the blockade, but we all felt we would have rather raised h--l and sunk the ships."

The *Chicora* as a Confederate photographer saw her. This shows that she had only two broadside gun ports and not three as the British artist who made the large engraving above seemed to think.

The *Queen of the West* rams the *Vicksburg.*

III. THE WAR ON WESTERN WATERS

FINAL OPERATIONS ON THE MISSISSIPPI

I. The Capture of the QUEEN OF THE WEST

At the beginning of 1863 the Confederates still held the Mississippi between Vicksburg and Port Hudson. Both places were well fortified, and work on them never stopped. Possession of this long stretch of the river enabled the Confederates to communicate with the trans-Mississippi area and bring in supplies from the West as well as manufactured goods run in through the blockade to Texas. Everyone in the Confederacy knew how important it was to maintain its hold on the river. As early as April 10, 1862, General Lee had telegraphed from Richmond to General John C. Pemberton: "IF MISSISSIPPI VALLEY IS LOST ATLANTIC STATES WILL BE RUINED."

Vicksburg was the key to the Mississippi. Grant realized this, and late in 1862 he began a long and bitterly fought campaign against the Confederate citadel which stood high on a bluff above a sharp bend in the river. Except for the never-ceasing attempts to take Richmond and Charleston, the more than six months' siege of Vicksburg was by far the most protracted and difficult campaign of the entire war. Although the battle for Vicksburg was fought mostly on land, there was also a great deal of activity on the rivers and bayous around the city as the Federal Army—with

the help of the Navy—tried to reach Vicksburg by oddly devious routes. The Union now had many armed vessels on the Western rivers; the Confederacy had very few. By this time the Richmond Government had apparently written off its western navy. Mallory's report for November 30, 1863, mentions only the recently completed ironclad *Missouri* in the Red River, although there were other ships in the west.

The most spectacular Confederate naval exploits on Western waters in 1863 were the capture of the Union vessels *Queen of the West* and *Indianola.* The *Queen of the West* was ordered to run past the much strengthened batteries at Vicksburg on February 2 and, on her way, to attack the Confederate steamer *Vicksburg,* known to be lying at a wharf there. Colonel Charles Rivers Ellet, the 19-year-old son of the man who had built the Union ram fleet, was in charge of the expedition.

The *Queen* struck the *Vicksburg* a glancing blow and fired blazing balls soaked in turpentine at her. Ellet doubtless did not want to wait too long under the guns of the powerful batteries above him, even though the *Queen* was protected by two layers of cotton bales. Both ships caught fire, but the flames on both were extinguished. Admiral Porter incautiously reported to Welles that the *Vicksburg* was "in a sinking condition" only to have his words proved false by Farragut who saw the allegedly damaged vessel two months later when she broke adrift and

The *Queen of the West* runs aground and is captured by the Confederates. Some of the crew are trying to escape by throwing bales of cotton overboard to serve as life rafts. Hot steam is pouring out of the stranded riverboat after shells struck boilers and steam drum.

floated down the river. "The boat was scarcely injured," he said indignantly.

The *Queen* kept on going and had a number of adventures when she encountered Confederate steamers whose captains could not believe that a Federal ram could be in that part of the river. Ellet captured and burned three such steamboats in rapid succession.

The Union command on the upper Mississippi was vitally interested in what Ellet could do once he got below Vicksburg. Authorities there gave him every assistance; they even loaded a barge with coal and set it adrift on the night of February 7 in the hope that it would reach him. By some miracle it went down the river without being grounded or captured. With a supply of coal from this, and accompanied by a small ferryboat called the *DeSoto* which the army had captured and turned over to him, Ellet set out on a raid up the Red River.

Pleased by the young officer's enterprise, Porter sent the new ironclad *Indianola* with two more coal barges to meet him. The *Indianola* was such a strange-looking vessel that Porter warned Ellet not to "mistake her for a rebel." She was high and wide, but certainly not handsome. Like others of the same quickly built class, she was badly designed and badly constructed, as inefficient as she was ugly.

Without waiting for the *Indianola,* Ellet went ahead on his own. On February 14 he captured the Confederate transport *Era No. 5* and foolishly employed her pilot to guide him up the Red River. When they came in sight of a battery, the pilot ran the *Queen* aground under its guns.

Within a short time shells struck the *Queen's* steam drum and penetrated her boilers. Men leaped overboard to reach the *DeSoto,* but many were shot, drowned, or captured. The *DeSoto* was soon disabled by a broken rudder, but Ellet let her drift downstream for 15 miles until they reached the *Era.* When they finally got to the Mississippi, the same pilot let the *Era* go aground. At this point, Ellet had the man placed under arrest.

Captain George Brown arrived with the *Indianola* in the morning. The *Era* was hastily repaired, and

the two steamers started for the Red River. Fog closed in. Looming up out of it came the very fast Confederate ram *William H. Webb.* Ellet blew his steam whistle to warn Brown, but the sound was heard on the *Webb,* which promptly turned around and disappeared into the fog.

When Brown reached the mouth of the Red River, he was informed that the *Webb* was accompanied by three other boats and that the Confederates were rapidly repairing the captured *Queen of the West.* He blockaded the mouth of the river for four days, but did not go up it because he could not find a trustworthy pilot. Ellet left to return to the Union fleet, after which the *Indianola* also started north.

On February 24, Brown saw four steamboats following him. He cleared the *Indianola* for action at 9:30 P.M. and prepared for a night battle. The *Webb,* the refitted *Queen of the West,* and two smaller cotton-clad steamers were soon close behind him. The *Indianola* had coal barges lashed to both sides and was clumsy to handle, but Brown turned her around to meet the attack. He ordered the two big bow guns fired, but both shots missed. Before he could reload, the *Queen of the West* hit him, smashing in the barge on the port side; then the *Webb* came at him, and the two boats crashed together, bows on, knocking down everyone on both vessels. The *Webb* drew away with the upper part of her bow stove in. Again and again the three rams hammered at one another in the darkness. The *Webb* destroyed the starboard barge and slammed against the *Indianola's* now unprotected side to crush her paddle wheel and rudder. Another blow on the stern started the timbers and let water pour into the hull. To avoid great loss of life, Brown ran the *Indianola's* bow on shore and surrendered the ironclad after a battle lasting one hour and 27 minutes. Officers and crew—more than 100 men—were taken prisoner and sent to Jackson, Mississippi. Despite the heavy damage to all three vessels, casualties were small—two killed and four wounded on the *Queen,* and only one man wounded on the *Webb,* while the *Indianola* had one man killed and one wounded. Except to fire occasional shots, the two small Confederate steamboats played no part in the battle.

133

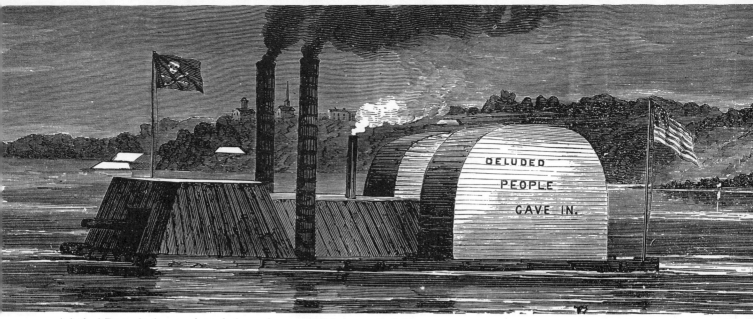

Admiral Porter's dummy ironclad running past Vicksburg at night.

FINAL OPERATIONS ON THE MISSISSIPPI

II.   The Destruction of the QUEEN OF THE WEST and the INDIANOLA

Since the east shore of the river was in Confederate hands, the *Indianola* was towed over there. She soon sank in about ten feet of water. The *Queen* went to get salvage equipment, and work on the valuable wreck began the next morning. Two 11-inch and two 9-inch Dahlgrens and many 24-pounders on the partly sunken ironclad made her a rich prize.

When word reached Admiral Porter of the loss of the *Indianola,* he promptly planned one of the most successful ruses of the war. He had his men build a dummy ironclad which was completed in the incredibly short time of 12 hours. According to Porter, they "made a raft of logs, three hundred feet long, with . . . two huge wheelhouses and a formidable log casemate, from the portholes of which appeared sundry wooden guns. Two old boats hung from davits . . . and two smokestacks made of hogsheads completed the illusion; on her wheelhouses was painted the following: 'Deluded Rebels, Cave In!' An American flag was hoisted aft, and a banner emblazoned with skull and crossbones ornamented the bow. . . . The mock ram was furnished with a big iron pot inside each smokestack, in which was [*sic*] tar and

The death of a tubby but gallant lady. The *Queen of the West* is shelled by Union gunboats.

oakum to raise a black smoke. . . . At midnight she was towed down close to . . . Vicksburg and sent adrift."

The batteries at Vicksburg fired furiously at the imitation ironclad as she drifted by during the night, but they wasted powder and shell. She ran ashore before morning, but some Union soldiers were on hand to push her back into the current. Down the river she went to be sighted by the *Queen of the West* as she came up for salvage material. A Confederate cavalry colonel tells what happened: "In a short time the *Queen of the West* came back in great haste, reporting a gunboat of the enemy approaching. All the vessels at once got underway in a panic and proceeded down the river, abandoning without a word the working party and fieldpieces on the wreck. The Federal vessel did not approach nearer than 2½ miles,

Another artist's less correct conception of the same dummy ram, LEFT, causing the destruction of the *Indianola*.

and appeared very apprehensive of attack. The position of the *Indianola* was such that her two 12-inch Dahlgren guns commanded the river above, and the two 9-inch guns could also have been brought in battery. With the assistance of our two vessels, the *Queen of the West* and the *Webb,* there is scarcely a doubt that we could have saved the *Indianola* and possibly have captured the other gunboat. . . . The lieutenant commanding the working party made some effort to free the vessel of water, but finding himself abandoned by our fleet, and the enemy's gunboat lying above him, he . . . burst three of the valuable guns on board, spiked the other, threw his fieldpieces overboard, blew up the vessel, and fled."

When Confederate newspapers found out about the hoax, they were furious. In faraway Richmond the *Examine*r said: "Laugh and hold your sides, lest you die of a surfeit of derision, O Yankeedom! Blown up because, forsooth, a flatboat, or mud-scow, with a small house taken from the back-garden of a plantation, put on top of it, is floated down the river."

The Confederates never changed the name of the *Queen of the West;* they repaired her again, gave her a coat of black paint, and sent her with two transports to Grand Lake, Louisiana. About 2 A.M. on April 14, 1863, when she was entering the northern end of the lake, the gunboat *Estrella* and two other Union gunboats hastened toward the Confederate vessels, firing as they went. A shell from the *Estrella* landed squarely on the *Queen*. It exploded, broke a steam pipe, and set fire to the cotton bulwarks. The stricken vessel blazed until the flames reached her magazine, which then blew up. It was the end for a fighting lady that had served in both navies.

The Union fleet running past the Vicksburg batteries on the night of April 16, 1863. The flagship *Benton* is in the lead with the *Louisville* and others following.

After the Union fleet went below Vicksburg other vessels had to follow. Here is how the tug *Rumsey* got past. Bales of hay on right; cotton bales on left.

"Whistling Dick," the Confederate gun at Vicksburg that made a whistling sound when its shells were fired.

A Union steamboat being taken through Steele's Bayou in the Vicksburg Campaign.

FINAL OPERATIONS ON THE MISSISSIPPI

III. *The Fall of Vicksburg*

At Vicksburg, ironclads and gunboats became tools in the hands of Grant and Sherman as their armies probed month after month to find a way to bring their troops nearer to the besieged city. A canal was cut through the narrow peninsula made by a sharp bend in the river opposite Vicksburg, but high water forced the project to be abandoned. Then another canal scheme at Duckport was stopped by low water. Four expeditions on the bayous in the backcountry were made in the spring of 1863 when steamboats were taken through the swamps in an effort to approach Vicksburg by water. It was hard work to get the clumsy river boats through the trees and densely tangled vines. Finally, the bayou expeditions also came to nothing. But Farragut's fleet came up the river, running past the Confederate batteries at Port Hudson on March 14 (SEE PAGE 122) and the batteries at Grand Gulf on March 31.

Vicksburg was short of food and everything else, but its citizens tried to carry on their usual life. They even held a ball on the night of April 16, but it was rudely broken up when Porter's fleet came down the river with guns roaring in the darkness. The gunboats had to get past the city to support the major army movement that was to be made farther south.

The Confederates left the ball and ran to their guns to send fire plunging down on the Union vessels. In order to light up the scene and enable the gunners on shore to see their targets better, wooden buildings and barrels of tar were burned.

Nearly every vessel in the Union fleet had a coal barge lashed to its starboard side to protect it, while leaving the port guns free to fire at the Confederate batteries. Heavy timber and bales of cotton or wet hay were used to cover weak spots, but some shells found their mark. The transport *Henry Clay,* struck in two vital places, was torn apart and quickly sank. Another transport, the *Forest Queen,* was badly damaged; but the *Tuscumbia* went to her assistance and towed her through while still under fire. It took two and a half hours for the fleet to file past Vicksburg. Despite the heavy firing, Union losses were remarkably light. Only 13 men were wounded, and the *Henry Clay* was the only vessel lost. On April 22, when six more transports ran the batteries, five got through.

The fleet was then ordered to reduce the Confederate batteries high upon the bluffs at Grand Gulf so Grant's army could cross without opposition, but after more than four hours of firing with little result, Porter had to order the vessels back. They were then run past at night to join Grant four miles below. Once the Union Army got across the river with the help of the Navy on April 30, Grand Gulf became untenable; its garrison evacuated it a few days later.

The Union fleet was called upon to cooperate several times during the land campaign against Vicksburg that followed, but it was probably most useful in supplying heavy naval guns which were mounted on shore and on scows.

Grant cut off Vicksburg's communications, brought in more and more men and guns, and slowly made life in the besieged city impossible. The Confederate commander, General John C. Pemberton, met with him on July 3 and surrendered the next day. After Vicksburg fell, Port Hudson also had to be surrendered and was given up on July 9. The Confederates then lost control of the Mississippi River. It was a serious blow, the first of several that were to dismember the Confederacy, as Union forces broke it into segments. And the only place on the western rivers where Confederate vessels were still in service was on the Red River where the ram *William H. Webb* was holding out. Some ports in Texas, notably Galveston, were under Confederate control and were to remain so until the end of the war. And Mobile was still Confederate. Its well-defended harbor entrance was being heavily mined to protect it against a Union attack which its people knew must come.

Along the Mississippi and its tributaries, Confederate opposition was reduced to guerrilla fighting and an occasional success in torpedo warfare. On July 13, 1863, the U.S. ironclad *Baron de Kalb* was blown up by a torpedo near Yazoo City.

The river guerrillas were held in great fear by the men on Union gunboats because it was impossible to remain undercover all the time, and one never knew when a sharpshooter's bullet might come whistling out of a thicket along the shore.

The Confederate Government made no provision for permitting privateering on inland waters. Those who wanted to operate armed riverboats were invited to join the Volunteer Navy in which they would be assigned to duty under an acting master and receive regular navy pay and subsistence. It was not a very attractive offer to partisans.

Sometimes the Confederates had trouble with their own guerrillas. After the *Arkansas* was blown up, its crew went to a guerrilla camp for aid but could not get within hailing distance of the suspicious freebooters, who promptly disappeared into the woods.

THE *ATLANTA* AND THE *WEEHAWKEN*

The original Ericsson *Monitor* had foundered while being towed past Cape Hatteras on December 31, 1862. But monitors as a class proved to be more seaworthy than was at first believed. The monitor *Weehawken* survived the gale of January 20, 1863; she then went through several more days of heavy weather while running outside from Newport News to Port Royal early in February.

In June, when Admiral DuPont learned that the Confederates were planning to use the ironclad *Atlanta* to attack the Federal fleet blockading the coast off Savannah he ordered the monitors *Weehawken* and *Nahant* to patrol Wassaw Sound. The *Atlanta's* iron-plated casemate had been built on the stripped-down hull of Bulloch's former blockade-runner *Fingal* (SEE PAGE 38). The converted ship drew nearly 16 feet of water because her heavy armor weighed down her deep oceangoing hull. The *Atlanta* was a formidable vessel with four rifled guns which could be quickly swung around to fire through eight portholes that could be protected by steel shutters. Federal naval men thought she was the best of the Confederate ironclads then in existence, although she was hurriedly and crudely built with little thought of comfort for her crew or fine finish for her guns and fittings.

With this floating fortress, Commander W. A. Webb planned to break the blockade between Savannah and Charleston, attack the Federal installation at Hilton Head, and perhaps recapture Fernandina, Florida. It was an ambitious scheme—the sort of bold raid people thought ironclads could carry out if they were able to stand the rough waters of the high seas.

Webb knew that the two Federal monitors were waiting for him in Wassaw Sound. At 3:30 A.M. on June 17 he started down to meet them with a spar torpedo projecting from the *Atlanta's* bows. When he entered the open waters of the sound shortly before 5 A.M., he saw the monitors and opened fire on them as soon as they came within range.

Before he could get near enough to either to use his spar torpedo, the *Atlanta's* deep hull grounded.

The *Weehawken* in a gale off the Atlantic coast on January 20, 1863.

The *Weehawken* and the *Atlanta* (with her spar torpedo raised) in combat on Wassaw Sound.

The tide was rising rapidly, and the powerful engines of the ironclad were able to pull her loose by backing off. But she would not answer her helm because there was not enough water under her. The swift tide swept her back on the bank. By this time the *Weehawken* was coming straight at her. The *Atlanta's* guns spat fire at the advancing monitor. Still the *Weehawken* kept advancing, holding her fire until she got very close.

John Rodgers, who had pioneered in establishing the Union Navy on western waters, was in command of the monitor, and he was out to make a kill. The *Nahant* did not have a pilot familiar with those shallow waters, so her commander had to follow Rodger's lead.

The *Weehawken's* 15-inch Dahlgren sent a heavy cored shot smashing through the armored casemate of the *Atlanta,* shattering the iron plating, and splintering the wood backing behind it. The terrible concussion knocked out 40 men, and the enormous wood splinters and fragments of iron wounded 16 more, one of whom soon died. The huge missile also drove solid shot out of the *Atlanta's* racks, turning the ironclad's own weapons against her crew with murderous effect.

A shot from the *Weehawken's* 11-inch gun then struck the *Atlanta's* knuckles, where the armor was only two inches thick. Water came in through the seam opened there. Then two shots from the 15-inch gun did more damage, one striking a corner of the pilot house and wounding its two occupants.

The badly damaged ironclad was now fast aground, and the two monitors had her cornered. Her commander had to surrender. The battle had lasted only a few minutes, during which the *Atlanta* had been

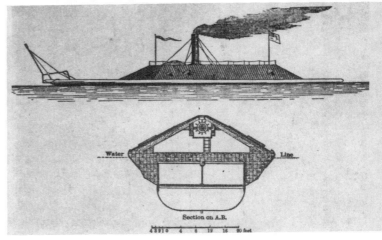

Profile and cross section of the *Atlanta*. Note the heavy wood backing for the armor.

able to fire only seven shots.

All 21 officers and 124 men—including 28 Confederate marines—were taken prisoner. Those not wounded were imprisoned in Fort Lafayette in New York Harbor, and the *Atlanta,* now called the USS *Atlanta,* was sent to the Philadelphia Navy Yard for repair. In February 1864 she became part of the North Atlantic Blockading Squadron based at Fort Monroe. The ship which had begun her career in commercial trade in the North of Scotland, had been a blockade-runner, and then an ironclad ram, was now used against the Confederates who had brought her hull to America.

A large supply of ammunition, various kinds of weapons, and stores of food were found on the *Atlanta* when she was captured. They had doubtless been put there in anticipation of what her commander hoped would be a triumphant cruise along the coast.

The *Atlanta* lying in the James River after her capture. A Union crew is on board.

"THE MOST BRILLIANT DAREDEVIL CRUISE OF THE WAR"

On May 6, 1863 (when Stonewall Jackson was dying of the wounds he had received at Chancellorsville), the *Florida,* while cruising off the coast of Brazil, captured the brig *Clarence,* bound from Rio to Baltimore. Lieutenant Charles W. Read, the twenty-three-year-old officer whom Maffitt had asked for because of his remarkable combat career on the Mississippi, thought that the *Clarence* could enter Chesapeake Bay because she had clearance papers for Baltimore. He asked for the brig and got her. With a boat howitzer, some small arms, 21 men, and a commission issued by Maffitt to operate as a Confederate raider, he sailed north along the outer rim of the West Indies.

The *Clarence* was too slow to overtake the first ships Read sighted. He did not make his first capture until June 6, when he took and burned the bark *Windward.* He then captured two other ships. From newspapers found aboard them and from his prisoners he learned that the entrance to Cheaspeake Bay was too closely guarded for him to get through. He decided to run along the coast instead.

On June 12 he captured the bark *Tacony* near Cape Henry and decided to use her as a raider because she was a better sailor than the *Clarence.* Before he could move his men and equipment, the schooner *M. A. Shindler* came along. Read quickly captured her and then started to transfer his crew and the howitzer to the *Tacony.* While the deck gun was being taken from one ship to the other, another schooner, the *Kate Stewart* came in sight. Read had nothing to threaten her with except a dummy wooden cannon on deck of the *Clarence,* put there to give the brig a more warlike appearance. The ruse worked, and the captain of the *Kate Stewart* surrendered without realizing how easily he had been gulled.

Read then burned the *Clarence* and the *M. A. Shindler,* bonded the *Kate Stewart,* and sent her off with all the prisoners he had taken. Between June 12 and June 24 he captured 14 more ships.

Meanwhile, the captain of the *Tacony,* who had reached shore on the *Kate Stewart,* hurried by train to Philadelphia to tell the owners of the second vessel what had happened. They promptly sent an indignant message to Secretary Welles.

Welles sent out ship after ship until all available naval vessels were hunting for Read. Commercial steamers and sailing ships were chartered and hurried to sea with orders to stop everything afloat and make a careful search. The Federal fleet rapidly picked up some of the ships Read had bonded and turned loose, so it was fairly well informed of his movements. But he was always one jump ahead of them.

His pursuers did not know that Read's single howitzer had run out of ammunition. When he captured the schooner *Archer* off the Maine coast on June 24 he had exhausted all his shot and powder. He decided to burn the *Tacony* and use the *Archer.*

He turned toward the shore and made Portland light on June 26. Near there, he picked up two local fishermen who thought the schooner was a pleasure vessel and offered to guide her into the harbor. They told Read that the revenue cutter *Caleb Cushing* and a New York passenger steamer were lying at the

Lieutenant Charles W. Read, CSN

docks. The ambitious young lieutenant wanted to seize them both. He had brought along an engineer from the *Florida* for just such a chance.

(At this time, Lee's Army of Northern Virginia was in Pennsylvania, spread out in a wide semicircle from Chambersburg to Harrisburg, while the Union Army was hurrying north. On July 1 they were to meet at Gettysburg.)

Read boldly sailed past the forts guarding the entrance to Portland Harbor and anchored in full view of the city. When he spoke to his engineer, he found him doubtful about being able to start the steamer's engines. Anyway, it would take time to get steam up, and Read knew he could not afford to wait several hours. He decided instead to cut out the revenue cutter *Caleb Cushing,* a well-armed sailing ship. With her eight guns he felt that he could fight his way through anything. Once at sea, he would not be dependent upon getting coal, which was hard for a hunted ship to obtain.

Shortly after midnight, two boats rowed by muffled oars and carrying men armed with revolvers and cutlasses moved silently across the water to the wharf where the *Caleb Cushing* was tied up. Most of the crew and all but one of the officers were at home asleep. A landing boom projecting from the side made boarding easy. Two men on deck were quickly subdued; then some of the Confederates dashed below, where a display of cutlasses enabled them to put irons on a lieutenant and eight or ten sailors. They lost time getting away from the dock because the cable could not be slipped. Worse still, the tide was coming in and the wind was dying down.

The *Archer,* with three of Read's men, had gone ahead. By the time he reached the forts at the harbor entrance the sun was rising. And the desperately needed wind was so slight that it did not even fill the sails.

A search of the presumably well-equipped *Caleb Cushing* turned up only five projectiles for the pivot gun. And there was hardly any gunpowder. More ammunition was certainly on board, but the captured Yankees, even under threats, refused to say where it was.

Two steamers with fieldpieces lashed on deck, and accompanied by three tugboats, were seen coming out of the harbor manned by volunteer crews. They headed straight for the becalmed revenue cutter.

Read's first shot went straight at the leading steamer. It ricocheted over the water but fell short. The steamer kept advancing. Read had the pivot gun fired again; again the shot fell short. He used all five projectiles hoping to scare off his pursuers. But they kept steadily coming on. When they got closer, Read ordered the gun to be loaded with scrap iron. The cannon made a loud noise, but the iron did not go very far.

One steamer looked as if she was going to ram them. Read hastily ordered everyone to take to the boats, and had the *Caleb Cushing* set on fire. White handkerchiefs were used as flags of truce as the two boats were rowed toward the nearest steamer. Soon after Read and his men surrendered and were taken on board, flames reached the revenue cutter's well-concealed magazine. She blew up with a great roar, scattering timbers over the water.

The captured Confederates were sent to Fort Warren in Boston Harbor. Read, whose exploit naval historian Richard S. West calls "the most brilliant daredevil cruise of the war," was exchanged in October 1864. He then served on the James River squadron. His last command was the ram *William H. Webb,* which he ran down the Mississippi in an effort to escape to the Gulf. He almost made it, but was headed off by the USS *Richmond.* He burned his ship before being captured. It was then April 26, 1865, seventeen days after Appomattox.

Read, in the *Tacony,* burning ships along the coast.

The U.S. revenue cutter *Caleb Cushing* just before she blew up.

Looking northwest from Fort Johnson toward the city and showing shipping activity on the inner harbor.

THE MILAN, FRENCH STEAM-SLOOP.   CASTLE PINCKNEY.   H.M.S. PETREL.   FORT

ABOVE: Looking northeast and showing visiting French and English warships at anchor.
BELOW: Looking toward the sea from Fort Johnson and showing Fort Sumter.

CHARLESTON HARBOR IN 1863

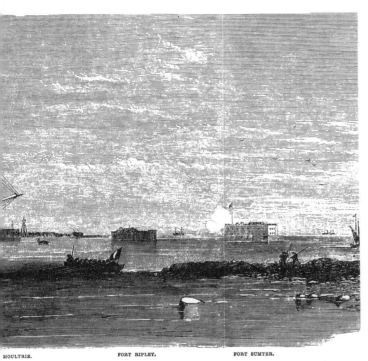

MOULTRIE.　　　　FORT RIPLEY.　　　　FORT SUMTER.

I. THE WAR ON CHARLESTON

Even before the *Palmetto State* and the *Chicora* successfully attacked the Federal blockading fleet off Charleston on January 31, 1863, Union naval authorities knew that wooden ships were not adequate for patrolling the coasts. Monitors and ironclads were sent down to reinforce the fleet. In order to test one of the first of the monitors, Admiral DuPont sent the *Montauk* to the Great Ogeechee River, west of Savannah, to attack Fort McAllister where the *Nashville,* now fitted out as a privateer, was ready to run to sea. After three attempts, the *Montauk* sank the well-known Confederate raider on February 28.

The Illustrated London News had sent the artist-correspondent, Frank Vizetelly, to America. Since he sympathized with the South, he spent most of his time in the Confederacy. Many of his drawings, from which wood engravings were to be made in London, were lost at sea or captured on blockade-runners and appropriated by Northern periodicals. These illustrations, printed in England, show Charleston Harbor as it looked during the winter of 1862–63.

The entrance to the harbor was covered by 76 large-caliber guns which could concentrate their fire from various points on any ship that tried to enter. More guns guarded the inner harbor; some of them were in the city itself. Torpedoes, rows of piling, and other hidden obstructions added to the difficulties that faced anyone trying to attack from the sea. Nevertheless, the Union kept sending ships, men, and supplies during the spring of 1863 for a massive assault.

II. Federal Ironclads Attack Fort Sumter

The Confederates lay torpedoes to stop the Federal fleet.

The Confederates continued to strengthen the defenses of Charleston; Fort Sumter now bristled with guns, and so did the forts around it. Three circles of fire were established by experiment, making it possible to place a projectile exactly where the gunner wanted it; the spot was then marked by a buoy. This meant that a ship trying to run past the forts would almost surely be hit when it passed near one of the marked target areas in the first circle. If it survived that, it would be struck again by other guns aimed at points in the second and third circles. More torpedoes were placed in strategic spots, and every precaution was taken to repel the attack which the defenders of Charleston knew must come.

It came on April 7, 1863, when Admiral DuPont on the *New Ironsides,* accompanied by seven monitors and the double-turreted armored vessel *Keokuk* (SEE PAGE 92), started toward the harbor entrance shortly after noon. The procession was led by the monitor *Weehawken,* pushing a 50-foot raft ahead of her as a guard against torpedoes. The other ships followed, moving ponderously as they went toward the menacing forts where Confederate gunners were waiting for a ship to arrive at a marked spot. Nothing could be heard but the pounding of the heavy marine engines and the sound of propellers churning the water. Forts and ships held their fire until the fleet got close. Then the sky was suddenly rocked by violent explosions when the guns roared out. Shells burst overhead, sent up columns of water, or smashed into iron armor.

Fort Sumter was the main target for the Federal fleet, which concentrated its fire on the massive pile that guarded the channel between it and Fort Moultrie. Sumter was an easy target to hit but a hard one on which to make an impression. Shots from the ironclads struck the solid brick walls again and again, doing visible but not serious damage.

But the rifled shells, bolts, and steel-pointed shot hurled at the fleet were hitting more vulnerable targets. The firing was so heavy that an officer on the

Passaic said he heard 15 shots go whistling past in a few seconds. These projectiles were the ones that missed. Those that found their mark shook the ships as they smashed into their not always invulnerable armor.

Under this dreadful rain of fire the *Weehawken* encountered several rows of casks floating on the water in the channel between the forts. Suspicious of what they might be, the monitor's commander, John Rodgers, hesitated. When a torpedo exploded near his bows, he ordered the *Weehawken* stopped. Following ships ran into trouble trying to stop behind him or turn aside in the narrow channel. Shot and shell began to take their toll. One of the monitors was hit more than 50 times, yet, although badly battered, was not knocked out. The misbegotten *Keokuk* ran in close to Fort Sumter but was riddled through before she could fire three shots. Her inadequate armor was no protection against projectiles which dented but did not penetrate the monitor's more solidly built iron walls. Nineteen of the 90 shots that struck the *Keokuk* went through her hull at or below the waterline. After 30 minutes, she had to be taken out of the battle. She kept filling with water all night and sank early in the morning.

The flagship *New Ironsides* was not able to get as close to Fort Sumter as the monitors did. It was not known until later, but the spot where she remained in the channel was directly over the biggest torpedo in the area. The Confederate who was frantically trying to explode it electrically from the shore was unable to make the detonation apparatus work because an ordnance wagon had run over the wires on the beach.

After the battered fleet withdrew, Admiral DuPont held a conference at which it was decided that it would be suicide to send the monitors in again, and the attempt to take Charleston from the sea was temporarily put off to await support by land forces.

During the battle, the Confederate ironclads *Palmetto State* and *Chicora* were in an inlet behind Fort Sumter, ready to take on any ship that might get past the forts. Their services were not needed.

One of the big guns in Fort Moultrie.

The Federal fleet in action. The *New Ironsides* and *Keokuk* at left, Fort Moultrie at right.

The *New Ironsides* and two Federal monitors firing at Fort Sumter.

A Confederate officer holds up the flag when a flagstaff is shot down in Fort Moultrie during the bombardment of April 7 by the Federal monitors.

The monitor *Weehawken,* while grounded in shallow water in September, lands a lucky shot on Fort Moultrie's magazine and blows up the powder stored there.

III. The Attack on Charleston Continues

No city in the South was more bitterly hated in the North than Charleston—"the font and head of rebel-

lion." When DuPont did not follow up his attack of April 7, he was relieved of command on June 3 and was to be replaced by A. H. Foote. But Foote died of Bright's disease three weeks after his appointment. Admiral John A. Dahlgren, Chief of the Bureau of Ordnance, inventor of the famous Dahlgren gun, and a friend of President Lincoln, was appointed in his place.

When the Confederates learned that an attack was to be made on Morris Island, they hurriedly strengthened their positions there. Federal troops had already established a foothold on neighboring Folly Island from which they were to direct their assault.

During July and August, Union forces made a series of combined attacks. Shelling of the harbor forts was almost incessant. The Confederates struck back on the night of August 21, when a steam torpedo boat tried to blow up the *New Ironsides*. It failed, but an attempt made on October 5 seriously damaged but did not sink the ship.

Confederate soldiers repair damage to Fort Sumter during the attack of April 7. BELOW: Charleston civilians watch the bombardment of April 7.

Shells bursting in the streets of Charleston when Federal guns were turned on the city.

The interior of Fort Sumter showing the effect of the Federal bombardment.

IV. Shells Rain Down on Charleston

So far, the city of Charleston itself had been spared the fury which had been raging around the outer rim of her harbor. She was, in fact, the only important Southern city which had not yet felt the effect of war. But her turn had now come.

Federal troops had built concealed batteries on Folly Island in preparation for an attack on Morris Island. Under the direction of General Q. A. Gilmore, they started their assault on July 10 (a week after Gettysburg) when 32 guns and 15 mortars began hurling shells while four monitors and four howitzer launches supported their fire from the sea. Boats carried troops across the narrow inlet which separated the two islands. The landing force was met with heavy fire but managed to get ashore in the shelter of some sand hills.

It drove back Confederate troops stationed on the southern end of Morris Island. The monitors then followed the Confederates along the shore, firing shells and grapeshot at them as they went. The men on the Federal ships were allowed to stop for lunch, but there was no rest for the harried Confederates retreating along the sandy beach in the hot sun. The Federal troops following them also had a difficult time. When the Confederates finally reached the shelter of Battery Wagner on the northern end of the island, their pursuers were too exhausted to attack, and the land battle halted while the assaulting troops dug in. The monitors, however, kept firing shells. Battery Wagner had only one gun powerful enough to

Federal shells exploding inside Fort Sumter in 1863.

reach the turreted ironclads. This was a 10-inch Columbiad, but its accuracy was so great that it hit the nearest monitor 60 times.

A Federal assault on Battery Wagner at dawn the next day also failed. After that, Union troops started building land batteries on Morris Island to reduce Wagner. While these batteries were under construction, the monitors kept firing at Wagner with businesslike regularity. The next big Federal assault came on July 18 when the newly placed guns on land and an enlarged fleet of monitors and gunboats lying off the coast began hurling shell and shrapnel at the sand and palmetto-log battery. They were joined by guns in the Confederate forts around the harbor, and the cannonading rose to a mighty roar that rocked the island and filled the sky with smoke. This went on for eleven hours, rivaling the great bombardment at Gettysburg on July 3 in intensity and exceeding it in noise and weight of metal.

The infantry attack began so late that night was falling when Federal troops advanced toward Wagner. Confederate casualties had been surprisingly light under 11 hours of shelling, but Union losses on the sandy beaches and in the ditches around the well-defended battery were staggering during the next few hours. In the morning, Confederates buried the bodies of 800 Union soldiers who had been killed that night.

Siege operations against Battery Wagner were now begun. While the monitors and Federal land batteries kept the northern end of Morris Island under a constant fire day and night, long trenches were driven forward toward Wagner. Men doing the excavating built the dead bodies of their comrades into the parapets, and the living and dead dwelt together under the hot summer sun.

While this engineering work went on, plans were made to place Fort Sumter under heavy bombardment by bringing up Federal guns to positions from which the fort could be shelled. The Confederates, foreseeing this, began to move all unneeded cannon and supplies from Sumter. On August 17 the Federal guns opened on the fort, firing 948 shots on the first day. The bombardment went on for weeks until the fort was reduced to a mass of rubble. But men still lived in the ruins. Finally only one gun remained in usable condition. The Confederate flag was kept flying defiantly and was hauled down every day at sunset when a salute was fired from the last gun to show that there was still life in the fort.

On September 5 a final effort was made to capture Battery Wagner. For 42 hours shells were dropped into the fort, driving the garrison into the bombproof shelters so they seldom had a chance to return the fire. During this intensive bombardment the trenches were driven forward with rolling saps at their heads to protect the men doing the digging. When morning came, and the Federals were ready to make their attack, they found that the long-defended battery had been evacuated by boat during the night.

As soon as Battery Wagner was occupied, an effort was made to capture Fort Sumter by sending in about 500 men in naval launches. The Confederates were ready for them with hand grenades and fireballs which they threw down while the other forts fired at the men trying to scale the walls. The attack failed, and more than 100 Federals were taken prisoner.

This drawing of a huge British gun was one of the first that Chapman made of the defenses of Charleston. It is dated October 29, 1863.

V. A Confederate Artist Records the Defenses of Charleston

Conrad Wise Chapman was the son of the artist who painted the well-known picture "The Baptism of Pocahontas" which still hangs in the Rotunda of the United States Capitol. His father took him to Rome at the age of six. He grew up there and studied art under his father's direction. In 1861 he went to Kentucky and enlisted as a private in the infantry. After being wounded at Shiloh, he was transferred to Richmond and then to Charleston. There General Beauregard commissioned him to make a series of paintings of the coastal defenses of the beleaguered city. Chapman worked on them during the winter of 1863–64 and made 31 finely detailed paintings as well as many black-and-white sketches. His work is by far the best of all Confederate artists; he was the only one who had formal training.

When Chapman went around the harbor to draw the Confederate defenses, he saw installations that

The well-protected casemate guns of Fort Sumter were mounted behind walls five to ten feet thick. Chapman shows them still in position.

In this Chapman painting, the Confederate flag still flies over the ruins of Fort Sumter where the last usable gun fired a salute to it every day at sunset.

had already been heavily bombarded by Federal naval and land guns. Many of the forts, particularly Sumter, were in a ruined condition, but their garrisons were still holding out in what remained. They held out until the end. Charleston was never taken by assault from the sea. It was evacuated in February 1865 when Sherman's army marched north from Georgia, cutting off the communications of the coastal towns along the way.

Chapman's paintings and sketches give us a vivid idea of what the defenses of Charleston looked like. Many of the huge guns were of English make and had been brought in through the blockade. They were still effective when Chapman sketched them, and their threat kept the Federal fleet from trying to enter the well-defended harbor again. But the city itself had been badly damaged by shells from Federal land-based guns. And when it was evacuated, cannon were blown up and the commissary depot and cotton warehouses were set on fire to prevent their falling into Union hands. As often happened in such cases, the flames rapidly got out of control and destroyed a good part of the city with much loss of life. When Union troops arrived on February 18, they found many buildings still burning and had to organize fire brigades to control the spread of the conflagration.

Chapman made this drawing of Battery Marion on November 14, 1863. Fort Sumter is at the right; at the left, smoke rises from Federal guns on Morris Island.

The *Alabama*, drawn from a description of her by a captain of one of the ships she captured.

THE *ALABAMA*
IN THE SOUTH ATLANTIC

The *Alabama* left Bahia, Brazil, on May 21, 1863, for the Cape of Good Hope. Semmes captured and burned several vessels on the way, but he found that Yankee ships were becoming scarce. Confederate raid-

THE PIRATE *ALABAMA*
John Bull (*furious*) "Hallo! there, Semmes; that's *my* Property. Fair play, you Rascal! If I'd suspected this, you'd never have *got out of Liverpool!*"
("Most of the property destroyed by the Pirate Semmes on board the vessels he has seized was insured in England, and the loss will consequently fall on Englishmen."—*Daily Paper*) A cartoon from Harper's *Weekly*.

ers were frightening their owners into transferring them to the flags of other nations or selling them abroad.

While crossing the South Atlantic, Semmes narrowly missed involving the Confederacy in a war with England. On July 2 he captured and burned the *Anna F. Schmidt* of Maine. When the *Alabama* parted from the flaming wreck that night, Semmes reported that "a large ship . . . passed us at rapid speed, under a cloud of canvas. . . . I conceived the idea that she must be one of the enemy's large clipper ships . . . and immediately gave chase, adding, in my eagerness to seize so valuable a prize, steam to sail. . . . By the time we were . . . in pursuit, the stranger was about three miles ahead. I fired a gun to command him to halt. In a moment or two, to my astonishment, the sound of a gun from the stranger came booming back over the waters. . . . I sent orders below to the engineer to . . . put the *Alabama* at the top of her speed. . . . About midnight we overhauled the stranger. . . . She was painted black, with a white streak around her waist, man-of-war fashion, and we could count . . . five guns of a side frowning through her

FACING PAGE: Consternation on board a ship when the *Alabama* approached. A drawing by Winslow Homer.

ports. 'What ship is that?' now thundered my first lieutenant through his trumpet. 'This is her Britannic Majesty's ship *Diomede!*' came back in reply very quietly. 'What ship is that?' now asked the *Diomede*. 'This is the Confederate States steamer *Alabama.'* 'I suspected as much,' said the officer, 'when I saw you making sail by the light of the burning ship.' A little friendly chat now ensued, when we sheared off and permitted her Britannic Majesty's frigate to proceed without insisting upon an examination of *her papers."*

The *Alabama* leaving Table Bay near Cape Town. A painting by Thomas Bowler, owned by Mr. William Fehr.

The ALABAMA Goes to the Far East

Semmes sighted the coast of South Africa on July 25, 1863, and the next day entered Saldanha Bay about 75 miles north of Cape Town. When he left there on August 5, he encountered the American bark *Sea Bride,* which he overtook and captured near Table Bay. According to Semmes, the ship was five or six miles offshore, but the American consul in Cape Town protested what he called a violation of British waters.

Semmes persuaded the local British authorities that the capture had been made on the open sea. He was allowed to keep his prize.

The chase had taken place in full view of the shore, where huge crowds gathered to watch this bit of drama of the far-off American Civil War. When the *Alabama* came to anchor, hundreds of people flocked to the ship in small boats to inspect the famous Confederate raider. Nearly everyone was friendly. Semmes granted an interview to newspaper reporters who printed detailed lists of the *Alabama's* many captures. And on August 12, photographers came on board to make pictures which were reproduced as wood engravings and printed in England.

Captain Semmes's secretary and Lieutenant Armstrong, photographed on the *Alabama* while at Cape Town.

Semmes, photographed at the same time.

On August 14 a ship arrived in Cape Town with news of what had happened at Gettysburg six weeks before. The next day Semmes left to go on a month's cruise of nearby waters. He was becoming bored with his work and noted in his journal, "How tiresome is the routine of cruising becoming!"

When he returned to Cape Town he was discouraged by word that Vicksburg and Port Hudson had fallen. And he learned that the well-armed Federal steamer *Vanderbilt* had been in port looking for him and was probably still in the vicinity. Semmes decided to go to the Far East; he left Cape Town on September 24 and started across the vast expanse of the Indian Ocean.

After nearly 3000 miles of sailing through nearly empty seas, he sighted the lonely island of St. Paul on October 12. He did not land but went on toward the East Indies, making a few captures on the way. From neutral ships Semmes learned that the USS *Wyoming*, a small bark-rigged steam gunboat, was patrolling the Sunda Strait between Sumatra and Java. Believing that the *Alabama* would be a good match for the gunboat, he resolved to attack her and sailed boldly into the strait. But the *Wyoming* had gone. Semmes, instead, met several American merchantmen which he captured and burned.

He then headed north and arrived at the French island of Puolo Condore, where he landed for supplies on December 3. On December 21 he sailed into the harbor of Singapore. The *Wyoming* had been there 20 days before him.

The *Alabama* remained in Singapore only three days. Then Semmes sailed west through the Strait of Malacca, capturing and burning another American ship a few hours after leaving port. He took still others on the way. On January 17, 1864, he made a brief landing at Anjenga on the southwest coast of India, to put his prisoners ashore. After that he sailed west to the Comoro Islands near the coast of Africa. In this Mohammedan settlement, Semmes found that slaves could be bought for five dollars. Yet there was no surplus of them. A local Negro church dignitary, who visited the ship, asked Semmes whether he belonged to the North or the South. On being told the South, he said, "We are slaveholders here. . . . The only trouble is that we cannot get slaves enough for our purposes. The English, who have no control of us, we being an independent government, are strong enough to interfere with everybody's business, and to us they say that we bring over . . . no more slaves."

Semmes gave his crew shore leave here, for no liquor was to be had on the Mohammedan islands. The men "looked rueful and woe-begone" when they returned. Four of them deserted but were soon brought back.

The *Alabama* left the islands on February 12 after a stay of several days. Semmes then headed for Cape Town, where he arrived on March 20 to be greeted with the unpleasant news that the British had seized the *Tuscaloosa,* the former Yankee bark which he had commissioned at sea in June.

Semmes immediately wrote a letter of protest to the British admiral in those waters. Correspondence had already begun between the local Governor and the Duke of Newcastle, Secretary for the Colonies, who had originally ordered the seizure. The Governor thought that it was unjustified, but a reversal of the decision did not arrive at the Cape until after Semmes had left there. When it did come, the war was nearly over, and the *Tuscaloosa* was eventually turned over to the local American consul.

Alabama destroys *Texan Star* in the Strait of Malacca.

155

SURGEON F. GALT

LIEUTENANT J. M. KELL

ENGINEER M. J. FREEMAN

Officers of the *Alabama*.

The Men Who Served on the ALABAMA

Semmes said that the crew of the *Alabama* "had been picked up promiscuously about the streets of Liverpool" and that they were a reckless, improvident, hard-drinking lot. But he kept them under rigid discipline which he seldom relaxed by letting them go ashore. His officers, however, were some of the best available.

The *Alabama's* first three lieutenants had served with Semmes on the *Sumter*. They were John McIntosh Kell, who later wrote a book about his experiences, Richard F. Armstrong, and Joseph D. Wilson. The fourth lieutenant was Arthur F. Sinclair, whose father and grandfather had been captains in the U. S. Navy. He, too, wrote a book about his two years on the *Alabama*. Lieutenant B. K. Howell was Jefferson Davis' brother-in-law; Acting Master Irvine S. Bulloch was the younger half-brother of James Dunwoody Bulloch; while Eugene A. Maffitt, a midshipman, was the son of the captain of the *Florida*.

There were about 120 seamen and 23 officers under Semmes's command. The muster roll kept changing as desertion, sickness or injury, and death took their toll. But enlistments along the way kept personnel up to normal.

THE CONFEDERATE COTTON LOAN IN EUROPE

Confederate agents in Europe were so successful in purchasing ships and military and naval supplies that the Richmond Government had trouble finding the cash to meet payments, which ran into many millions of dollars. The heads of the Government knew that they could get money for cotton, for Europe was now running short of that essential staple. But their cotton was in storage in the South, and the Federal blockade was growing tighter every day.

Slidell, the Confederate Commissioner in France, had met Emile Erlanger, who offered to lend the Confederacy money against cotton as collateral. Slidell wrote to Mason that the Erlangers were "one of the richest . . . banking houses in Europe, having extensive business relations throughout France and free access to some very important men about the Court. They will . . . exert themselves in our favor and enlist . . . persons who will be politically useful."

The Erlangers sent agents to Richmond who offered to lend $25,000,000, but the Confederate Treasury was reluctant to accept more than $15,000,000. And the terms which the Erlangers proposed were so steep that Judah P. Benjamin, then Secretary of State, felt obliged to persuade the French firm to reduce its demands. As finally settled, the Erlangers were to lend £3,000,000 ($15,000,000) against cotton bonds which were to be offered for sale in Europe at 90 per cent of par, and which were to pay 7 per cent interest. The bonds were to be exchangeable for cotton at sixpence a pound (it then sold for 21 pence in England) or were to be redeemable at par in 20 years. A contract with the Erlangers was signed on January 28, 1863, and was approved by the Confederate Congress.

When the bonds were put on sale in Europe on March 19, the issue was heavily oversubscribed, with many highly placed people eagerly buying the securities. The bonds promptly rose above their issue price and for a few days did very well. But on April 1, the price began to sag. It was feared that Charles Francis Adams, the American Minister, was using Federal funds to beat the market down, but this has never been proved. A more likely bearish influence was the fact that the British Government was at this time about to seize the *Alexandra,* a ship which had been built in Liverpool for the Confederate Government.

To let the bonds drop in value on the European market would have had a disastrous effect on the Confederacy's financial standing there. Confederate agents in Europe had to use £1,500,000 during the next few weeks to keep the bonds at par. It has been estimated

that the Richmond Government finally received only about $2,600,000 from the $15,000,000 loan.

Europe was still willing to advance credit. The Erlangers again offered money, but after the Confederate Congress approved their proposed contract on February 17, 1864, it rejected the loan and started negotiations for setting up a Franco-Confederate Bank in Europe which was to have cotton delivered there to use as collateral. But the war ended before such a bank could be put into operation.

Although these financial difficulties made it hard for Confederate agents to purchase war material in Europe, they were never at an utter loss to get what was needed. Right up to the very end of the war, a fairly steady supply of much-needed goods was obtained for shipment to the Confederacy. It was the closing of Southern ports that stopped supplies from getting through.

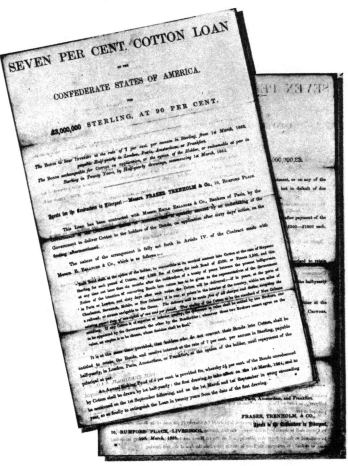

The prospectus for the Erlanger European Cotton Loan.

THE LAIRD RAMS

The Confederates knew that their only hope of doing serious damage to the fast-growing Federal Navy was to obtain at least a few ships that were better armed, better armored, and more seaworthy than their adversaries' far more numerous vessels. The Union had concentrated on monitors, which were excellent fighting ships but which were too slow, too unmaneuverable, and too low in freeboard to withstand heavy seas. They also had the disadvantage of not being able to be sailed and were dependent on getting coal at frequent intervals.

The European type of armored warship like the *Gloire,* the *Warrior,* and the improved models which had followed them, seemed more suitable to the Confederates' purposes—especially since ships intended for

One of the Laird rams as it looked when nearing completion in the Birkenhead yard.

them had to be brought across the Atlantic. When Bulloch went to Richmond after running the *Fingal* through the blockade in November 1861, he had been told how urgent the need for ironclads was. On his return to England he went to the Lairds in Birkenhead, who had built the highly successful *Alabama* for him, and in July 1862 he contracted with them to build two ironclads for the Confederacy.

The Laird rams differed from other French and British ironclads in that each had two revolving turrets designed by Cowper Coles. One of them was the first ship to carry Coles's tripod masts. These three-legged masts were forerunners of the basket masts later used on heavy battleships. They served the same purpose in being less liable to be shot down by enemy gunfire, and on these early cruisers, which needed sail more than steam, such masts also permitted wider arcs of fire from deck cannon than standing rigging did.

Bulloch knew that he now faced a far greater legal problem than he did when he got the *Florida* and the *Alabama* safely to sea. It was possible to pretend that those ships were intended to be used as merchantmen, but the two vessels now under construction in the Laird yards were to be armored and carry formidable 7-foot underwater rams. There was no concealing the ships' obvious purpose. But in order to stay within the letter of the British law, Bulloch not only refrained from putting guns on board; he also told the Lairds not to provide powder magazines or racks for shot and shell.

While under construction, the rams were known only by their shipyard designations No. 294 and No. 295.

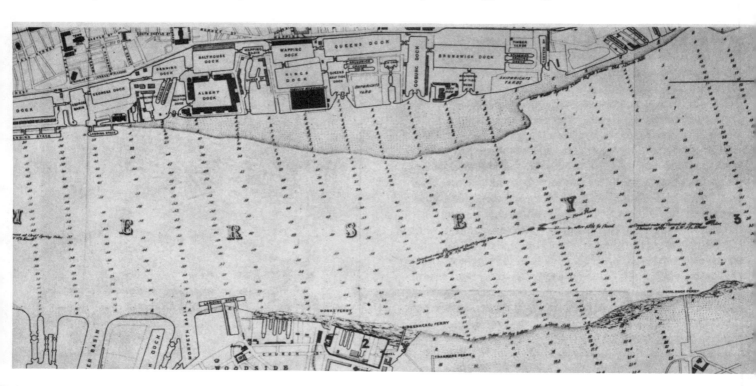

The first was to be ready in March 1863; the second in May. Except for guns and magazines, they were to cost £93,750 each.

The 230-foot ships were to be bulkheaded, and armored from 3½ feet below the waterline, while the hulls were to be plated with iron tapering from 4½ inches amidships to 2 inches at stem- and sternposts. This armor was to be backed with teak tapering from 12 to 6 inches. Each one of their two armored turrets was to carry two 9-inch rifles.

On November 7, 1862, Bulloch wrote to Mallory that the two ironclads were coming along well despite some delay caused by bad weather. He mentioned a plan he had for getting them out of England, but said that the need for secrecy prevented him from describing it in a letter which might be captured on the high seas.

But the indefatigable American Minister, Charles Francis Adams, was hard at work, and the British were becoming wary about offending the United States. On February 3, 1863, Bulloch sent a cipher dispatch to Richmond in which he said: "Think British Government will prevent iron ships leaving. . . . Object of armored ships too evident for disguise." He soon received instructions to sell the two ironclads to a French citizen. They could then be completed in France, loaded with supplies for the French Army in Mexico, and after that be resold to the Confederate Government. Bulloch made arrangements for such a

deal with Messrs. A. Bravay et Cie. of Paris, who were supposed to be agents for the Pasha of Egypt. The ships were then given the Arabic-sounding names *El Tousson* and *El Mounassir*.

Bulloch's hopes for the ironclads' future were rising. On July 9, five days after the first ram was launched, he wrote to Mallory suggesting that the presumably invincible armored ships be used to break the blockade, go up the Potomac to "render Washington untenable," and proceed to Portsmouth, New Hampshire, to destroy the navy yard there. He said that the ships were too big to navigate the crooked channels of the Mississippi, but that they could do so with help from smaller vessels. They could then run up the river to defend Vicksburg. It was an ambitious scheme. But Bulloch did not know that Vicksburg had been surrendered five days before he wrote.

Adams now brought so much pressure on the British that they ordered Custom House officials to examine the ironclads and question the Lairds about their ownership. The Lairds got permission from Messrs. Bravay to say that the French firm had title to the ships. Events moved swiftly after this. On September 1, Earl Russell sent a long letter to Adams in which he said that much of the evidence against the ironclads was hearsay; that they were built for the French or perhaps the Viceroy of Egypt; and that there was no proof that Bravay was not acting in good faith. He then said that "under these circumstances . . . Her Majesty's

EL TOUSSON   HMS MAJESTIC EL MOUNASSIR

HMS *Majestic* keeps watch over the Laird rams.

LEFT: The Birkenhead and Liverpool waterfronts in 1863. The initials EM and ET (at right center) show the location of the rams in the river.

CHARLES FRANCIS ADAMS

Government cannot interfere in any way with these vessels."

On the same day, Thomas H. Dudley, American Consul in Liverpool, notified Adams that one of the ironclads was ready to go to sea.

Even before he received Russell's letter, Adams wrote to the Earl on September 3 to say that "there is not any reasonable ground to doubt that these ves-

sels, if permitted to leave . . . Liverpool, will at once be devoted to the object of carrying on war against the United States." And then, when Russell's letter of September 1 finally arrived on the fourth, Adams, determined to prevent a recurrence of the way the *Florida* and the *Alabama* escaped, replied to Russell the next day with a phrase that was to create an international sensation. After pointing out that he had good reason to believe that at least one Confederate ironclad was about to depart "on a hostile errand to the United States," the American Minister quoted a Confederate publication as saying that an armored ship could easily enter any Northern port to inflict a vital blow and that this publication had also said that "the destruction of Boston alone would be worth a hundred victories in the field." Boston had been the center of the Adams family's activities for generations, and it was Charles Francis Adams' native city. Undoubtedly this influenced him when he wrote the famous phrase: "It would be superfluous in me to point out to your Lordship that this is war."

His words evidently had a profound and immediate effect upon Her Majesty's Government, for Adams noted in his journal on September 8 that there was a short article in the *Morning Post* that day announcing that the government was detaining the ironclads. Later the same day he received a brief statement from Russell confirming this.

The British Government's decision to detain the rams immediately depressed the price of Confederate cotton bonds. They had lost only two points when news of Lee's failure to win the Battle of Gettysburg arrived in England on July 16, but now they fell to 70 and dropped to 65 a month later when the Government officially seized the two rams, marked them with its symbolic broad arrow, and anchored the warship *Majestic* between them to make sure they could not get away.

Meanwhile, the British, with characteristic political sagacity, were trying to find a reasonable way out of their difficulty. On September 22, a British naval officer called on Bravay and Company in Paris to inquire about the ownership of the rams. After satisfying himself that Bravay had taken title to the vessels, he "mentioned that the British Government might be inclined to purchase them." Bravay said he would be glad to sell them, but that he would first have to clear the matter with the new Pasha of Egypt who allegedly had prior claim.

The British Foreign Office promptly went into action. Word came back from Cairo that when the Pasha had ascended the throne—several months before—he had notified Bravay that he would not honor any contracts made with his predecessor.

"Old Marm Britannia, as she will catch it one of these fine days from her own Rams." A contemporary cartoon from Harper's *Weekly*.

One of the Laird rams photographed in 1865 after being sold to the British Navy and commissioned as HMS *Wivern*. (*Crown copyright reserved*)

After protracted negotiation, the British bought the two ironclads in 1864 for £220,000, and made them part of Her Majesty's Navy. They were the first of that navy's turret ships—not to reach the water but to be designed as such and to start building. The series of long legal delays had held up their completion. When commissioned, they were named the *Scorpion* and the *Wivern*. The *Scorpion* spent 30 years as a harbor ship in Bermuda; in 1901 she was condemned to be used as a target and was sunk by shellfire. Her hulk was raised the next year and sold in 1903 for scrap. She foundered while being taken to Boston to be broken up.

The *Wivern* (which had the tripod masts) had an even longer career. After serving for 15 years as a coast-guard ship in British waters, she was sent to Hong Kong in 1880 to act as a harbor-defense ship. Much later she was sold and made into a distilling ship.

These two pioneer ironclads had many ingenious features. The bulwarks in front of each turret were hinged so they could be dropped down when the guns were ready to fire. When the bulwarks were raised, they prevented heavy seas from breaking on deck. In battle, the sailors' canvas hammocks could be piled around the tops of the turrets to protect riflemen posted there. Both these features can be seen in the photograph shown above.

When Bulloch had begun his dealing with Bravay and Company in March 1863, he had been introduced to them by L. Arman, a shipbuilder of Bordeaux, who was then constructing two iron-cased floating batteries for the French Navy. Arman was close to the Minister of State and had access to the Emperor. According to him, Napoleon III was willing to have warships built in France. They would then be sent out under the French flag for delivery to any agreed-upon place.

It was well known that the Emperor favored the South, and now that he was engaged in establishing an empire in Mexico he would certainly prefer to have the Confederacy as a neighbor rather than the United States, which, ever since the Monroe Doctrine of 1823, was known to be opposed to efforts by foreign powers to extend their influence into the Western Hemisphere.

Bulloch began by contracting with Arman for four wooden corvettes which were to be armed with 6-inch rifled French guns. Arman's yards were busy, so he subcontracted two of these vessels to shipbuilders in Nantes. The corvettes were ostensibly intended for the China trade where such armed vessels were in common use.

But eager as Bulloch was to obtain the wooden corvettes, he wanted ironclads even more. The French had led in the development of armored ships, and their yards knew how to build them. Iron, however, was in short supply in France at this time—so short, in fact, that it was holding up the construction of that country's own navy. Despite this drawback, Bulloch was determined to try to persuade the French shipyards to build ironclad rams for the Confederacy.

161

The launching of an ironclad ram in a French shipyard.

THE FRENCH-BUILT IRONCLADS

Even before he ran into trouble trying to get the Laird rams out of England, Bulloch had been convinced that the French would be easier to deal with than the British. Certainly, their Emperor was friendly. Impressed by the work Arman was doing for the French Navy, Bulloch signed a contract with him on July 13, 1863, for two ironclads tentatively named *Sphinx* and *Cheops*. These were to be smaller and lighter in draft than the Laird rams because Mallory wanted to use them in the Mississippi River.

Work on the four wooden corvettes and the two ironclads was proceeding nicely when, on September 10, 1863 (just after Russell had notified Adams that the Laird rams would not be allowed to leave England), the confidential clerk of one of the Nantes' shipbuilders called on John Bigelow, the American consul in Paris, and offered to sell correspondence that revealed the Confederates' plans to have ships built in France. Bigelow informed William L. Dayton, the

American Minister to France, who promptly addressed a protest to the French Government.

Bulloch was kept well informed of what was going on. On November 23 he wrote to Mallory, giving full details of what had happened. In this letter he said: "The extent to which the system of bribery and spying has been and continues to be practised by the agents of the United States in Europe is scarcely credible. The servants of gentlemen supposed to have Southern sympathies are tampered with, confidential clerks, and even the messengers from telegraph offices are bribed to betray their trust." Bulloch, however, was still optimistic; he told Mallory that whether or not the ships would be allowed to leave France depended on the fortunes of the Confederacy at the time they neared completion. When that time arrived, Bulloch said, "the course of the Civil War . . . took an unfavorable turn for the Confederate States, and the South began to show signs of exhaustion, which were painfully manifest to those

of us who were conscious of the strain and the inadequacy of the means to resist it." Napoleon III, whose spies were everywhere, undoubtedly knew this.

Bulloch wrote to Mallory on February 18, 1864, to tell him how matters stood. The Emperor had changed his mind, as he often did. He had notified the builders that the ironclads were not to sail and that the corvettes must be sold abroad.

It was a crushing disappointment. But Bulloch felt that if the ships were sold in Europe and not to some distant purchaser, he might still have a chance to re-buy them. He tried to exert what influence he could to have them sold locally. But the Emperor demanded that all the ships be disposed of quickly and to *bona fide* customers. One ram (the *Sphinx*) was to be sold to Denmark; the other to Prussia, which also bought two of the corvettes. The other two corvettes were purchased by the Peruvian Navy.

By a stroke of luck, it suddenly seemed possible late in 1864 to buy back the ram that was going to Denmark. Bulloch concentrated all his efforts on this (SEE PAGE 246).

A model of the French-built ironclad ram that was sold to Prussia and renamed the *Prinz Adalbert*. Owned by Friedrich Joberg, Berlin.

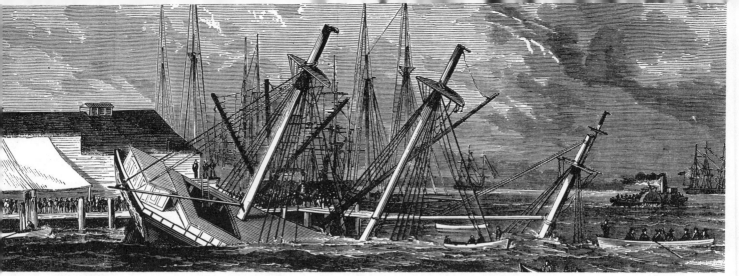

The wreck of the *Aquila,* sunk with the parts for the monitor *Camanche* on board.

CONFEDERATE EFFORTS
IN THE PACIFIC

On January 19, 1861, months before Sumter was fired on, and even before the Confederate Government was formed at Montgomery, word reached Washington that "a piratical expedition is on foot to proceed to the isthmus for the purpose of seizing the California steamers with their treasure." Nothing further was heard of this scheme. But the gold of California, which was shipped to the East in vast amounts, was a tempting prize to men who wanted to operate Confederate privateers. Plans were made to outfit ships to seize the gold steamers, but such efforts never got beyond the planning stage or were stopped by vigilant Federals. The only serious attempt to outfit a privateer in the Pacific came in 1863, when Asbury Harpending went from California to Richmond to obtain a letter of marque. On his return to San Francisco, he purchased a small schooner, the *J. M. Chapman.* Arms, ammunition, and uniforms were bought and put aboard, and a crew of 15 was recruited.

The expedition was scheduled to sail from San Francisco to Mexico on March 15, 1863, but on that day several boats from an American warship in the harbor came alongside. A frantic attempt was made to destroy all incriminating documents, but enough evidence remained for the owners of the *Chapman* to be arrested, brought to trial for treason, fined and sentenced to jail terms.

After this abortive attempt, repeated demands were made to Washington for naval protection for California. Accordingly, orders were issued to send a monitor there. The *Camanche,* then under construction in Jersey City, was put aboard the *Aquila* in sections,

which were to be assembled on arrival in California. She sailed for San Francisco in the summer of 1863.

The *Aquila* went around Cape Horn and arrived at Hathaway's Wharf in November. A storm came up soon after her arrival, and she sank in 37 feet of water. There were charges of Confederate sabotage, but nothing was proved. A professional wrecking crew with four divers brought up the various parts of the sunken monitor which were cleaned for reassembly. The *Camanche* was finally launched before a huge audience on November 14, 1864; she was commissioned on May 24, 1865—after the war was over. But she remained in service until 1899. It has been said that the *Camanche* is the only ship that ever sank before being launched.

Although another attempt to seize the gold steamers was about to be made in November 1864, its chief actors, Thomas E. Hogg and a group of Confederates, were arrested on the mail steamer *Salvador.* Still another was detected in January 1865.

The only time San Francisco was actually in danger of a Confederate naval attack was in July 1865, when the Confederate raider *Shenandoah* came down the Pacific Coast after a successful cruise against New England whaling ships in the Arctic Ocean (SEE PAGE 252). Her captain was long out of touch with Richmond and did not know that the war was over. He thought of running through the Golden Gate to attack San Francisco, but fortunately for him, he did not try to do so. If he had, he would have found the newly commissioned ironclad monitor waiting for him. And his wooden ship would have been no match for her.

THE CAPTURE OF THE *CHESAPEAKE*

Capturing a ship by a raiding party disguised as passengers had been tried successfully early in the war when Zarvona, posing as a French lady, had taken the *St. Nicholas* on Chesapeake Bay in June 1861 (SEE PAGES 39, 110). Now an attempt was to be made on the high seas—with international complications that almost brought on a war with England.

On December 5, 1863, the steamer *Chesapeake* left New York bound for Portland, Maine. (By coincidence, the *Chesapeake* had taken part in the capture of the daring young Confederate raider Lieutenant Charles W. Read at Portland earlier that year (SEE PAGE 140). Sixteen men dressed as civilians had boarded the steamer as passengers, bringing with them a heavy trunk. Their leader was John C. Braine, who had spent six months in a Northern jail for being a member of the secret pro-Confederate organization, the Knights of the Golden Circle. When the steamer was passing Cape Cod, they took their weapons from the trunk and forced the captain to surrender the ship. The second engineer was killed during the brief struggle for control; two other officers were injured.

The ship was taken to Grand Manan Island near the border between Maine and Canada, where the passengers were put in a small boat to row ashore. There Braine was joined by Vernon Locke, a Canadian who had a letter of marque which had been issued to another ship and was therefore not valid. Locke and Braine wanted to take the *Chesapeake* to Bermuda, but they needed coal for the ocean run. They tried to get some in Saint John, New Brunswick. The passengers, however, had rowed nearly 60 miles to Saint John to give the alarm.

The *Chesapeake* was hurriedly run across the Bay of Fundy and then taken around Nova Scotia toward Halifax. Braine went ashore at Petite Rivière, while two Federal warships caught up with her near Halifax, and the USS *Dacotah* took possession of her in British waters. A telegram from the Navy Department in Washington ordered the captain of the *Dacotah* to turn the ship and all prisoners over to the Nova Scotian authorities. When he delayed, there was talk of having the land batteries fire on the American warship. A shot from either side might have precipitated a war. No firing took place, but a long drawn-out legal battle followed which ended in the *Chesapeake* being returned to her owners in March 1864.

John C. Braine went on to seize still more Northern vessels. On September 29, 1864, he captured the *Roanoke* at sea and took her to Bermuda, where he put his passengers ashore and burned the ship. He was arrested but escaped to seize two schooners on Chesapeake Bay in the late spring of 1865. He ran one of them, the *St. Mary's,* to Jamaica, where he again escaped and went to Liverpool. He died penniless in Tampa, Florida, in 1906.

The steamer *Chesapeake,* after her capture, landing passengers in the Bay of Fundy.

CONFEDERATE SHIPS
AND BRITISH LAW

Bulloch was a good businessman who knew that he was working in the shadowy fringe areas of international law, British version. His first move had been to get the best possible advice from one of England's top legal authorities (SEE PAGE 36). Keeping firmly in mind the fact that British law permitted ships to be constructed in England but not armed within its borders, Bulloch had the *Florida* and the *Alabama* built there and later armed at sea. When Her Majesty's government bought the Laird ironclad rams for its own navy in order to placate the United States, things looked bad for Confederate ships under construction in English yards. One of them was the *Alexandra* which the Confederacy's financial agents, Fraser, Trenholm and Company, were having built at their own expense with the intention of presenting her as a gift to the Confederate Government. Bulloch had no connection with this ship, but he naturally knew a great deal about what was going on. He said that she was to be sent across the ocean unarmed and run through the blockade to Charleston. The United States attempted to prove that she was designed to be a gunboat.

The American consul in Liverpool, Thomas H. Dudley, had the ship watched closely to gather evidence about her. Charles Francis Adams sent this evidence to Lord Russell. As a result, the *Alexandra* was seized on April 5, 1863. An elaborate trial began on June 22 in the Court of Exchequer, at which the Crown tried to prove that the "vessel was built for the purpose of a warlike equipment . . . and that she was intended . . . for the service of the Confederate States."

Adams and Dudley had collected a great deal of evidence against the ship, but their case was weakened by the character of their witnesses who were professional spies, waterfront drifters who had to be paid to testify, or former Confederates who had deserted their cause. One of the latter, a paymaster named Clarence R. Yonge, after being dismissed from the *Alabama* in disgrace, had gone to Dudley to tell him what he knew about the Confederacy's secret naval plans.

The court decided the case against the Crown and ordered the ship to be restored to her owners with £3700 for damages and costs. The Crown applied for another trial and again lost. The *Alexandra* was released in April 1864. Her name was then changed to *Mary,* and she sailed to Halifax, Bermuda, and Nassau as a commercial vessel. She was seized again on December 13, 1864, in Nassau. This time, the case

The *Alexandra* lying alongside a dock in Liverpool after being seized by the British.

ABOVE: The *Pampero* after being seized in Glasgow. RIGHT: An original drawing of a contemporary cartoon found in the Public Record Office, London. (*Crown copyright reserved*)

against her dragged on so long that the war was over when she was finally released in May 1865.

The extensive legal documentation on the case of the *Alexandra* helped to define the position of Her Majesty's government toward the building of Confederate ships in England. The official British attitude toward the subject kept changing as the fortunes of war changed. During the spring of 1863 the Confederacy's prospects seemed good; England therefore tended to favor the South. News of Gettysburg and the fall of Vicksburg reached London on July 22. The full significance of these events apparently was not immediately understood even by the leaders of the British government, for its Prime Minister, Lord Palmerston, speaking in the House of Commons the next day, said: "I cannot . . . concur . . . in thinking that there is any distinction in principle between muskets, gunpowder, and bullets on the one side, and ships on the other. These are things by which war is carried on, and you are equally assisting belligerents by supplying them with muskets, cannon, and ammunition, as you are by supplying them with ships that are to operate in war. . . . Therefore I hold that on the mere ground of international law belligerents have no right to complain if merchants—I do not say the Government, for that would be interference—as a mercantile transaction, supply one of the belligerents not only with arms and cannon, but also with ships destined for warlike purposes." Despite this broad interpretation of the law by the British Government's Prime Minister, however, it became increasingly more difficult for the Confederates to get ships out of England.

The case of the *Pampero* (or *Canton*) is a good instance of this. The ship had been ordered in the summer of 1862 by Lieutenant George T. Sinclair of the Confederate Navy and was under construction on the Clyde. She was seized in December 1863, but did not go to formal trial. The Scotch builders were willing to make any reasonable compromise, but did not regain possession of their ship until September 1865.

In their effort to stop the building of any ship that might possibly be intended for the Confederacy, Dudley and Adams sometimes called British attention to vessels that were obviously not designed to carry guns. The *Phantom* was being built for use as a blockade-runner, but she was privately owned, and the Confederate Government had no financial interest in her. Most amazing of all was the case of the *Hector*, which Adams had been told was intended for the Confederate Navy. The British Foreign Office rather huffily informed him that the ironclad was being constructed for Her Majesty's Navy.

A companion drawing to the one shown above caricaturing the case of the *Phantom*. (*Crown copyright reserved*)

THE *COMMODORE BARNEY*
HITS A TORPEDO

On August 4, 1863, four Federal ships left Newport News to go up the James River on reconnaissance. The next day the senior officers boarded the *Commodore Barney,* which then went ahead of the other vessels. At Cox's farm, about six miles below Fort Darling, a large torpedo fired electrically by an observer on the shore exploded directly under the bows of the ship, lifting the front end ten feet into the air and sending up an enormous column of water. About 20 men were knocked overboard, two of whom drowned.

The damaged ship was taken in tow and brought down the river. The next day it had to pass through a barrage of artillery and musketry fire, for the Con-federates had had time to rush in troops and haul up guns to oppose the Union fleet's return. Thirty artillery shells hit the vessel; it was also riddled with bullets. And the tug towing the injured ship was struck many times. Yet both got back to Newport News. Except for one man injured by splinters, the two drowned men were the only serious casualties.

Hereafter, the Union Navy's ships navigated the James River with greater caution. Nevertheless, the *Commodore Jones* was blown to pieces on the James by an electric torpedo on May 6, 1864. The ship was a total loss with 69 casualties. She was dragging the river for torpedoes, and was over one when it exploded.

The *Dunderberg* under construction in 1863 in New York.

THE UNION NAVY BUILDS A HUGE IRONCLAD

While the Confederacy was having great difficulty having ironclads built in Europe, the Union had the material, the shops and yards, and the skilled labor to build plenty of them at home. But the North's most ambitious armored vessel was so slow in construction that the formidable *Dunderberg* was not launched until after the war (on July 22, 1865), although the big ship had been contracted for on July 3, 1862. W. H. Webb and the Aetna Iron Works of New York City were her builders, and she was put together at the foot of Sixth Street on the East River.

This "Thunder Mountain" was 373 feet long with a beam of 73 feet and a draft of 23 feet. She carried a 50-foot, very sharp ram backed with heavy timbers, and she was pierced for 21 guns. Two gigantic engines were to drive 21-foot propellers that were to speed her along at 15 knots. She was designed as a wooden-framed casemated ship, but she was also intended to carry two revolving turrets as well, although they were never put in place.

The *Dunderberg*, which was by far the biggest ironclad ever completed in America up to that time, had many unusual features. She had such advanced protective devices as a double bottom, collision bulkheads, watertight bulkheads enclosing the engines and boilers, and her 13-foot-wide smokestack had armor gratings inside it to prevent grenades, shells, or the debris of battle from falling down to choke the boiler fires.

It took 1000 tons of coal to fill the *Dunderberg's* enormous bunkers, and she ate up fuel like the snorting monster she was. Since she was completed when there was no longer any need for her, and the Union Navy was then being cut back to peacetime size, the great ship, which had been contracted for at a price of $1,250,000, was sold to her builders for the $1,092,887.73 which had already been paid to them. They in turn sold her to the French Navy, in which she served under the name *Rochambeau*. On her first run across the Atlantic she proved to be an excellent ship. Had she been put into operation sooner, she might have done a great deal of harm to the Southern cause. But time lost in construction invalidated her for use against the Confederacy as effectively as if she had been sunk in battle.

The former *Dunderberg's* hull shape influenced French naval design for a generation to come, because their architects admired her exaggerated ram bows and home-sloping top sides and copied them for their own warships.

France had been building a powerful navy ever since *La Gloire* was launched at Toulon in 1859. But when the Franco-Prussian War broke out in 1870, the Germans struck from the east by land. Their navy was so far inferior to the French that its five ironclads took refuge in Wilhelmshafen and the Elbe, where they remained for the duration. Three German armies overran France so swiftly that there was no time for naval action of any consequence before the brief but devastating war was over. French marines helped defend Paris, the Loire, and Brittany, but the main fighting was done on land, not on sea, and all the careful French naval preparation went for nothing.

THE *ALABAMA* MEETS
THE *KEARSARGE* IN BATTLE

The Civil War's most important naval engagement on the
high seas took place off the coast of Cherbourg, France,
on June 19, 1864, when Semmes accepted a challenge to

The year 1864 was a turning point for the Confederate Navy—and for the Confederacy. The year began well enough. The Confederate's Hunley was the first submarine in the world to sink an enemy ship. The North's Red River Campaign that spring was a dismal failure, while the Confederate ram Albemarle was a great success in the Carolina sounds. Confederate torpedoes continued to do their deadly work. But in June the Alabama was sunk; then the Florida was captured, and the Albemarle was blown up in a daring raid. At the close of the year the Federals launched their first attack on Fort Fisher. It was the beginning of the end.

1864.

JANUARY								JULY						
Sun.	M.	T.	W.	T.	F.	Sat.		Sun.	M.	T.	W.	T.	F.	Sat.
..	..	..	..	..	1	2		..	..	..	..	..	1	2
3	4	5	6	7	8	9		3	4	5	6	7	8	9
10	11	12	13	14	15	16		10	11	12	13	14	15	16
17	18	19	20	21	22	23		17	18	19	20	21	22	23
24	25	26	27	28	29	30		24	25	26	27	28	29	30
31	..	..	..	..	..	..		31	..	..	..	..	..	..

FEBRUARY								AUGUST						
..	1	2	3	4	5	6		..	1	2	3	4	5	6
7	8	9	10	11	12	13		7	8	9	10	11	12	13
14	15	16	17	18	19	20		14	15	16	17	18	19	20
21	22	23	24	25	26	27		21	22	23	24	25	26	27
28	29	..	..	..	..	..		28	29	30	31	..	..	..

MARCH								SEPTEMBER						
..	..	1	2	3	4	5		..	..	..	..	1	2	3
6	7	8	9	10	11	12		4	5	6	7	8	9	10
13	14	15	16	17	18	19		11	12	13	14	15	16	17
20	21	22	23	24	25	26		18	19	20	21	22	23	24
27	28	29	30	31	..	..		25	26	27	28	29	30	..

APRIL								OCTOBER						
..	..	..	..	..	1	2		..	..	..	..	..	..	1
3	4	5	6	7	8	9		2	3	4	5	6	7	8
10	11	12	13	14	15	16		9	10	11	12	13	14	15
17	18	19	20	21	22	23		16	17	18	19	20	21	22
24	25	26	27	28	29	30		23	24	25	26	27	28	29
..	..	..	..	..	..	..		30	31	..	..	..	..	..

MAY								NOVEMBER						
1	2	3	4	5	6	7		..	..	1	2	3	4	5
8	9	10	11	12	13	14		6	7	8	9	10	11	12
15	16	17	18	19	20	21		13	14	15	16	17	18	19
22	23	24	25	26	27	28		20	21	22	23	24	25	26
29	30	31	..	..	..	..		27	28	29	30	..	..	..

JUNE								DECEMBER						
..	..	..	1	2	3	4		..	..	..	..	1	2	3
5	6	7	8	9	10	11		4	5	6	7	8	9	10
12	13	14	15	16	17	18		11	12	13	14	15	16	17
19	20	21	22	23	24	25		18	19	20	21	22	23	24
26	27	28	29	30	..	..		25	26	27	28	29	30	31

come out and fight the USS *Kearsarge*. It was an unequal combat, for the *Alabama* was a tired ship badly in need of repair. She was riddled by shellfire and went down.

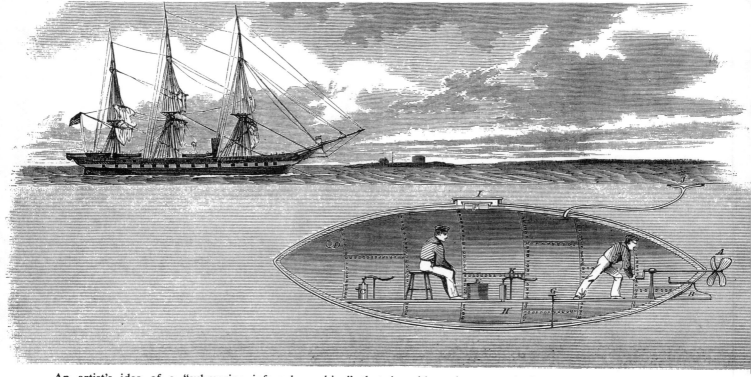

An artist's idea of a "submarine infernal machine" that is said to have attacked the USS *Minnesota* near Fort Monroe in October 1861.

CIVIL WAR SUBMARINES: REAL AND FANCIED

Although a working submarine is said to have been in existence at the beginning of the seventeenth century, the first undersea boat attack on an enemy ship took place in New York Harbor during the Revolution when David Bushnell's primitive little *Turtle*

made several unsuccessful attempts to blow up a British warship. He was followed by Robert Fulton, who invented several submarines at the beginning of the nineteenth century. After Fulton, there was so much activity in submarine design that a score or more were

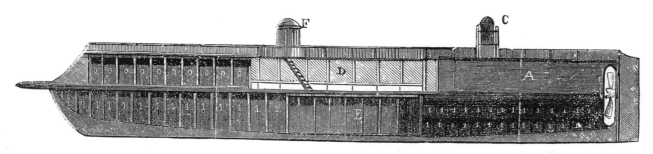

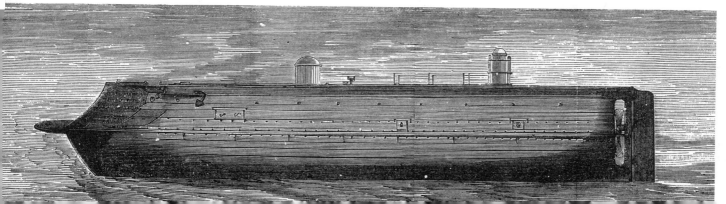

built and tried out in various parts of the world before 1861. They were all experimental; none sank a ship. That was left for the Confederate Navy to do.

During the early years of the Civil War all sorts of rumors were circulated about death-dealing undersea monsters supposedly being built in both the North and the South. The rumors had some basis in fact. The Union had employed a French engineer early in the war to design a submarine, the *Alligator,* which was built in Philadelphia. Forty-seven feet long and made of steel, it had such advanced features as a system for purifying air, a watertight compartment in the bow from which a diver could exit and return, and it carried a torpedo at the end of a long spar. But it was still a very primitive war machine, for its screw propeller was operated by 16 men turning hand cranks. The Federal Navy wanted to use this new undersea weapon against the *Merrimack-Virginia,* then being built at Norfolk, but it was completed too late. The *Virginia* had already been destroyed by its own crew when the *Alligator* was towed from Philadelphia toward the entrance to Chesapeake Bay in June 1862. It was lost in a storm on the way.

In the 1850s, the French had been world leaders in naval design, so it was not surprising that they turned their thoughts to undersea warfare. A remarkable submarine named the *Plongeur* was developed there from plans made by Charles Brun. When completed on April 16, 1863, she was 146 feet long, by far the largest ship of her kind yet attempted. She was driven by a compressed-air engine which drove a propeller. Among other improvements she carried a small escape boat in an outside chamber. Like most submarines built before the self-propelled torpedo was invented, this one depended on a spar torpedo as its chief weapon. The *Plongeur* was cranky and difficult to keep level when immersed. She was not successful, but much was learned from her. After two years of experimental work, the big submarine was scrapped.

About 2 A.M. on January 26, 1865, a moving object came out of the darkness and appeared alongside the U.S. armed paddle-wheel steamer *Octorara.* The captain of the afterguard grabbed it by the smokestack and tried to hold it fast, meanwhile calling for ropes. But the pipe was hot, and he had to let go. The nearly submerged vessel rapidly steamed away.

Other countries could afford the luxury of building trial vessels and taking time to improve them. They were not at war. The Confederacy was. It had neither the time nor the money to spend on theoretical experiments. It needed working submarines, and it needed them fast. It was even willing to settle for boats which were not completely submersible, but which could run low in the water and creep up unseen to a ship under the cover of night.

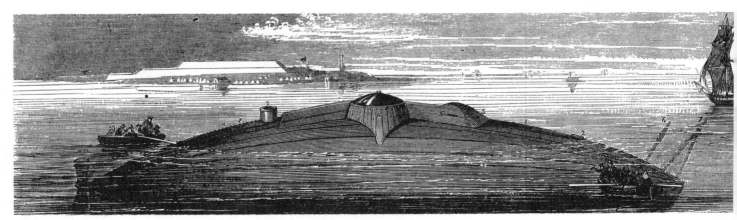

This fanciful picture of another Mobile-built Confederate steam-powered submarine appeared in *Le Monde Illustré* in 1864.

LEFT: Confederate submarines were being built in Mobile in 1863, but they were far simpler than this dream version which appeared in *Le Monde Illustré.*

Confederate Submarines and Davids

The *Pioneer* was aptly named, for she was the first submarine built in the Confederacy. The ironclad turtle-shaped ram *Manassas* looked as if intended to be submersible, but she was not. Like the *Manassas,* the *Pioneer* was the product of New Orleans builders who constructed the novel little vessel for use as a privateer. More is known about her origins than her later career, because the application her owners made on March 29, 1862, for a letter of marque has been preserved. This document states that "said vessel is commanded by John K. Scott. . . . is a propeller; is 34 feet in length; is 4 feet breadth; is 4 feet deep. She measures about 4 tons; has conical round ends and is painted black. She is owned by Robert R. Barrow [also named as Robin R. Barrow], Baxter Watson, and James R. McClintock, all of . . . New Orleans. She will carry a magazine of explosive matter, and will be manned by two men or more." The letter of marque was issued two days later. One of the men listed as sureties was Horace L. Hunley, who was soon to make history in submarine warfare.

The *Pioneer* is said to have blown up a barge during her trials, but she was destined never to see action. There are several stories about the way she was lost —some highly improbable. The most believable account says that she was purposely sunk to prevent capture when Farragut came up the Mississippi to take New Orleans. Another version states that she went to the bottom on a trial run and drowned her three-man crew.

About 16 years later, the *Pioneer* was accidentally found by some boys who were swimming; the sunken wreck was then brought to the surface by a sand dredge. She lay near the shore until 1907, when she was presented to the Camp Nicholls Home for Confederate Soldiers. There she was mounted on a concrete block to become a minor curiosity for tourists. An amazing sea change seems to have taken place during her long immersion. When she was measured in 1926 by William Morton Robinson, Jr., he found that she was hardly 20 feet long. Yet the application for a letter of marque described her as being 34 feet long. It is possible that the original overall dimensions included some part—such as a long spar—which might have been missing after weather and vandals had worked their mischief on her. It is also possible that the little submarine, which is now on display in the Presbytere, is not the *Pioneer,* and that the original is still at the bottom of Lake Ponchartrain.

In his book, *The Confederate Privateers,* Robinson described the *Pioneer* as she was when he saw her: "She is fabricated of ¼-inch iron sheets, fastened with ⅝-inch countersunk rivets. The deck plates are curved to conic surfaces. The little vessel seems the product of true craftsmanship; and . . . a recognized authority on submarine design . . . said that her form indicated that she should have been very stable and successfully navigable under water.

"The propeller—the blades are now broken off— was turned by cranks operated by two men sitting on little iron brackets fastened, opposite, on each side of the vessel, immediately under the hatchway. There were rudders on either end, connected for single control. The bow rudder is gone, the stock being snapped off just below the rudder-post. The stern rudder is buried in the concrete base, but a photograph taken before the emplacement shows it to be an equipoise-rudder. The diving was accomplished by two side vanes, or fins, 35 inches long by 16 inches wide,

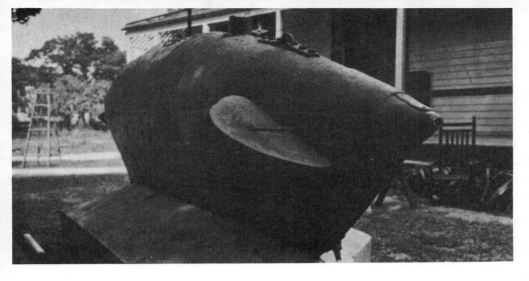

placed about on the level of the propeller and over the forward rudder. They both worked on. the same shaft, rotated by a lever arm, which directly pointed the angle of the dive. The port vane has been twisted off.

"The sole entrance to the vessel is through the 18-inch hatchway amidships. The edge of the opening is reinforced with an iron collar, 3/8 of an inch thick and 2½ inches wide. The cover is gone, but the indications are that it was simply a lid hinged aft and closing on a gasket fastened directly to the curved roof or deck; for the rivet holes surrounding the hatch are only ⅛ of an inch in diameter. It does not seem probable that the cover stood high enough . . . to serve as a conning tower with eyeports. In fact, little provision seems to have been made for light or observation. In the roof, forward of the hatch, there are two groups of eight ¾-inch holes, each, arranged in circles one foot in diameter. These holes may have been glassed, serving as small light ports. Surmounting the center of the more forward set of holes is a cuff, five inches in height and in diameter, which seems to have been a stuffing box through which an air shaft passed. This pipe was not more than an inch and three-quarters in diameter; and . . . was probably rather short and intended only for the intake of air when the vessel was operating near the surface—at which time it resembled the present-day periscope traveling through the water. An interior stopcock would prevent the admission of water when the submergence was deep. There is in the prow or nose of the vessel a two-inch circular opening, which, I am inclined to believe, was used for forward observation rather than as a socket for a torpedo spar.

"There is little doubt that the torpedo, or 'magazine of powder,' as it was called in the letter of marque, was carried on a tow-line, the attack being made by the submarine diving under the enemy craft and the floating torpedo exploding upon being trailed into contact with its hull. . . .

"The station of the commanding officer of the *Pioneer* was well forward and within easy reach of the diving lever, the rudder control, the depth gauge, and the air cock. The course was laid on the surface, and held by a set screw on the rudder-head. A magnetic compass, lighted by a candle, was used to detect variations from the desired direction."

After the capture of New Orleans, Hunley went to Mobile with McClintock and Watson to experiment further with submarines. Mobile was a good place for such work. Iron was available in Alabama, and the shop of Parks and Lyons on Water Street, where the construction was done, was unusually well equipped for its time and place. Their second vessel had a short life; she foundered while being towed to the harbor entrance to attack the Federal blockading fleet lying outside. But their third undersea boat achieved world fame, for she was the first submarine to sink an enemy ship.

Two engineers from the 21st Alabama Infantry were sent to the Parks and Lyons shops to give technical assistance. One of them, Lieutenant George E. Dixon, was to be in command when the new submarine went on her historic mission.

While the Hunley submarine was under construction in Mobile, long, low, cigar-shaped, steam-powered torpedo boats were going into action at Charleston. They looked like submarines, but they were not intended to operate under water. They depended on their hardly visible silhouette to escape detection, especially in poor light. Their major weapon was a torpedo carried ahead on a long spar. Because of their small size and lethal punch, they were called "Davids."

On the night of October 5, 1863, one of them went out of the harbor to hunt down the big armored Federal ship *New Ironsides*. J. H. Tomb, acting engineer on the David, wrote this official report of the attack: "At 9 P.M., everything being favorable . . . we headed for the *Ironsides*. When within 50 yards of her we were hailed, which was answered by a shot from

The David that attacked the *New Ironsides,* drawn by a Harper's *Weekly* artist from description.

a double-barreled gun in the hands of Lieutenant Glassell. In two minutes we struck the ship (we going at full speed) under the starboard quarter, about 15 feet from her sternpost, exploding our torpedo about 6½ feet under her bottom. The enemy fired rapidly with small arms, riddling the vessel, but doing us no harm. The column of water thrown up was so great that it recoiled upon our frail bark in such force as to put the fires out and lead us to suppose that the little vessel would sink. The engine was reversed for backing, but the shock occasioned by the jar had been so great as to throw the iron ballast among the machinery, which prevented its working. During this delay, the vessel, owing to the tide and wind, hung under the quarter of the *Ironsides,* the fire upon us being kept up the whole time. Finding ourselves in this critical position and believing our vessel to be in a sinking condition, we concluded that the only means of saving our lives was to jump overboard, trusting that we would be picked up by the boats of the enemy. Lieutenant Glassell and the fireman swam off in the direction of the enemy's vessels, each being provided with a life preserver. . . . The pilot stuck to the vessel, and I being overboard . . . concluded it was best to make one more effort to save the vessel. Accordingly, I returned to her and rebuilt my fires; after some little delay got up steam enough to move the machinery. The pilot then took the wheel and we steamed up channel, passing once more through the fleet and within 3 feet of a monitor, being subjected the whole time to one continuous fire of small arms, the *Ironsides* firing two 11-inch shot at us."

The shot fired from the handgun on the David struck Acting Ensign C. W. Howard, who was standing on the deck of the *New Ironsides,* and wounded him so badly that he died a few days later. When divers were sent down to investigate the wreck, they found that planking had been shattered and that some damage had been done to the inside of the hull.

The men who had escaped from the sinking David swam to a Union ship. They were interrogated by their captors, who obtained enough information about the mysterious little attacker to send rough sketches and descriptions of it to Washington. Admiral Dahlgren re-

corded in his diary that "nothing could have been more successful as a first effort, and it will place the torpedo among certain offensive means."

Defensive devices, such as outriggers or hawsers with netting attached, were used to protect Union ships at anchor, and the fleet was kept on a round-the-clock alert to watch for further attacks. The ironclads were guarded by fenders which supported weighted nets.

The Mobile-built submarine had been named the *H. L. Hunley.* Since she was badly needed in Charleston, she was shipped there by rail on two platform cars and was launched early in September 1863. Unfortunately, the *Hunley* had a great affinity for water, as her luckless crews found out, and she could not be operated below the surface by steam, since there was no way of getting enough air to feed oxygen-hungry boiler fires once she was submerged. Much time was lost trying to develop an electromagnetic engine for her, but it was finally decided to propel the primitive submarine by eight men working cranks that rotated a shaft turning a helical screw.

At first the *Hunley* was supposed to drag a torpedo behind her at the end of a long line. She was to dive under her target, and the torpedo would then be exploded by contact when it brushed against the bottom of the ship to be destroyed. But the long cable caused so much trouble that the customary method of using a spar torpedo had to be resorted to instead.

Long before the *Hunley* was ready for action, her trial runs proved her to be cranky and dangerous. Known also as the "American Diver" (which she certainly was), her beginnings were described by a Confederate deserter who had seen her in Mobile and Charleston. Since he told the Union Navy about her on January 7, 1864, it had some idea of what to expect. The deserter, originally a mechanic from Michigan, said that "she has had bad accidents hitherto, but was owing to . . . not understanding her. Thinks . . . she can be worked perfectly safe by persons who understand her. . . . Has drowned three crews, one at Mobile and two here, 17 men in all."

The *Hunley* sank again on October 15, drowning another crew and the man whose name she bore. The Confederate Journal of Operations said that she "left the wharf at 9:25 A.M. and disappeared at 9:35. As soon as she sank, air bubbles were seen to rise, and from this fact it is supposed the hole in the top . . . by which the men entered was not properly closed." General Beauregard saw her brought up. He said that "the spectacle was indescribably ghastly. The unfortunate men were contorted into all sorts of horrible attitudes, some clutching candles . . . others lying in the bottom tightly grappled together, and the blackened faces of all presented the expression of their despair and agony."

Despite the *Hunley's* murderous record, the two engineers from the 21st Alabama Infantry Regiment who had given technical assistance in Mobile, now volunteered to take her out. One of them, Lieutenant George E. Dixon, was in command when the little submarine left Charleston on the night of February 17, 1864. The *Hunley's* ordinarily slow progress was helped by an ebb tide which carried her out to sea. Visibility was improved by a bright moon which lacked only a few days of being full. Running along the surface, the small, low-lying craft was able to approach the 207-foot-long armed screw-steamer *Housatonic* without being noticed until very near.

There are no Confederate witnesses as to what happened. J. R. Crosby, Acting Master of the *Housatonic*, reported that about 8:45 P.M., he "discovered something . . . about 100 yards from and moving toward the ship. It had the appearance of a plank moving in the water. . . . The chain was slipped, engine backed,

The torpedo explodes under the *New Ironsides*. The men in the small boat are said to have accompanied the David from Charleston.

and all hands called to quarters. The torpedo struck forward of the mizzenmast, on the starboard side, in a line with the magazine. Having the after pivot gun pivoted to port, we were unable to bring a gun to bear upon her. About one minute after she was close alongside, the explosion took place, the ship sinking stern first and heeling to port. . . . Most of the crew saved themselves by going into the rigging."

Five Union sailors were killed or drowned. And the *Hunley* and her crew went down with the *Housatonic*. Their lives must be added to those which the "veritable coffin" had already claimed.

A contemporary sketch of the *Housatonic* when blown up by a torpedo from the *H. L. Hunley*.

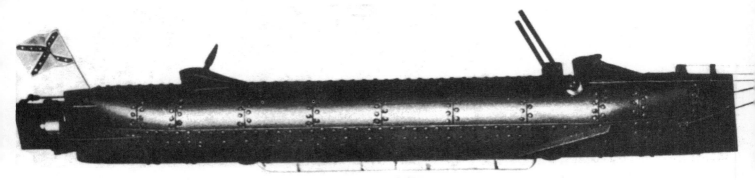

A modern scale model of the *H. L. Hunley,* showing its spar for carrying a torpedo; its iron keel, which was detachable in sections; and its diving fins. The rivet heads are probably larger in proportion than they should be.

Amidships sections of the *Hunley* drawn by W. A. Alexander showing position of one of the eight men who supplied motive power by turning cranks.

The interior of the *Hunley* as a Northern artist imagined it to be. It is incorrect in almost every detail. BELOW: Mechanical details of the *Hunley's* interior, drawn by W. A. Alexander.

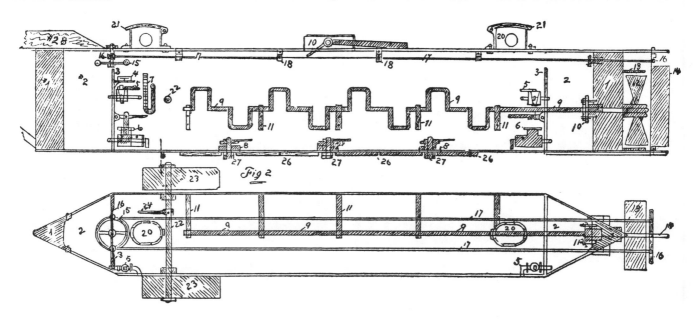

The World's First Successful Submarine

Although it is not known whether the *H. L. Hunley* was actually submerged or not when she torpedoed the *Housatonic,* she was built to be a submarine. As such, she claimed what was to be the first of many victims sent to the bottom by undersea craft. No more ships were sunk by submarines until the First World War began in 1914. Submarines had been improved enormously by that time, but there had not been much chance to use them in warfare.

The *Hunley* was described in some detail by the deserter previously mentioned. He said that she was "about 35 feet long; height about the same as 'David' (5½ feet); has propeller at the end . . . has two manholes on the upper side, about 12 to 14 feet apart. The entrance into her is through these manholes, the covers being turned back. . . . Manholes are about 16 inches high and are just above water. . . ."

Fortunately, the Confederate artist, Conrad Wise Chapman, saw the *Hunley* lying on a dock when he was sketching the defenses of Charleston. The pencil drawing he made on December 2, 1863, is an authentic representation of the world's first submarine. He used this drawing later as the basis for a painting, but it is reasonable to assume that the original sketch made on the spot is more correct in detail than the painting derived from it. Chapman's exterior view

agrees amazingly well with what we know about the interior. And the diagrammatic sketches made by W. A. Alexander, which appear in Volume 15 of *Official Records of the Union and Confederate Navies,* are also in reasonable accord with Chapman's picture of the hull.

Admiral Dahlgren, who was a weapons inventor himself, understood the importance of the torpedo boats the Confederates were using against his fleet. In a report announcing the sinking of the *Housatonic,* he said: "The Department will readily perceive the consequences likely to result from this event; the whole line of blockade will be infested with these cheap, convenient, and formidable defenses, and we must guard every point. The measures for prevention may not be so obvious. I am inclined to the belief that in addition to the various devices for keeping the torpedoes from the vessels, an effectual preventive may be found in the use of similar contrivances. I would therefore request that a number of torpedo boats be made . . . to float not more than 18 inches above water. . . . I have already submitted a requisition . . . for some craft of this kind . . . which, with the great mechanical facilities of the North, should be very quickly supplied. I have also ordered a quantity of floating torpedoes, which I saw tried here and thought promised to be useful. . . . I have attached more importance to the use of torpedoes than others have done, and believe them to constitute the most formidable of the difficulties in the way to Charleston. Their effect on the *Ironsides* . . . and now on the *Housatonic,* sustains me in this idea. . . . I desire to suggest to the Department the policy of offering a large reward . . . for the capture or destruction of a 'David'; I should say not less than $20,000 or $30,000 for each. They are worth more than that to us."

Conrad Wise Chapman's drawing of the *Hunley.*

ARMORED SHIPS IN 1864

Because the urgencies of war require production in quantity rather than just improvement of quality, the North and the South both tended to freeze the development of ironclads where it was when they built the first ones. The North, with the exception of the casemated *Dunderberg* (SEE PAGE 169), concentrated largely on monitors, while the South continued to build casemated ironclads.

The loss of the original *Monitor* off Cape Hatteras.

The monitor *Weehawken* sinking near Charleston.

Monitors were gradually improved, but their basic defects were showing up. Their chief fault was that they were easily swamped because of their low freeboard. The original *Monitor* had foundered in a storm at sea on the last day of 1862. And then, on December 6, 1863, the monitor *Weehawken* sank suddenly near Charleston with a loss of 31 lives. She went down in a few minutes broad daylight "with the ship fully under the observation of her officers." At the time, the water was relatively calm. A court of inquiry found that the monitor had been overloaded with ammunition and was badly trimmed, so that water had come in through the hawse hole and the windlass-room hatch. Admiral Dahlgren was not satisfied with the court's findings, and the mystery of the sinking has never been fully explained.

The design of deep-draft ocean-going armored ships was static in the United States because there was no great need for such vessels. They could not invade the shallow Southern ports, and they had very few worthy Confederate opponents on the high seas.

But ironclad design was rapidly going ahead in Europe. The Royal Navy's first turreted ship was completed on August 20, 1864. She was the *Royal Sovereign,* which was built upon the cut-down hull of a 131-gun old-style wooden sailing ship just completed at Portsmouth. She had four Coles-type turrets, one with two guns, and three with one each. A true steamship, her stubby masts were intended only for steadying sails. She was far ahead of any ship in any other navy. And while the *Royal Sovereign* was being built on a wooden hull, a similar British ship, the *Prince Albert,* was being constructed entirely of iron.

The *Royal Sovereign* with bulkheads lowered to expose four turrets.

THE CONFEDERATE MARINE CORPS

Relatively little is known about the Confederate Marine Corps because the largest collection of records of its activities was lost shortly after the war when the home of its commandant, Colonel Lloyd J. Beall, was destroyed by fire. We do know that the Corps's existence was authorized early in the war, that by October 30, 1864, it numbered 539 (of whom 62 were then prisoners of war) plus 32 in training. A larger Corps than this was evidently planned, for on May 9, 1861, Bulloch was instructed to order 2000 outfits of clothing in England. Since the enlisted men were paid $3 a month less than their army counterparts, it must have been difficult to get recruits.

Yet Marines served on almost every cruiser that roamed the seas, and they took part in many engagements on inland waters. A list of the ships and Marine personnel can be found in *Official Records of the Union and Confederate Navies,* Series II, Volume 1, pages 273 ff., where the muster rolls are printed.

The largest Marine unit to see active service on a ship was the group of 55 officers and men who helped to serve the guns of the *Virginia* when she fought at Hampton Roads in March 1862. After she was blown up, they went to Drewry's Bluff on the James River to man the shore batteries there. This same outfit marched with Lee in April 1865 when Richmond was evacuated. They were part of the naval brigade that fought in the Battle of Sayler's Creek on April 6.

This sadly neglected arm of the Confederate service deserves a full-length study. A good book on the subject would be a welcome addition to the literature of the Civil War. It will, however, be hard to illustrate, for a long search for pictures of anything that had to do with Confederate Marines turned up only these two.

The original Confederate Marine uniform worn by Second Lieutenant Harry L. Graves who was in command of 20 Marines on the CSS *Savannah*. It is now in the possession of the Atlanta Historical Society.

A rare contemporary picture of Marines in their camp at Drewry's Bluff.

CONFEDERATE TORPEDOES

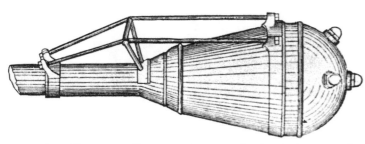

DRIFT-CONTACT TORPEDO. A number of these homemade devices were found in the Stono River, South Carolina, on August 16, 1863. The upper cylinder is a hollow float; the lower one contains 60 pounds of gunpowder. Contact with a ship's side pushes in one of the four wooden vanes to trip the trigger of a sawed-off musket. The musket's hammer detonates a percussion cap which fires into a powder-filled iron tube leading to the lower chamber. These torpedoes were sent down the river in roped pairs to drift against a ship. One exploded under the stern of the USS *Pawnee,* blowing up her launch, and shaking the entire vessel; others went off when they touched sandbars. The one shown here was pulled out of the water by the mortar schooner *C. P. Williams.*

SPAR TORPEDO. Contact points on the head detonate the charge in the copper or iron container. The braces support weight of the head when lifting it out of water.

A UNION DEMOLITION SQUAD at work in Mobile Bay disarming 440-pound Confederate iron torpedoes mounted on a raft. This was part of the effort to clear the bay for ship traffic after the battle.

A nation with little capital and inadequate manufacturing facilities has to devise new and inexpensive means of warfare to contend with a more powerful enemy. Since a few hundred pounds of gunpowder in a watertight container could blow up—or at least seriously damage—a ship costing many thousands of dollars, the poorly armed Confederates naturally turned toward the use of underwater mines, then called torpedoes.

On July 7, 1861, two weeks before Bull Run, an "infernal machine," BOTTOM RIGHT, was seen floating in the Potomac. The sailors who found it, extinguished its 40-foot-long, coiled-up fuses before they could ignite the gunpowder in the two lower metal containers.

Matthew Fontaine Maury, the great Confederate scientist, is believed to have been the inventor of this first Civil War torpedo. He superintended another attempt at Hampton Roads with a similar device, but it too was unsuccessful. Maury then went seriously to work to solve the problem of exploding an underwater mine by electricity.

Torpedoes intended to explode on contact were also constructed. The bottom of a vessel brushing against a triggered mechanism set them off. And spar torpedoes, exploded by manual control from a boat or ship carrying them mounted ahead on a long rod, came into use. All these mechanically operated mines were rather primitive, uncertain in their operation, and as likely to damage their operator as the enemy. Only the electrically exploded torpedo, which could be set off by a distant observer closing a switch, seemed to offer real possibilities.

Electricity was then a still little-understood force, but it had been put to work to operate telegraph lines which sent current from wet batteries for long distances over wires. And insulated cable, sufficiently waterproof to be used for submarine transmission, had already been invented, although its insulation was often defective. But the Confederacy had very few batteries and hardly any submarine cable. Some was secured in the spring of 1862, when a Federal attempt to install such cable from Fort Monroe to Eastville was abandoned. With this, the channels of the James River were mined by torpedoes.

Hunter Davidson was placed in charge of the Torpedo Bureau in Richmond in June 1862; Maury left to go to England in October. Under Davidson, the Torpedo Bureau blew up the *Commodore Barney* and the *Commodore Jones* (SEE PAGE 168) and placed the torpedoes which, in combination with sunken barriers and heavy artillery, defended the James River until the end of the war.

The James River torpedo experts were sent to Fort Fisher late in 1864 to mine the channels leading to the Cape Fear River. They placed nine very large torpedoes near the bar and in the river and attached them to electric batteries on shore. But neither they nor smaller land mines were effective in the battle. The ones on land were quickly put out of commission by heavy fire from the Federal fleet; two in the river were prematurely exploded when the connecting wires were hit by lightning; and the seven big ones near the bar were rendered useless because Union ships did not try to come in until the fort was taken.

A spar torpedo badly damaged the USS *Minnesota,* the flagship of the Federal fleet, as she lay in Hampton Roads on the night of April 9, 1864.

The harbors of Charleston and Mobile were mined to guard them from attack. In some cases, however, certain areas were planted with empty casks or other floating objects to give the appearance of being mined because the Confederates were so short of materials that they could never make all the torpedoes they needed. This was particularly true of the electrically controlled ones, for they required rare metals like platinum and mercury for their detonating devices. At the beginning of the effort to mine the James River only four or five feet of fine platinum wire was available in the entire Confederacy. More material was ordered abroad to be sent in through the blockade, but it was only toward the end of the war, when most of the Confederacy's important ports had already been lost, that insulated wire, batteries, and other electrical equipment began to be shipped.

Torpedoes were introduced into the Western rivers early in 1862 when the Confederates stretched a chain across the Mississippi between Belmont, Missouri, and Columbus, Kentucky, with a number of torpedoes attached to it. They were never of any practical use because the area had to be evacuated after Forts Donelson and Henry were captured. Torpedoes undoubtedly would have been more widely used in the Mississippi Basin if it had not been for the fact that the Confederates lost control of the river after the fall of Vicksburg and Port Hudson in July 1863. Before that, the Union ironclad *Cairo* was sunk by a torpedo in the Yazoo River in December 1862; so was the USS *Baron de Kalb* in July 1863. (SEE PAGE 107).

According to the most recent list of ships sunk or damaged by torpedoes (compiled by E. B. Canfield in 1960), 34 Federal vessels were hit.

WESTERN RIVER TORPEDO. These large glass demijohns filled with gunpowder were exploded by a man on shore who pulled a long cord which operated a friction primer.

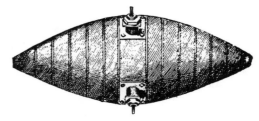

KEG TORPEDO. Large numbers of beer kegs were shipped to Charleston in 1863 to be loaded with powder, armed with contact points, and equipped with conical ends.

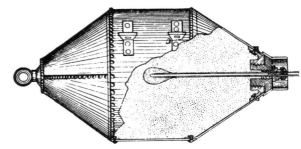

ELECTRIC TORPEDO. A container made of ¾-inch boiler plate was filled with powder and sunk into the water. Insulated wires connected it to a detonating switch on shore. When an observer closed the circuit, current from batteries on land heated a fine platinum wire inside a waterproof quill packed with highly unstable fulminate of mercury which exploded the charge instantaneously.

DRIFT TORPEDO. These were sent downstream in pairs tied together so they would catch across a ship's bows or stern. This early unsuccessful example was used on the Potomac River in July 1861.

Confederate troops attack the Federal fleet on the Red River.

THE RED RIVER CAMPAIGN

The Red River Campaign of 1864 is the stepchild of Civil War history. To the North it was merely an expedition that failed when all the odds seemed to be in its favor, while the South has probably preferred to forget the wanton destruction and senseless loss of life that took place during the invasion of the bayou country of Louisiana. After the campaign was over no one on the Federal side was willing to admit that he had originated it. Grant, who became commander of all the Union armies on March 10, 1864, wrote in his *Memoirs* that he "had opposed the movement strenuously." The idea for such a campaign seems to have started with Halleck, who had suggested it to General Banks in November 1862. There were still plenty of reasons for the move to be made in 1864. Now that the Mississippi River was under Federal control, only two major areas of resistance were left along the Gulf Coast. One was Mobile, Alabama, the other was the "Trans-Mississippi Department" which included Louisiana and Texas. The region nearer the Mexican border called for immediate action to offset the growing power of Napoleon III, whose army had entered Mexico City the year before and who was about to make the Austrian Archduke Maximilian emperor there.

There was at least one other reason for the expedition, although it was hardly of a military nature. More than 100,000 bales of cotton were said to be stored along the Red River. Admiral Porter, who was in charge of the Union fleet, stated bluntly that "the whole affair was a cotton speculation . . . a big cotton raid."

An army under the command of the political general Nathaniel P. Banks was to march overland while Porter's fleet went up the Red River. Troop transports started out from Vicksburg, Mississippi, on March 10 and met Porter's ironclads the next day. So powerful did the invading forces seem that the Confederates at

first did little to oppose them. They fell back from a poor position aptly called Fort Humbug and left only 300 men to defend Fort De Russy farther north. This was easily captured on March 14; two days later the Union fleet reached Alexandria, Louisiana, where General Sherman had been superintendent of a military academy before the war. Six Confederate steamers retreated when the Federal fleet approached. All but one—the *Countess*—were able to get through the rapids that were to give Union boats trouble.

So far the Federals had had everything their way; matters now changed rapidly. Confederate reinforcements were being rushed to the area, and troops from Missouri, Arkansas, Texas, and even Arizona were to fight against the invaders. And the Union Army, instead of following the road along the west shore of the Red River where they would be close to the guns of the fleet, apparently did not even know that such a route existed. (Oddly enough, this road does not appear on the Union map for the campaign in the *Atlas* for *Official Records*, Plate LII, but is shown on the Confederate map, Plate LIII, 1.) This lack of knowledge about the terrain was the first error in what was to be a series of fatal blunders.

After a long delay, caused by the difficulty of getting the Federal gunboats through the rapids north of Alexandria—and by an eager search for cotton—the fleet reached Grand Ecore early in April. There was much complaining along the way that the Confederates were burning cotton and everything else as they withdrew. But they soon stopped retreating and made a stand west of the river along the road between Pleasant Hill and Mansfield, Louisiana, where they badly defeated Banks's troops on April 7–9. "It was the worst managed affair that I have ever heard of," wrote Porter in a report to Gideon Welles.

Contrary to seasonal expectations, water on the river was falling instead of rising. On April 10 the fleet got as far as Springfield Landing, about 30 miles below Shreveport, where they found that the Confederates had sunk a large steamboat across the channel. On it was a big sign inviting the invaders to a ball in Shreveport—an invitation which, as Porter said, he was never able to accept. No attempt was made to clear the river, for a courier arrived that day with word of the army's rout. Troops and transports were ordered to turn back to Alexandria.

The Confederates, freed from having to fight the Union Army, made the fleet's passage down the Red River a continual nightmare. Fieldpieces were hauled from place to place to fire at the slow-moving steamboats as they came down the winding curves of the muddy stream. Thousands of riflemen crept from thicket to thicket to shoot at anyone in the fleet unwary enough to venture on deck. When one of the clumsy vessels ran aground or hit a snag, as they often did, men had to work out in the open to free the stranded boat. It was an exceedingly dangerous job, and many a sailor or soldier died in the muddy waters of the river aptly named Red.

To make matters worse, the unpredictable stream kept falling. Porter hurried his biggest gunboats to Alexandria so they could try to get through the rapids above the city while there was still enough water to float them. During this rush down the river the most powerful ironclad in the fleet, the USS *Eastport,* hit a torpedo and sank. She was raised, and a long struggle to save her took place while men labored under fire to keep her going. She finally ran hard aground and had to be blown up.

Far more terrible was what happened to the transport *Champion No. 3,* which was carrying a large number of Negroes removed from the plantations. When a shell pierced her boiler, steam quickly killed more than a hundred of them and scalded 83 others so badly that most of them died.

The fleet suffered heavy casualties in its run down the river, while the Confederates had only one man killed and one wounded. Driven out of northwestern Louisiana, the Federals concentrated their forces in Alexandria, which they fortified strongly. The fleet was still above the rapids and for a while it looked as if it might have to be destroyed there.

Then an engineer officer from the Wisconsin logging country, Lieutenant Colonel Joseph Bailey, suggested that the river be dammed to raise the water level so the gunboats could be run through the rapids. His scheme was scoffed at but was finally adopted. For ten days thousands of men felled trees and hauled stone and bricks to construct a barrier across the 758-foot-wide river. When the water behind the dam rose, the 177-foot side-wheel steamer *Lexington* (which

drew six feet of water) was ordered to run down an opening in the barrier wall. She got through safely; then three other gunboats followed. But more were stranded above the rapids when the level of the water behind the dam fell.

In three days of hard work, wing and bracket dams were constructed in order to turn the water into the channel and so raise its height there. The rest of the fleet was brought through by May 13 and sent down to the Mississippi.

Troops then began to evacuate Alexandria. As they marched out, scores of buildings and great quantities of cotton were set on fire by incendiaries. Negroes, soldiers from the western armies, and unidentified persons were all blamed for starting the flames which destroyed the town.

While the Union Army was leaving the bayou country it had ravaged, Confederate troops kept up a running attack on it. Confederate artillery, much of it captured during the campaign, blocked the way on an open plain at Mansura, where a spectacular duel between ranked guns took place. But the Confederates were too few to stop the progress of the Federals who were desperately eager to get out of Louisiana, a state which most of them now wished they had never seen. On May 19 they crossed the Atchafalya River, and the disastrous Red River Campaign was over. It had lasted more than two months. During that time Federal casualties were more than 5000, about a thousand greater than Confederate losses.

Gideon Welles said in his *Diary:* "The whole affair is unfortunate. Great sacrifice of life and property has been made in consequence of an incompetent general in command."

No one on the Confederate side understood better than General Richard Taylor—who had done much of the fighting—that the Red River Campaign could have been an even greater triumph for the South if enough reinforcements had been sent in to destroy Banks's army rather than tamely let it escape. He also pointed out that Porter's fleet could not have gotten away if thousands of Union soldiers had not been at Alexandria to build the dam that got the gunboats over the falls. Taylor felt the halfway victory could have been a decisive one.

The dam near Alexandria that raised the water in the Red River and saved the stranded Federal fleet.

The Confederate cruiser *Georgia*.

THE MAURY CRUISERS

In 1839, Matthew Fontaine Maury, then a young naval officer who might have had a brilliant career at sea, injured his knee in a stagecoach accident. The badly set fracture made him lame for life and prevented him from continuing an active career in the Navy's operations on the high seas. After the accident, Maury devoted himself to science and the administration of the Naval Observatory in Washington. As a result of his separation from active service, he was not able to develop as wide a knowledge of ships and shipping as that practical administrator, James Dunwoody Bulloch. When Maury was sent to England late in 1862, he was one of nine Confederate Naval officers stationed abroad who had the authority to buy ships.

Maury also had the disadvantage of arriving late on the scene when most of the more desirable fighting ships had been contracted for by one of the many navies then eager to acquire them. Furthermore, Maury's chief duties concerned the further development of electrically exploded torpedoes.

In March 1863 he bought a newly built iron screwsteamer designed to be a merchant ship. Originally named the *Japan,* she was rechristened the *Georgia* when she was armed and outfitted off the coast of France a month later. Under the command of William L. Maury, a cousin of the Confederate scientist, the *Georgia* went to Brazil and from there to the Cape of Good Hope, capturing nine Northern ships, of which she burned five.

The skimpily built and scantily rigged *Georgia* proved to be a poor sailer, and while she cruised in the warm waters of the South Atlantic her hull became foul with sea growth. She limped into the port of Cherbourg during the night of October 28–29, 1863, to get her bottom cleaned and her engines overhauled. Although the French were more hospitable to a Confederate ship than the British had been, it took several months to have everything put in order.

While the work was going on, another Maurybought ship entered a French port for repairs. This was the *Rappahannock,* a former British Navy dispatch boat previously known as the *Victor.* She was in appallingly bad condition and had neither masts nor rigging when purchased on November 14, 1863. But the British permitted the hulk to be taken to Sheerness Dockyard for masts and essential fittings to be put in. While she was there, Maury had reason

COMMANDER WILLIAM L. MAURY, captain of the *Georgia*.

The *Rappahannock,* sketched at the pier in Calais.

to suspect that the British were not going to let his ship go to sea. On November 24 a young lieutenant from the Confederate Navy appeared at the dockyard dressed in civilian clothes and bearing a letter from the ship's purchasers authorizing him to make a thorough inspection. Her engines had steam up when he went on board. He seemed to be particularly interested in the steering gear and insisted that the ship be taken out into the stream for a few trial turns. As soon as he got her safely away from the dock, he headed out to sea, hoisted the Confederate flag, and took the ship across the Channel to Calais. The *Rappahannock's* poor condition and French governmental red tape kept her in that port for a long while. But she was usefully employed as a depot and as a hostelry for Confederate officers and men who were needed in France.

In February 1864 the *Georgia,* having been judged unfitted to be a cruiser, left Cherbourg for a secret rendezvous with the *Rappahannock* off the coast of Morocco. She was to give that ship her guns, ammunition, and part of her crew. But the *Rappahannock* never showed up. The French refused to let her leave Calais, and she had to remain there until the end of the war.

The *Georgia* waited for several weeks at the appointed rendezvous for the *Rappahannock* to arrive. While near the coast of Morocco some of her crew were allowed to go on shore where they were met by "hundreds of Moors armed with spears and old-fashioned guns. . . ." There were no casualties on the desolate beach, but there was a general melee from which the *Georgia's* sailors escaped by hurriedly taking to their boats. When they got back to the ship, the drummer was ordered to beat to quarters, the guns were cast loose and fired at the mob on shore. The

surprised Moors vanished immediately, disappearing into cave dwellings cut into the cliffs that lined the beach. The shelling probably did no damage, but the incident became known among the young officers on the *Georgia* as "the Confederacy's only Foreign War."

The ship then sailed back to France, entering the port of Bordeaux, where she was ordered to leave within 24 hours. Two Federal warships had been summoned to blockade the Garonne, but the *Georgia* slipped past them in the night and went to Liverpool. It was her last port as a cruiser. She was ordered out of commission and hauled down her flag on May 10, 1864.

The *Rappahannock* caricatured. Public Record Office, London. (*Crown copyright reserved*)

THE *ALABAMA'S* LAST DAYS

Immediately after the *Alabama* arrived at Cape Town on March 20, 1864 (SEE PAGE 155), Table Bay was swept by a gale, but the veteran ship which had weathered heavy winds on the oceans of the world, had no trouble riding out the storm. Semmes remained at Cape Town just long enough to catch up with the news from America. What he heard was discouraging —the blockade of the Southern coast was growing tighter, the Mississippi River had been lost, and Confederate finances were going from bad to worse.

The *Alabama* left Table Bay on March 25. Sailing out, she passed the Yankee steamer *Quang Tung,* which was on her way to China. Semmes decided that she was inside the marine league and regretfully had to let her go. He wanted no trouble with the British at this time, for he had to go into an English or French port to get his ship overhauled.

But this did not stop him from capturing two other Northern ships once he was on the high seas. In April he burned the *Rockingham* and the *Tycoon.* These were Semmes's last prizes, although he was still to overtake and examine the papers of nearly a score of ships. All these proved to be of foreign origin and had to be let go.

The most significant thing about Semmes's last two captures was that target practice on the abandoned *Rockingham* showed that the *Alabama's* gunpowder had deteriorated. Long storage and exposure to widely varying climatic conditions had weakened it so much that one shell out of three did not explode, while others went off with less than full force.

Early in May, Semmes crossed the equator and was on his old cruising grounds, where he had captured many prizes. But the *Alabama,* he said, "was not now what she had been then. She was like the wearied foxhound limping back after a long chase, footsore, and longing for quiet and repose. Her commander, like herself, was well-nigh worn down. Vigils by night and by day, the storm and the drenching rain, the frequent and rapid change of climate, now freezing, now melting or broiling, and the constant excitement of the chase and capture, had laid, in the three years of war he had been afloat, a load of a dozen years on his shoulders. The shadows of a sorrowful future, too, began to rest upon his spirit."

The *Alabama* sailed on, heading ever northward. She passed the Azores where she had begun her career. She went along the coasts of Portugal and Spain and then, on June 11, entered the harbor of Cherbourg. This was to be her last port; the far-traveled ship had only eight more days to live.

When the *Alabama* ended her long cruise, Semmes figured that she had burned $4,613,914 worth of Yankee ships and had bonded others valued at $562,-250.

Stationed off the French coast to make sure that the CSS *Rappahannock* did not try to escape from Calais was the USS *Kearsarge,* a third-rate armed screw-steamer commanded by Captain John A. Winslow. Semmes and Winslow had been room-mates on the *Raritan* in the old Navy and had fought together in the Mexican War. They were exact opposites in character. Winslow, although Southern born, had been educated in New England and had married a Boston girl. He had become an ardent abolitionist who felt that it was his moral duty to help exterminate slavery and subjugate the South. After serving on the Mississippi River, he was given command of the *Kearsarge* and sent to European waters. He was so zealous in patrol work that he lost the sight of one eye because he refused to go ashore long enough to have it treated when it became inflamed.

The *Kearsarge* was at Flushing when Winslow received a telegram on June 12 from the American Minister to France saying that the *Alabama* had put into Cherbourg. He telegraphed to Lisbon to ask the commander of the USS *St. Louis* to join him at Cherbourg and sailed immediately for that port.

Semmes was certainly not surprised to see a Yankee warship arrive. He immediately sent a challenge to Winslow, saying that "my intention is to fight the *Kearsarge* as soon as I can make the necessary arrangements. I hope these will not detain me more than until tomorrow evening or after the morrow morning at the furthest. I beg she will not depart before I am ready to go out."

Semmes put ashore his captured chronometers, all the *Alabama's* gold, the payroll, and the ransom bonds he had issued. As a matter of pride, however, he kept about 100 flags he had taken. The *Alabama* was then made ready for battle. The magazine and shell rooms were overhauled, and the guns and their equipment were prepared for firing.

About ten o'clock on the morning of Sunday, June 19, the *Alabama* steamed out of the harbor of Cherbourg. When she got outside, Semmes saw the *Kearsarge* lying six or seven miles off the coast. Both commanders knew that they had to stay well outside the marine league in order not to trespass on French territory.

The shores near Cherbourg were crowded with some 15,000 people who had come to watch the great spectacle. Several smaller ships were also on hand to see the battle. Among them was the yacht *Deerhound,* owned by John Lancaster, a pro-Southern British gentleman of Lancashire.

A clipper with all sails set trying to escape from the *Alabama*.

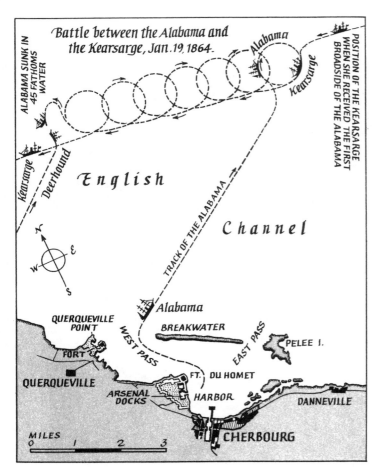

Battle between the Alabama and the Kearsarge, Jan. 19, 1864.

ALABAMA SUNK IN 45 FATHOMS WATER

POSITION OF THE KEARSARGE WHEN SHE RECEIVED THE FIRST BROADSIDE OF THE ALABAMA

Alabama

Kearsarge

Kearsarge

Deerhound

English

Channel

TRACK OF THE ALABAMA

N
E
W
S

Alabama

QUERQUEVILLE POINT

BREAKWATER

EAST PASS

PELEE I.

WEST PASS

FORT

FT. DU HOMET

QUERQUEVILLE

ARSENAL DOCKS

HARBOR

DANNEVILLE

CHERBOURG

MILES
0   1   2   3

THE BATTLE COURSES OF THE *ALABAMA* AND THE *KEARSARGE*.

The ALABAMA and the KEARSARGE

When the *Alabama* stood out to sea, she was accompanied by the French ironclad *Couronne* which stayed with her until she was past the three-mile limit. The yacht *Deerhound* went with them because the Lancaster family had voted to see the battle. Their nine-year-old daughter had cast the deciding ballot.

The *Alabama* and the *Kearsarge* seemed evenly matched. The *Alabama* was armed with six 32-pounders, one 68-pounder, and one 100-pounder pivot rifle, while the *Kearsarge* had four 32-pounders; one 28-pounder rifle, and two powerful 11-inch Dahlgren shell guns mounted fore and aft on pivots so they could be swung around to either side. The ships were about the same size—a little more than 200 feet long. Both had two engines, although the *Kearsarge's* developed 400 horsepower to the *Alabama's* 300. The *Kearsarge* had 163 officers and men to the *Alabama's* 149.

But the odds of battle favored the Federal ship. The *Alabama* was travel-worn, her foul bottom slowed her down, and her gunpowder was stale. Most important of all, the middle section of the *Kearsarge*, where the engines were, was protected by heavy iron chains draped along her sides and fastened to the

One of the 11-inch shells from the *Kearsarge's* two Dahlgrens hits the *Alabama*. The Dahlgren shell guns were smooth bores of limited range, but they were used to deadly effect as the ships came closer to each other on their seven successive concentric circular courses.

The forward pivot gun on the *Kearsarge* in action.

planking—a method of defense which had originated on the Mississippi River. And since the chains had been neatly boxed over with boards painted the same color as the rest of the hull, Semmes did not know that he was about to go into combat with a ship that was partially armored.

The sun was shining, the sea was nearly calm, and the air was warm. The wind was coming from the west, but it was not strong enough to blow away a mist which was so thin that it hardly affected visibility.

As soon as Winslow saw the ship come out of Cherbourg, he ordered the *Kearsarge* to steam away from the coast so as to be well outside the three-mile limit. The *Alabama* followed. Both vessels had been made ready for combat with decks holystoned, bright-work polished, hammocks stowed along the rails, and officers and crew dressed in their best uniforms as they went to their battle stations. Magazines and shell rooms were opened, the decks were sanded down to prevent them from becoming slippery with blood, while tubs of water were placed at convenient locations for putting out fires—or for washing blood and fragments of flesh overboard. Overhead, the yards had been slung in chains, stoppers were prepared for the rigging, and preventer braces had been rove. This was to keep the stuff aloft from coming down on the heads of the men when shells broke it loose. And down below, where it was so dark that one could see only with the help of a candle or a lantern, surgeons were setting out their instruments. Such routine preparations for a naval battle had evolved over the centuries and had changed very little since Trafalgar or even since the days of the Spanish Armada.

While the *Alabama* was steaming north to meet her adversary, Semmes mounted a gun carriage to address the crew. He reminded them that this was the first time they had had a chance to go into combat since they sank the USS *Hatteras* and told them that all Europe would be watching them. The commanders of both ships were fully aware of the fact that they were in the English Channel where so many historic naval engagements had been fought.

Semmes expected to use his starboard guns in broadside and had shifted a 32-pounder from the port side to strengthen the battery. This caused the ship to list about two feet to starboard, which hampered speed and maneuverability but was supposed to be an advantage because it cut down the area exposed to the enemy's guns. Since Winslow also wanted to use his starboard battery, the ships met each other while going in opposite directions. In order to keep from drawing apart, they had to circle around a common center. (SEE DIAGRAM.) The *Kearsarge* wheeled suddenly as the two ships approached each other and presented her starboard guns.

The *Alabama* fired first at 10:57 A.M. when she was about a mile away, sending solid shot across the water three times before the *Kearsarge* replied. As the ships steamed around each other in ever narrowing circles, solid shots were soon replaced by shells. Since the *Alabama's* guns were of longer range, she had an initial advantage. In the first 15 minutes, the battle might have ended in her favor because a shell from her 100-pound bow gun lodged in the wooden sternpost of the *Kearsarge*. It made the ship stagger, but the fuse was defective, and the shell did not explode. If it had, it would have blown the steering apparatus to bits and made the vessel unmanageable. Even as it was, the rudder became so stiff that it took four men to move it.

The ALABAMA in Battle

Semmes, who was standing on the horse block watching the effect of his guns through his spyglass, quickly saw that shots which struck the *Kearsarge's* chain-armored sides fell into the water, leaving the hull unharmed. He ordered the gunners to aim higher. One shell went through his opponent's smokestack, tearing a huge hole in it when it exploded on target. Another sheared off the top of the engine-room hatch. Only one shot caused injury to personnel. This was a 68-pound Blakely shell which exploded on the quarterdeck, wounding three men of the crew of the after pivot gun, one of them so badly that he died.

For the first 18 minutes, the *Alabama* did very well. Semmes wanted to bring his ship in close in order to board his opponent and overwhelm her by hand-to-hand fighting. But Winslow was wary, and his ship was faster and more maneuverable than Semmes's. He kept his distance, always making sure that he was not too far away for his limited-range guns to do their deadliest work.

Shells from the two 11-inch Dahlgrens now began to smash into the highly vulnerable *Alabama*. Lieutenant Arthur Sinclair said that "our bulwarks are soon shot away in sections; and the after pivot gun is disabled. . . . The spar deck is by this time being rapidly torn up by shells bursting on the between-decks . . . and the compartments below have all been knocked into one. . . . An 11-inch shell enters at the waterline and explodes in the engine room. . . . Our ship trembles from stem to stern. Semmes at once sends for the engineer on watch who reports the fires out and water beyond the control of the pumps."

But terrible as the effect of the gunfire was on the wood and metal of the *Alabama,* it was even more terrible on the flesh and blood of her crew. One of the guns "had just been loaded and run out to fire . . . when an 11-inch shell struck full in the middle of the first man on the port side of the gun, passing through the entire lot, killing or wounding them, and piling up on the deck a mass of human fragments." The one man in the gun crew who had remained unhurt shoveled the shapeless flesh overboard and then calmly resanded the deck.

Shells from the *Kearsarge* were rapidly destroying everything on, above, and below the main deck. Worst of all, they kept blasting away at the hull, tearing planking apart and making huge holes in the sides. The *Alabama* was noticeably low in the water and was listing badly to starboard. When Sinclair went below he saw that the water was waist-deep. The ship was sinking fast, for he could hear huge air bubbles rise to break with loud gurgles when they surfaced. Dr. D. H. Llewellyn, the *Alabama's* British-born surgeon, was standing in the water waiting for help to get the wounded up on deck.

Semmes, whose right arm had been hit, now tried to reach the French coast under sail. As soon as he realized that he could not make it, he ordered the colors struck and sent the dinghy to the *Kearsarge* to notify Winslow that he was ready to surrender. He claimed that the Federal ship continued to fire upon him after his colors had been lowered and a white flag displayed. Winslow was equally positive that the *Alabama* had fired two port guns at him after striking her colors.

The yacht *Deerhound* (center) rescuing the crew of the *Alabama.* The *Kearsarge* at left.

The last moments of the *Alabama.*

The battle had lasted hardly more than an hour. Winslow reported that his ship had fired exactly 173 shots and that the *Alabama* had fired about twice that many, 28 of which had hit the *Kearsarge.* Stale gunpowder had prevented them from being fully effective.

The *Alabama* was now far down in the water. Semmes ordered the signal "All hands save yourselves" to be piped. All but two of the *Alabama's* boats had been smashed, and one of these had been damaged. They were not enough to take off the survivors. Many were jumping overboard to swim away from the ship before she went down. Semmes entrusted his papers to a sailor who was a good swimmer. He then hurled his sword into the sea before plunging overboard himself.

The *Deerhound* now approached the *Kearsarge* and, according to the yacht's owner, Winslow shouted: "For God's sake do what you can to save them." The *Deerhound's* boats were lowered to join those of the *Kearsarge.* Several French pilot boats also came up to help.

The *Alabama's* 21 wounded were saved because they were placed in the stricken ship's own boats and sent to the *Kearsarge.* Young Dr. Llewellyn, who could have accompanied them as their surgeon, refused to do so and was drowned. Semmes estimated that nine men had been killed outright by gunfire and that another ten were drowned. It was impossible to determine the exact figures, for the survivors were rescued by several boats and taken to different ports.

The *Deerhound* picked up 42 men, including Semmes and his executive officer, Kell. Kell said that when her owner asked Semmes where he wanted to be

landed, he replied, "I am under English colors; the sooner you land me on English soil the better." The fast yacht steamed toward the British coast to put Semmes and his men ashore at Southampton.

Winslow was greatly incensed at the *Deerhound's* owner for not turning the Confederates over to him as prisoners of war. It was especially galling for him to see the famous raider get away to safety. And when England lionized Semmes, Charles Francis Adams wrote a letter of protest to Lord Russell. To this, Russell replied indignantly: "It appears to me that the owner of the *Deerhound* performed only a common duty of humanity in saving from the waves the captain and several of the crew of the *Alabama.* They would otherwise, in all probability, have been drowned, and thus would never have been in the situation of prisoners of war. It does not appear to me to be any part of the duty of a neutral to assist in making prisoners of war for one of the belligerents."

DR. DAVID H. LLEWELLYN, the *Alabama's* surgeon. He could not swim, so several empty shell boxes were tied to his waist to serve as makeshift life preservers. These raised the middle of his body higher in the water than his head; he was drowned only a few minutes before a rescue boat reached him.

The *ALABAMA* Goes Down

While survivors were being picked up from the sea, the *Alabama* was in her death throes. Sinclair said that "her wounded spars are staggering in the steps, held only by the rigging. The decks present a woeful appearance, torn up in innumerable holes, and air bubbles rising and bursting, producing a sound as though the boat was in agony. . . ." The surgeon of the *Kearsarge* also described her last moments: "She was severely hulled between the main and mizzen masts and settled by the stern; the main mast, pierced by a shot at the very last, broke off near the head and went over the side, the bow lifted high from the water; then came the end. Suddenly assuming a perpendicular position caused by the falling aft of the battery and the stores, she went down, the jib boom being the last to appear above water. . . . As she disappeared to her last resting place, there was no cheer [on the *Kearsarge*]; all was silent."

The *Alabama* sank in 250 feet of water some time between 12 and 1 P.M. (The log of the *Kearsarge* says 12:24; the *Deerhound's* 12:50.)

When Semmes and Kell were taken on board the rescue yacht, the seaman who had carried the *Alabama's* papers returned them to her captain. Semmes found that the master's mate who had been sent to the *Kearsarge* in the dinghy to offer to surrender had conveyed the message and then had backed away to reach the *Deerhound.* He now told the two officers about the chain armor on the *Kearsarge.* He had seen how the *Alabama's* shells had torn holes in the wood covering but had been unable to pierce the heavy iron chain underneath. Kell said later that if they had known about the armor, the unequal battle would never have been fought.

While the *Deerhound* was on her way to Southampton, some of the officers of the *Alabama* thanked the yacht's owner for saving them from the sea. In reply, Lancaster said: "Gentlemen, you have no need to

ÉDOUARD MANET, the French artist who was later to achieve world fame as one of the founders of the Impressionist School, was at the beginning of his career when he journeyed from Paris to Cherbourg to watch the much-publicized battle between the *Alabama* and the *Kearsarge.* He managed to get a place on one of the French pilot boats. On its deck he drew on-the-spot sketches from which he made this painting of the battle. It is now in Philadelphia in the John G. Johnson Collection.

give me any special thanks. I should have done exactly the same for the other people if they had needed it."

An attempt was made to get the Royal Yacht Squadron to censure Lancaster for taking the men he had rescued away from the scene of action to put them ashore in neutral England, but nothing came of the move. Lancaster wrote to *The Daily News* saying that "as to my legal right to take away Captain Semmes and his friends, I have been educated in the belief that an English ship is English territory, and I am, therefore, unable even now to discover why I was more bound to surrender the people of the *Alabama* whom I had on board my yacht than the owner of a garden on the south coast of England would have been if they had swum to such a place and landed there, or than the mayor of Southampton was when they had lodging in that city, or than the British government is now that it is known that they are somewhere in England." In a letter to Earl Russell, Lancaster admitted "that in leaving the scene of action so quickly, I was animated with a wish to save from captivity Captain Semmes and the others whom we had rescued from drowning." He went on then to repeat what he had told the officers of the *Alabama*: "But I should have done the same for the people of the *Kearsarge* if they had been placed in similar jeopardy."

The fact that the *Alabama* was a British-built vessel which had never touched Confederate soil and which was operated by a crew that was largely British undoubtedly had something to do with the great enthusiasm shown in England for Semmes and his men. (By an odd coincidence, both the *Alabama* and the *Deerhound* had been built by the Laird yards in Birkenhead.) But the British had less reason to be proud of the guns they had supplied. The battle between the *Alabama* and the *Kearsarge* was the first test of British and American weapons since the War of 1812, and the outcome showed that American guns were better. The stale powder which the *Alabama* had to use, put her at a disadvantage; but the fact remained that the *Kearsarge's* two 11-inch Dahlgrens won the day. An Englishman who visited the *Kearsarge* soon after the battle said they were so far superior to the British guns on the *Alabama* that officers from the French Navy came to the *Kearsarge* to take exact measurements of the big Dahlgrens. In the United States, where war was rapidly forcing the development of all kinds of weapons, the Dahlgrens were already considered out of date.

It may be wondered why Semmes deliberately chose to fight his sea-weary ship rather than remain safely in Cherbourg Harbor for the duration of a war which

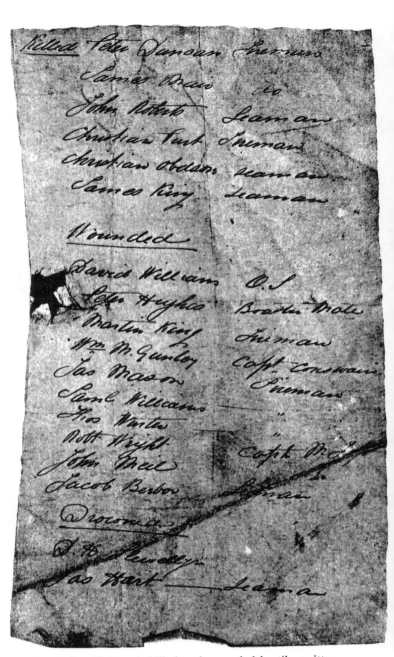

A list of the *Alabama's* killed and wounded hastily written by one of her seamen and given to the captain of the *Deerhound* while on the way to Southampton.

he knew could not last much longer. It was probably a matter of pride. Semmes had been capturing and burning unarmed merchant ships because it was his job to do so. But there was no glory in it. No one—least of all a man of Semmes's background—could like such work. And he may very well have felt that a victory would give the hard-pressed Confederacy new prestige in Europe. But he never explained his reasons or confided to anyone why he had invited an encounter with a fully armed Federal warship.

Looking down on a scale model of the gun deck of the *Alabama*.

Postscript to the ALABAMA Story

The fate of the *Alabama* seized the imagination of the world. Poems and songs were written about her, and newspaper editorials commented on the American naval battle that had been fought on Europe's doorstep. Each writer, of course, interpreted the story as his own sympathies dictated. In England, the press was largely pro-Southern; the British favor a gallant loser. The august *Times* ran a long editorial on June 21 which said in part: "Fathoms deep in Norman waters lies the good ship *Alabama,* the swift sea rover, just so many tons of broken-up iron and wood, and wearing away in the huge depository of that genuine and original marine store dealer, Father Neptune!

"Should any painter conceive a fantasy of the ocean . . . the famous Confederate cruiser would be one of the first ships that his imagination would summon from the depths of the sea, and amongst the spectral fleet of high-beaked Danish galleys, of antique Spanish caravels, of bluff and burly British three-deckers and saucy British frigates, there would be room for this quick and cunning craft that raced so swiftly and roamed the deep so long. The waves wash to and fro about her as if in mockery of the dead mass that could once almost outstrip the hurricane, and the fish swim in and out of the portholes and round the muzzles of the guns that will never again burn powder. For yet a day or so to come corpses of brave men killed in battle or miserably drowned will float to and fro on the summer waves—a strange and horrible sight, perchance, to French fishers busy with their nets or English yachtmen taking their pleasure in the Channel. . . . The *Alabama* could have found no more fitting grave, for she had lived on the waters, their child and playmate. She hailed from no Southern harbor, she was warned off from many a neutral port and went away to her wild work amid the loneliness of the watery waste. It was well, then, that she was not destined to be laid up in ordinary, or daubed with dockyard drab at Charleston or Savannah while idle gossips wandered over her and talked glibly about her deeds. . . . She was a good ship, well handled and well fought, and to a nation of sailors that means a great deal.

"The *Alabama* seemed ubiquitous. If suddenly on the Indian Ocean a red light was seen in the distance, and dim clouds of smoke rolled away before the wind, men knew that Semmes was at work and was boarding and burning some Yankee trader to the water's edge. . . . The Federals tried hard to catch her. . . . She had many a narrow escape, had often to show a clean pair of heels and run for it, often to change her guise to give her sides a fresh coat of paint and hoist some foreign flag. In all the sea subtlety and stratagem Semmes was as cool and crafty as even old Francis Drake himself, but also like Drake he could fight when fighting was required. Gradually men came to think that the *Alabama* bore a charmed life, that nothing could hurt her, that to all purposes she was like Vanderdecken's barque—a phantom ship . . . never to be caught. No really mortal ship, however, can keep the sea forever. . . . Beaten in fair but unequal combat by a gallant foe she has disappeared from the . . . ocean to take her place in history. . . . So ends the log of the *Alabama*—a vessel of which it may be said that nothing in her whole career became her like its close!"

Cover of the sheet music of a Northern song.

The 11-inch after pivot gun of the *Kearsarge*.

Semmes and Kell with their English hostesses.

The 100-pound shell that lodged in the sternpost of the *Kearsarge* but that did not explode.

CAPTAIN JOHN A. WINSLOW of the *Kearsarge*, the North Carolina-born officer who was promoted to commodore after his ship sank the *Alabama*. He was eventually made a rear admiral.

THE SOUTH TRAINS NAVAL OFFICERS

When officers resigned from the United States services at the beginning of the war, 286 out of 1036 (27.6%) left the Army, whereas only 322 out of 1300 (24.8%) resigned from the Navy. The Army was then twice as large as the Navy, but the Navy had a much larger percentage of officers to enlisted men. In either service an officer could resign; an enlisted man could not, for he would be charged with desertion and might be executed. Southern-born men and officers remaining on United States naval vessels during the war were watched carefully and were often kept at sea.

A few days before South Carolina seceded from the Union in December 1860, Harper's *Weekly* published an article on the Marine School which had been established in March 1859 under the auspices of the Charleston Port Society. The Society bought the brig *Lodebar* in May for use as a training ship for 16 pupils. Attendance was soon increased to 25, who were to serve as apprentices for three years.

The Confederate Government needed young officers for its growing Navy, but it did not establish an academy until 1863, when the *Patrick Henry,* then in the James River, was made into a school ship. The first class of about 50 midshipmen was increased later to 60, while 13 teachers and administrators were in charge of instruction.

A Confederate law limited the number of acting midshipmen to 106. Only about half of these could be trained on the *Patrick Henry,* so the cadets spent part of their time on the school ship and part on vessels in service. This gave them practical experience and a chance to see action, but it broke up the course of instruction. Plans were made to remedy this in 1864 by erecting cabins on Drewry's Bluff to house more students. Mallory requested that their number be increased to 150.

Staff and students at this Southern counterpart of Annapolis lived under combat conditions, but the 500 midshipmen in training at the United States Naval Academy were far from the conflict. The Academy had moved to Newport, Rhode Island, for the duration because it was felt that Annapolis might be captured. The old *Constitution* and the more modern *Santee* served as school ships. And the *Macedonian,* which had been captured from the British during the War of 1812, was also stationed at Newport.

Cadets on the *Patrick Henry* sometimes had to leave the schoolroom to fight on the James River fleet or in the shore batteries. The training ship came to an abrupt end on April 2, 1865, when the Confederates evacuated Richmond. The ship was set on fire, and the cadets were ordered to guard the public treasure of the Confederacy and the private treasure of the Richmond banks. About $500,000 in bullion was put on one of the trains which were to take the members of the Confederate Government to Danville. The young boys accompanied the rapidly diminishing treasure as far as Abbeville, South Carolina, where they were given $40 in gold to help them reach their homes, and were disbanded on May 2.

Charleston cadets at their studies on the *Lodebar*. ABOVE: They practice furling a sail and literally learn the ropes.

The Confederate training ship *Patrick Henry*. She was in the *Virginia's* raid on Hampton Roads in 1862.

SUPPLIES FOR
THE CONFEDERATE NAVY

The South had difficulty manufacturing arms and munitions for its Army and Navy because it did not have enough mines, smelters, factories, or skilled mechanics. Nor were enough supplies ever brought in through the blockade to satisfy the needs of the combat forces. It took much improvisation and much hard work to establish sources of supply inside the Confederacy.

The most important drawback was the shortage of skilled labor. An attempt was made to import trained artisans from Europe, but relatively few were willing to come to a war-torn nation. The South had raw materials, but it lacked the means to process them. By 1864, however, a great deal had been accomplished to establish iron foundries, gun factories, powder mills, lead smelters, and the other technical facilities needed to fight what has been called the first modern war.

In some instances, supplies for both the Army and the Navy were manufactured in the same place. This was especially true of heavy goods, because a foundry that could make castings for railroads or field artillery could also produce material for the Navy. Nevertheless, by the end of 1864, the Confederate Navy had been able to set up a number of establishments that specialized in work for its own needs. A powder mill modeled after Britain's Waltham Abbey Work was built by the Army at Augusta, Georgia, but the Navy had a mill at Columbia, South Carolina, for making cannon powder for its guns. It also had ordnance works at Charlotte, North Carolina, Atlanta, and Richmond. At Selma, Alabama, it had a foundry large enough to cast seven heavy guns, five fieldpieces, and the projectiles for them on a theoretical weekly schedule, but actual production was far less than capacity because skilled labor was always scarce.

The South had plenty of wood for making charcoal for manufacturing gunpowder. It also had enough sulphur, but it sorely lacked the most important ingredient—potassium nitrate, or niter, as it was called. A Niter and Mining Bureau was created to organize the work of digging out earth from caves rich in nitrate deposits. This earth was then refined by leaching it with wood ashes. Another source of niter was the offal collected from outhouses and chamber pots —a necessary but odd enterprise that inspired ribald songs and poems.

Another problem which the Confederate Navy had to solve was the modernization of the old-style 32-pounders it had obtained when it took over Federal arsenals and navy yards at the beginning of the war. Chief Engineer Michael Quinn invented a machine to rifle the barrels, and Commander Archibald B. Fairfax supervised the work of strengthening the breeches of these guns with bands.

But the Navy went far beyond merely improving or improvising. Many of its more scientifically minded officers did experimental work on ordnance and armor. Mallory encouraged the building of the laboratories and workshops which were established at Richmond, Charlotte, Atlanta, and Selma.

The important cannon foundry and rolling mill at Selma was originally a joint Army-Navy enterprise, but in 1863 it was transferred to the Navy. Experiments were made there on Alabama iron to determine how to use it for casting cannon. In the days before metallurgy became an exact science, trial and error had to be employed to build up a body of knowledge in what was still a little-known field. In many civilian products, such things as tensile strength, density, or the fracturing of metal may not have been especially important, but it was literally a matter of life or death to protect the men behind the guns. And the constant improvement in gunpowder and projectiles called for ever stronger gun barrels. Only by firing cannon under observed conditions with larger and larger loads of powder could the bursting point be determined. Studies also had to be made of the effect of various types of projectiles on armor.

The shortage of skilled labor for the foundries and mills that were making weapons and ammunition for the Confederate Navy was still further aggravated by the shortsighted measure adopted by the Confederate Government in April 1864 which made workers in Navy projects subject to Army draft. Mallory asked that mechanics be allowed to enlist for naval work rather than have to be assigned to it after they were in the Army, but before any solution could be reached, Union armies overrunning the deep South were capturing one plant after another. Efforts were made to ship machinery out of the way of the advancing armies, but heavy equipment was slow to move, and the invading troops were quickening their pace as they sensed that the end was near.

The *Tallahassee* sketched in Liverpool at the end of her career.

THE *TALLAHASSEE* RAIDS THE ATLANTIC COAST

Like Raphael Semmes, John Taylor Wood served as an officer in both the Confederate Army and Navy. Trained as a naval officer, he fought on the *Virginia* at Hampton Roads and then made many adventurous expeditions against Northern ships in Chesapeake Bay. Jefferson Davis appointed him a colonel of cavalry in January 1863 so he could do liaison work between the two services.

Wood soon became bored with what he was doing, so he applied for active service again. He returned to raiding on Chesapeake Bay and captured a number of Federal ships, some of them by hand-to-hand conflict. After seizing and destroying a Union gunboat at New Bern early in 1864, he was made a commodore in the Confederate Navy. He also took part in the siege of Plymouth, North Carolina.

The *Tallahassee* had been built in England "ostensibly for the Chinese opium trade" but actually to operate as a blockade-runner under the name *Atlanta*. She was armed as a raider and commissioned at Wilmington on July 20, 1864, when she was renamed the *Tallahassee*. Seventeen days later, Wood took her through the Union fleet, which at that time was thoroughly experienced in stopping blockade-runners. He ran past the Federal warships, which fired as he passed, and he was then chased by four other patrol vessels stationed offshore, but he managed to elude all pursuit.

He headed for the New Jersey coast and made his first capture near Long Branch. Then he went toward Fire Island Light on the south shore of Long Island where he seized a pilot boat which he used to decoy other ships to come near the *Tallahassee's* guns. He captured 20 ships along the Long Island coast and

acquired so many prisoners that he had to send them ashore on one of his prizes.

When he captured another pilot boat he wanted to pay or force its master to take him into New York Harbor so he could "go on up the East River, setting fire to the shipping on both sides, and when abreast of the [Brooklyn] Navy Yard to open fire, hoping some of the shells might set fire to the buildings and any vessels that might be at the docks, and finally to steam through Hell Gate into the Sound." Since he could not obtain a pilot willing to undertake such an ambitious project, he was forced to abandon it.

Wood sailed from Montauk Point to Boston Bay and then went along the New England coast, capturing and destroying 26 ships in ten days. What he did was similar to what Charles W. Read had done the year before (SEE PAGE 140), but he did not repeat Read's mistake of going into a port. A number of Federal naval vessels were sent in pursuit of Wood, but he avoided them. The most dangerous Yankee he encountered was a middle-aged married woman taken as one of the prisoners from the Maine ship *Glenarvon*. Wood said that "she came on board scolding and left scolding. Her tongue was slung amidships and never tired. Her poor husband, patient and meek as the patriarch, came in for his full share. Perhaps the surroundings and the salt air acted as an irritant, for I can hardly conceive of this cataract of words poured on a man's head on shore without something desperate happening. . . . At rare intervals there was a calm, and then she employed the time in distributing tracts and Testaments. When she left us to take passage in a Russian bark, she called down on us all the imprecations that David showered on his enemies. And as a final effort to show how she would serve us, she snatched her bonnet from her head, tore it into pieces, and threw it into the sea."

Since the *Tallahassee* needed steam for quick maneuvering, she had to keep looking for coal to fill her ever emptying bunkers. She was able to get some from a few of the ships she captured, but it was never enough. And she had lost her mainmast and all its rigging when she accidentally collided with one of her prizes. Wood decided to take her into the neutral Canadian port of Halifax for coal and repairs. The Queen's Proclamation of Neutrality declared that such a ship could stay only 24 hours, but the Lieutenant Governor granted 12 hours more so a new mast could be put on board.

A local pilot guided the *Tallahassee* at night through the difficult passages leading to the open sea, and the Confederate raider then headed south for Wilmington. Wood took time out to capture a few prizes on the way, but his ship was running out of coal when she neared her home port. She had to run through the blockade under fire again, but she reached her destination on August 26, having been away only 20 days.

In 1953, while James Horan was examining Civil War secret service records in National Archives which had just been opened for public inspection, he discovered the fact that the *Tallahassee* cruise was not an ordinary raiding voyage. The ship was supposed to take part in a Confederate conspiracy to invade the State of Maine. Topographers, pretending to be artists, had been sent ahead to chart the coast, and blockade-runners were to put trained guerrillas ashore who were to be reinforced by more troops from Canada. The *Florida* was also supposed to play a part in the invasion. But the whole scheme suddenly collapsed when three of the men who were to participate in it held up a bank in Calais, Maine, and were arrested. One of them confessed. The inquiry into the plot was conducted in such secrecy that nothing was known about it until Horan's book came out in 1954.

Another officer took over the *Tallahassee* after she returned to Wilmington, but her career was by no means finished. She underwent another change of name and was called the *Olustee* after the Confederate victory in Florida in February that year. She ran through the blockade again on October 29, 1864, receiving some damage from a few well-aimed shells, but this did not prevent her capturing and destroying seven more ships along the Delaware and New Jersey coasts. On November 5, off Cape Henry, she was attacked by the Federal gunboat *Sassacus* in a running battle that went on for 26 hours.

The next day while nearing Cape Fear River she

was sighted by four Federal ships, which came after her, firing as they ran. But again she outdistanced them and reached Wilmington safely.

Her name was then changed to the *Chameleon,* an appropriate appellation for a ship which had undergone as many rechristenings as she had. She left Wilmington as a blockade-runner on December 24 for Bermuda to pick up badly needed supplies for Lee's army. The British seized her there, but her owners were able to prove that she was a merchant ship so she was released. But she was never able to reach the Confederacy, for all ports had been captured. She arrived at Liverpool the day Lee surrendered and was seized there and sold. She ended up as a cruiser for the Japanese Government.

The *Tallahassee* escapes from Wilmington . . .

. . . and burns ships along the Atlantic coast.

Gideon Welles, Secretary of the Navy, was often caricatured in Northern newspapers. Since the artist did not know what the *Tallahassee's* commander looked like, he gave him Semmes's face.

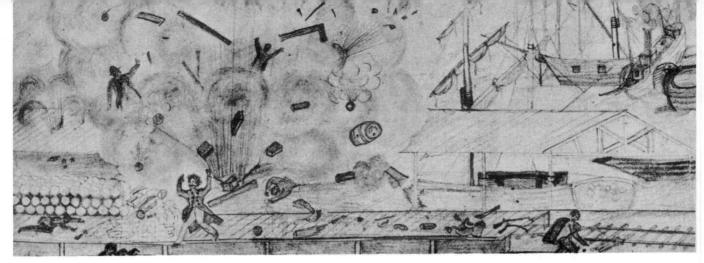

An amateur's contemporary drawing of the City Point explosion.

ABOVE: A "horological torpedo" or clockwork bomb. The one illustrated here was used in evidence at the Copperhead trials in Indiana. BELOW: Harper's *Weekly* makes front-page news of the City Point explosion.

ACTION ON
THE JAMES RIVER

Because the James River was a vital artery leading to the heart of the Confederacy, action along that essential waterway never stopped, although it sometimes had to be suspended for a while. In May 1864, while Grant was making his massive drive against Richmond, Union strategy called for General Benjamin F. Butler to move up the south bank of the James to attack the Confederate capital. Instead, he allowed himself to be bottled up in a bend of the river on a level stretch of land called Bermuda Hundred. On May 6 the Confederates blew up the Union gunboat *Commodore Jones* near there by using an electrically exploded torpedo. As part of the Confederate river defenses, a battery had been built at Howlett's to command a broad stretch of open water known as Trent's Reach, where a fleet of Federal gunboats and monitors was gathered. Big guns were so scarce in the Confederacy by this time that the battery could be armed only by bringing in heavy artillery from other places where it was also badly needed.

In the middle of June, when Grant's armies, after being turned away from Richmond, were assailing Petersburg, the James River squadron was ordered to go downstream and make an effort to take the pressure off the army. Obstructions blocked the way, so it was decided to bombard the Federal fleet in Trent's Reach by firing at it from a distance, sight unseen. The Confederate ships went to within a mile and a half of their targets and began firing in concert with the guns at Howlett's. A lot of gunpowder was burned, and much heavy metal was flung into the air, but no damage was done. "The whole affair was a mortification to us of the navy," said one Confederate officer.

A long drawn-out stalemate ensued. It was planned to bring the Confederate fleet down, again, but low water, a series of mechanical failures, malaria, and other misfortunes prevented it from going into action during the rest of the summer. Union and Confederate lines on land moved so close together that they almost met at Howlett's, and shots were often exchanged between them, the battery, and the Federal ships, but no decisive move was made by either side. Action along the James became subordinate to the final military movements at Petersburg.

Later in 1864, Federal engineers began to cut a passage through the narrow neck north of Trent's Reach so Union ships could avoid having to run past the formidable battery at Howlett's. This was the famous Dutch Gap Canal, which was built under such heavy artillery fire from Confederate guns that the new channel could not be opened to traffic until after the war was over.

At Petersburg a vast network of earthworks and trenches protected that city and Richmond from attack. In an effort to break through the Confederate fortifications, the Federals exploded a huge land mine south of Petersburg on July 30. The follow-up attack was so badly coordinated that it failed, with terrible slaughter on both sides. It has ever since been known as the Battle of the Crater, and a big hole in the ground still marks the site of the mine.

This use of concealed explosives at Petersburg may have inspired a successful Confederate act of sabotage against City Point, Grant's supply depot, which was located at the confluence of the Appomattox and James rivers. There, on August 11, less than two weeks after nearly 300 Confederate soldiers had been killed or wounded by the explosion of the giant mine at Petersburg, a secret agent from Richmond placed a "horological torpedo" (clockwork bomb) on a ship lying alongside a wharf where tons of munitions were stored.

An hour later the spring-wound mechanism detonated a percussion cap that fired 12 pounds of gunpowder in the candle box housing the device. The ship on which the bomb had been hidden was loaded with about 25,000 rounds of artillery ammunition and nearly 100,000 rounds of ammunition for small arms. When this vessel blew up, it set off a series of explosions and started fires on nearby wharves and on other ships. Since many of those who were killed were blown to bits, there was no way of determining the total loss of life.

Earlier in the war the American consul in London had sent word to Washington that infernal machines of European manufacture were about to be sent through the blockade. These were ingenious devices intended to destroy ships lying at anchor. A small float, designed to lie deep in the water, was to carry three boxlike bombs provided with waterproof fuses leading down to glass globes filled with a mysterious green liquid. The fuses were lighted and the float was then allowed to drift toward the target ship. When it reached the ship, the time fuses ignited the green fluid and simultaneously released a powerful steel spring which hurled a mass of burning liquid and small explosive spheres filled with poisonous, inflammable matter at the ship to set it on fire and spray anyone on deck with the deadly green fluid. "This is a capital idea," said the consul admiringly when he sent a model of the device and a sample of the liquid to Washington.

The apparently deadly device, however, does not seem to have been used successfully against ships anywhere in the world. The exact estimate of timing needed to fire the explosives when the float neared the target probably made the seemingly clever weapon too difficult for practical use.

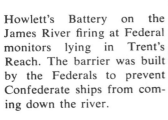

Howlett's Battery on the James River firing at Federal monitors lying in Trent's Reach. The barrier was built by the Federals to prevent Confederate ships from coming down the river.

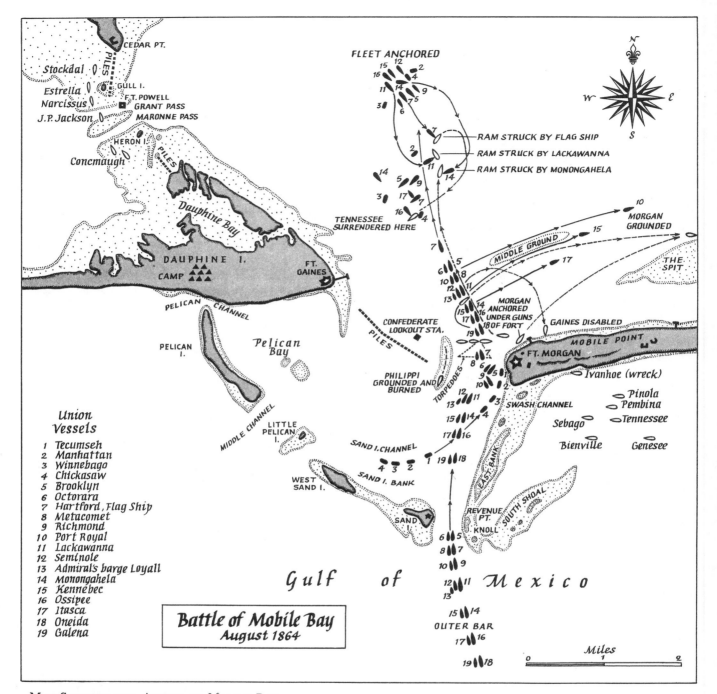

MAP SHOWING THE ACTION AT MOBILE BAY

THE BATTLE OF MOBILE BAY

BELOW: THE DECK PLAN OF THE *TENNESSEE*. Although the big ironclad ram had only six guns, those in the stern and bow were mounted on pivots so they could be swung around to fire through any of the three ports on which each one was centered.

Farragut wanted to move against Mobile after he captured New Orleans, but two years passed before the Union Navy was willing to let him make the attempt. Meanwhile, the Confederates had greatly strengthened Mobile's harbor defenses and had planted nearly 200 torpedoes on the west side of the entrance bay, forcing

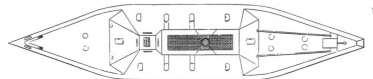

all ships to pass close to the guns of Fort Morgan. Several small ironclads in various stages of construction were farther up the bay, but they could take no part in the coming battle. Near the entrance were three paddle-wheel gunboats, the *Selma, Gaines,* and *Morgan,* all unarmored except for protection around their boilers. The chief guardian of the harbor was the huge ram *Tennessee,* one of the most powerful ironclads ever built in the Confederacy. She had been constructed in Selma and then towed down the Alabama River to have her guns and armor put on at Mobile. She carried only six guns, but they were big Brooke "rifles." And her armor was six inches thick. On May 22, Admiral Franklin Buchanan, who had been the *Virginia's* first commander, made her his flagship.

Farragut was watching what was going on inside the bay. On May 25 he ran inshore to take a good look at the new ironclad and wrote the next day that "she is a formidable thing." Formidable she was, so much so that Farragut decided to wait for ironclads to support his wooden ships.

He had to wait until late in July when he got the single-turreted monitors *Tecumseh* and *Manhattan* and the double-turreted *Chickasaw* and *Winnebago.* He put them at the head of the fleet and lashed his 14 wooden ships together in pairs to protect the weaker vessels from Fort Morgan's guns. Since Fort Gaines was more than two miles away, it could be ignored.

At 5:30 A.M. on April 5 the long line of vessels started moving up with the incoming tide. The *Brooklyn* led the wooden ships; then came the smaller *Octarora,* followed by Farragut in his flagship, the *Hartford,* with the *Metacomet* lashed to her port side. The Union ships carried 199 guns, while the four Confederate vessels steaming down to meet them had only 22.

The *Tecumseh* fired the first two shells which exploded over Fort Morgan at 6:47 A.M. Then the monitor's turret was turned around to protect the gunners while they reloaded. The *Tennessee,* followed by the three Confederate gunboats, approached the oncoming Union fleet. Firing from Morgan and both fleets soon became general.

A wholly fanciful picture of "a Rebel ram at Mobile" printed in Harper's *Weekly* for February 20, 1864.

Then something happened that proved forever the effectiveness of underwater mines in naval combat. The *Tecumseh* struck one or more torpedoes which tore a hole in her bottom. The monitor sank in 25 seconds, and all but 21 of her 114 officers and men were killed or drowned. It was a bad beginning for the Union fleet. And the sudden accident halted the progress of the long line of vessels. They lay motionless for a while under devastating fire from Fort Morgan and the *Tennessee.* During this, the *Hartford* was badly hit. A signal officer on her said: "Shot after shot came through the side, mowing down the men, deluging the decks with blood, and scattering mangled fragments of humanity so thickly that it was difficult to stand on the deck, so slippery was it. . . . The bodies of the dead were placed in a long row on the port side, while the wounded were sent below until the surgeons' quarters would hold no more. A solid shot coming through the bow struck a gunner on the neck, completely severing head from body. One poor fellow . . . lost both legs by a cannon ball; as he fell, he threw up both arms, just in time to have them also carried away by another shot."

Smoke from the guns was so thick that Farragut climbed aloft to see better. There he was lashed to the futtock shrouds to prevent him from falling if wounded or if part of the rigging was shot away. He ordered the flagship to pass the *Brooklyn* and when warned about the minefield, he is said to have uttered the famous words: "Damn the torpedoes! Go ahead."

Amazingly enough, none of the torpedoes exploded, although men on the Federal fleet swore they could hear the ships' sides brush against them. Long exposure to salt water may have corroded the detonating mecha-

The CSS *Selma,* the wooden gunboat that played an important part in the battle.

Farragut's fleet entering Mobile Bay on August 5, 1864.

A BIRD'S-EYE VIEW OF THE UNION FLEET ENTERING MOBILE BAY. Looking south. Fort Morgan is at the left, Fort Gaines at the right. The *Tecumseh*, leading the fleet, has struck a torpedo and is sinking. The CSS *Tennessee*, followed by two of the three Confederate gunboats, is at the lower left. The 14 wooden ships of the Union fleet, beyond the four monitors, are strung out diagonally from left to right.

The *Tecumseh* sinking after having struck a torpedo.

nisms. The torpedoes that sank the *Tecumseh* had been placed in the water only a few days before.

The *Selma* now attacked the *Hartford* and the *Metacomet* lashed alongside her. The *Metacomet* was quickly cut loose and, since she was very fast, she turned around and went after the Confederate gunboat. When the *Selma's* chief officers were killed or wounded by the *Metacomet's* gunfire, she was forced to surrender. Meanwhile the *Hartford* shot up the

Gaines, which was run aground near the fort and burned. The *Morgan* also grounded in shallow water beyond the fort. This left only the *Tennessee* in action. The big ram was well protected by her armor, but, like nearly all Confederate ironclads, she was underpowered, and her inadequate engines made her slow and clumsy. Singlehanded and without support she took on the whole Union fleet, but the much faster wooden ships were able to avoid her lumbering attempts to ram them.

Since the monitors were too slow to ram, the wooden Union ships *Monongahela* and *Lackawanna* tried to run down the Confederate ironclad. Both vessels nearly wrecked themselves by striking the heavy mass of metal without doing any noticeable damage to it.

The *Hartford* now tried to ram, but fortunately for her wooden sides, she did not meet the *Tennessee* head on. The two big ships grated along each other's port sides while a broadside fired from the *Hartford* bounced off the *Tennessee's* iron walls. So far the great ram seemed invincible.

The entire Union fleet was now concentrating all its efforts on destroying a single ship, ramming the *Tennessee* again and again. During the confused movements that followed, the *Hartford* was struck by the *Lackawanna*. The three Union monitors now closed in, although they were all damaged by shellfire. The *Chickasaw,* which was in the best condition, remained near the *Tennessee,* firing more than fifty solid shots into her. It was believed to be her guns that did the most to cripple the mighty Confederate ironclad. The *Tennessee* had a major weakness: her rudder chains ran across the after deck and were soon shot away, making it impossible to steer. Another weakness was the fact that her port covers revolved on pivot bolts, and some of the covers now jammed under fire. When the after port shutter was hit, two men behind it were instantly killed, and Admiral Buchanan was badly wounded and carried below.

Commander J. D. Johnston then took over. His report to Buchanan tells what happened: "The enemy was not long in perceiving that our steering gear had been entirely disabled, and his monitors and heaviest vessels at once took position on each quarter and astern, from whence they poured in their fire without intermission for a period of nearly half an hour, while we were unable to bring a single gun to bear, as it was impossible to change the position of the vessel, and the steam was rapidly going down as a natural consequence of the loss of the smoke pipe. Feeling it my duty to inform you of the condition of the vessel, I went to the berth deck for this purpose, and . . . asked if you did not think we had better surrender, to which you replied: 'Do the best you can, sir, and

when all is done, surrender,' or words to that effect. Upon my return to the gun deck, I observed one of the heaviest vessels of the enemy in the act of running into us on the port quarter, while the shot were fairly raining upon the after end of the shield, which was now so thoroughly shattered that in a few moments it would have fallen and exposed the gun deck to a raking fire of shell and grape. Realizing our helpless condition at a glance, and convinced that the ship was now nothing more than a target for the heavy guns of the enemy, I concluded that no good object could be accomplished by sacrificing the lives of the officers and men in such a one-sided contest, and therefore proceeded to the top of the shield and took down the ensign, which had been seized onto the handle of a gun scraper and stuck up through the grating. While in the act, several shots passed close to me, and when I went below to order the engines to be stopped, the firing of the enemy was continued. I then decided, although with an almost bursting heart, to hoist the white flag."

It took some time for the Union vessels to see what was happening, for heavy smoke obscured the view. While Johnston was putting up the white flag to indi-

The CSS *Selma* surrenders to the *Metacomet* after her chief officers were killed or wounded.

The *Hartford* and the *Tennessee* at close quarters in the Battle of Mobile.

cate surrender, the USS *Ossipee,* which was running in to ram the *Tennessee,* had too much headway to be stopped. She hit the ironclad on the starboard quarter but did no damage. Her commander, William E. Le Roy, called out an apology and greeted Johnston warmly, for they had been close friends in the Old Navy. Then he sent a boat alongside to bring Johnston to his cabin, where he treated him to some ice water and "navy sherry." Farragut demanded Buchanan's sword, but when he sent the wounded admiral to the hospital at Pensacola, he permitted the Confederate fleet surgeon and naval aides to accompany him.

The battle to put the *Tennessee* out of commission had lasted hardly more than an hour. When she surrendered about 10 A.M., the Union fleet had 145 killed and 170 wounded, whereas the Confederates had only 11 killed and 19 wounded. The disastrous sinking of the *Tecumseh* accounted for more than half of the Union deaths.

Fort Gaines surrendered on August 17; Fort Morgan on the twenty-third. During the Union's efforts to bring the area under its control, its navy lost more ships when they ran into torpedoes. The Confederate Navy had been driven from the lower bay, but it still held out in the upper part and in the rivers around Mobile.

On the night of the battle of August 5, some 129 men and officers from the *Gaines* reached Mobile by rowing up the harbor in six small boats. On the same night, the CSS *Morgan* also arrived there after having been aground for most of the day. And several ironclads, then still building, were later available for the defense of the city. Chief among them was the 271-foot CSS *Nashville.* She was a strange-looking vessel that was more like one of the Union's converted Mississippi riverboats than a Confederate ironclad. Two semicircular boxes covered her huge side wheels, over which a high smokestack towered. Her armor was only two inches thick, so she was highly vulnerable in serious combat. She saw some action at the end of the war when she took part in a battle near Spanish Fort and Fort Blakely during the Union campaign to capture Mobile. The struggle lasted beyond Appomattox, for the city was not occupied until April 12, 1865. Then the Confederate naval vessels were taken up the Tombigbee River and were not surrendered until May 4.

After the capture of Mobile, only a few Texas ports remained in Confederate hands. Sabine Pass was surrendered on May 25; Galveston on June 2. On that day, the Confederate Navy's career on the rivers and bays of America was finished. But the Confederate flag was still flying at sea. When Galveston surrendered on June 2, the commerce-raider *Shenandoah* was running north along the coast of Siberia bound for the Arctic Ocean to capture Yankee whalers.

ABOVE: The Union fleet closes in on the *Tennessee*. BELOW: Diagram showing how the Union ships rammed the *Tennessee*. The little *Kennebec* was lashed alongside the *Monongahela* when the larger ship first rammed the *Tennessee*. She was cast off later. Note that the actions shown on the diagram were widely separated in time.

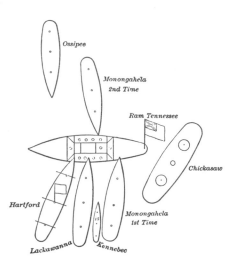

The *Tennessee* is ready to surrender. The *Winnebago* is at left; the *Ossipee, Hartford,* and *Richmond* at the right. Drawing by Xanthus Smith.

Log of C.S.Str. Florida — Commander C.M. Morris

At Sea
4th July 1864

H.	K.	F.	Courses.	WIND Direct.	WIND Force	Wea.	Bar.	Ther.
1.								
2.								
3.	1							
4.	1							
5.	2							
6.	2							
7.	2							
8.	2							
9.								
10.								
11.								
12.								
1.								
2.								
3.								
4.								
5.								
6.								
7.								
8.								
9.								
10.								
11.								
12.								

Log of C.S.Str. Florida — Commander C.M. Morris

At Sea
1st July 1864

Remarks.

Commences & till 4 A.m.
At 2 squared yards to light easterly breeze. S. G. Stone
4 to 8
As per col. At 4.30 made a barque on starboard beam, hauled up in chase — hoisted the English Ensign — fired a shot from howitzer & hove her to when she hoisted the Yankee flag, shot a boat aboard of her. Saml Barron Jr

8 to Meridn
As per col. At 9 hove to and sent Lt Floyd with Midn in cutter's boat crew to board the vessel which proved to be the American Barque "Harriet Stevens" of New York & from Portland bound to Cien Fuegos. Hauled down her colors & sent her Captain, two mates, & six men with papers on board. Wrecked prize brought on board a number of stores belonging to the Master's, Boatman's, Sailmaker's, Paymaster's, & Medical departments, among which was 285 ℔ 16 oz of Smyrna Opium. J. R. Porter.

Meridn to 3. As per col. All lowered propeller & called all hands to General Quarters. Practised at prize with light guns. Powder, Shell & Master's Divisions ready in 2 m. 3rd div in 2½ m. 2nd in 3 m & 1st in 6 min. 1st shot of # 1 Pivot amidship & over. 2nd ahead. 3rd over & ahead. 4th in. No 2 Pivot 1st over her. 2nd astern. 3rd over her. 4th ricochet. 5th the same. 6th over amidships. No 1 Broadside 1st ahead. 2nd astern. 3rd ahead. After Broadside first three shots over her. 4th shot a piece of shell struck her. 5th astern. 6th exploded midway. 7th over her. 8th astern near water line. 9th exploded alongside 10th over her. At 2.15 set fire to prize & hoisted boats. At 2.50 stood in chase of a sail to the S.d & E.d. G. D. Bryan Act Mr

3 to 6. In chase of a barque. Hoisted Yankee ensign & exchanged it for Confederate. Barque hoisted Danish. S. G. Stone
6 to 8.
As per col. At 6.20 boarded Danish barque "Fredrica" from Hayti bound to Cork. Doctor went aboard at the request of her Captain. Gave him 1 Bbl beef 1 of flour & 2 of bread for the subsistance of our prisoners all of whom he agreed to take. Sent prisoners aboard of him. At 7.20 stood in our course with steam on our boiler. Saml Barron Jr

8 to Midt
Steaming N N W. Burning prize in sight during the whole watch.
R. S. Floyd

The *Florida* portrayed in a highly romanticized European lithograph. (She had two smokestacks.)

THE LAST DAYS OF THE *FLORIDA*

The captains of the *Florida* were apparently destined to have poor health. Maffitt had turned command of the famous raider over to J. N. Barney when he asked to be relieved at Brest in August 1863 because of illness (SEE PAGE 129). Now Barney's health failed before he could take the ship to sea. He was replaced on January 5, 1864, by Lieutenant C. M. Morris, who took the *Florida* from Brest on February 10 and sailed her to Funchal, Madeira. He got a hostile reception there. Confederate ships were no longer welcome in many ports. Pressure exerted by American consuls on local authorities was having its effect.

On March 29, Morris captured and burned the *Avon* from Boston. But Union ships were becoming scarce. The *Florida* obtained coal at Martinique on April 26 and then went on to Bermuda where the British were still cordial. She remained near Bermuda until July 1, when she made the capture described in the ship's log shown on the opposite page. According to the entry the ship "proved to be the American Barque *Harriet Stevens* of New York." In her cargo were 285 pounds of opium, a drug badly needed for the Confederate Medical Department. This was transferred to the steamer *Lillian* and run through the blockade. The captured ship was used for a target and was then set on fire. A little later in the day, a Danish

bark was boarded. Her captain agreed to take the *Florida's* prisoners to port in exchange for enough food for their subsistence. The *Florida* then sailed on with the burning hulk of the *Harriet Stevens* in sight until long after midnight.

When Morris had put in at Bermuda on June 19, he remained at anchor there for more than a week. During this time he received an important letter of instruction which Mallory had mailed to him from Richmond on June 2. It authorized him to draw up to $50,000 from Bulloch for cruising funds. Then Mallory said: "A dash at New England commerce and fisheries has always seemed to offer peculiar attractions, as you will see by the instructions to your predecessors, on referring to them."

The suggestion was probably tied in with similar instructions issued to the *Tallahassee*. Both vessels were supposed to take part in a Confederate conspiracy directed from Canada to invade the state of Maine (SEE PAGE 200).

After planting the idea of making a raid on New England shipping in Morris' mind, Mallory then went on to indicate something else that was to influence the *Florida's* fate: "The practice of placing their commercial vessels under foreign flags to avoid capture has become very general with Federal shipowners, and re-

NAPOLEON COLLINS, USN

CHARLES M. MORRIS, CSN

quires increased vigilance on our part to detect and defeat it. With an earnest desire to treat with all proper respect the rights of neutrals, this practice is an abuse of neutral flags which justice to them, no less than to our own, calls upon us to correct; and in all cases where the voyage, the build, the officers and crew, or the papers create suspicion of colorable transfer for this purpose you will not hesitate to scrutinize closely and act upon your judgment. It is represented that the Brazilian flag is generally used fraudulently to cover American shipping between Brazil and the United States."

The *Florida's* movements during the next three months show that Morris literally obeyed the "suggestions" in Mallory's letter. He did not make the projected raid in the Gulf of Mexico; he did start to run north along the Atlantic coast to New England, and then when he had to abandon this cruise, he headed for Brazil, evidently intent on finding out more about the way the flag of that country was being used on ships that were really of American ownership.

First he started for New England and made several captures along the Atlantic coast. On July 10 he took four ships in a single day. One of them, the *Greenland,* was being towed by a fast steam tug, the *America.* When the tug hurriedly cut loose and ran for the nearest port, Morris tried to overtake it, but it was too fast for the *Florida.*

Morris knew that the tug would alert the Federal Navy and make it impossible for him to carry out the projected raid on New England. A few hours later he captured the mail steamer *Electric Spark* bound from New York to New Orleans. This was a rich prize, not

only in value but in information, for the ship was carrying newspapers and—more important—secret diplomatic correspondence from the Washington Government. This was sent on to England for Mason to see.

It is possible that something in the captured documents also influenced Morris' decision to abandon the New England cruise, although he said nothing about the contents of the correspondence in his report to Richmond. There he merely stated that his "plans were all disarranged by the escape of the steam tug."

At any rate, he burned the *Electric Spark* that night and then turned east to run across the Atlantic Ocean to Santa Cruz de Tenerife in the Canaries. He arrived there on August 3, obtained coal, and left the next day, heading southwest to reach the coast of Brazil. On September 26 the *Florida* made her last capture, the bark *Mondamin.* On October 4 she entered the port of Bahia (now Salvador), so late in the day that it was dark when she came to anchor. During the evening a boat approached; after being challenged, a voice from the night-shrouded prowler replied that it was from the British steamer *Curlew.* When morning came, no such ship was in the harbor. But anchored nearby was the USS *Wachusett,* with her black sides and deck bristling with guns.

A Brazilian officer boarded the *Florida.* Morris told him that he needed coal and repairs. The officer said that he would convey the message to the President of the Province of Bahia and warned him not to communicate with the shore. That afternoon, Morris called on the President, who informed him that he would be allowed forty-eight hours to refit and repair and would be given more time if the port engineer decided that it was needed. Morris, in his official report, wrote that President Gomez "was most urgent in his request that I would strictly observe the laws of neutrality (implying by his manner, and, in fact, almost in as many words, that he had no fears on account of the United States steamer, but that I was the cause of uneasiness to him, lest I should attack the *Wachusett* in port), at the same time stating to me that he had received most solemn assurances from the U.S. consul that the United States steamer would do nothing while in port contrary to the laws of nations or of Brazil, and that he desired the same from me, which I unhesitatingly gave. The Brazilian admiral, who was present at the interview, suggested that I had better move my vessel between his ship and the shore, as our proximity to the *Wachusett* might cause some difficulty."

Morris accordingly moved the *Florida* nearer shore. The Brazilian engineer then told him that he would be allowed four days for repairs. Reassured by what had happened, Morris gave some of the crew shore leave. That evening a boat from the *Wachusett* came alongside with a message addressed to the captain of "the sloop *Florida*." The lieutenant to whom it was handed refused to accept it, saying that it was improperly addressed, since the ship was the CSS *Florida* and not a nationless sloop. The next day a Brazilian came on board with a letter from the United States consul enclosing the refused message. Morris returned the message unopened but was told by the bearer that it was a challenge from Commander Napoleon Collins of the *Wachusett*.

Collins was a fifty-year-old officer who had served in the Mexican War and who doubtless felt that if he was ever to achieve distinction he would have to act quickly. (The name "Napoleon" must have been burdensome to live up to.) Welles said of Collins later that he was "an honest, straightforward, patriotic man" but that he did not have any "particular love or aptitude for the service."

Morris told the bearer that he would not violate the neutrality of Brazil but that if he met the *Wachusett* outside he would do his best to destroy her. He then made the mistake of going ashore for the night.

At 3 A.M., lookouts on board the *Florida* saw the *Wachusett* moving rapidly toward them. Collins, apparently mad with dreams of glory, was trying to ram the Confederate raider and sink her in defiance of Brazil's neutrality. But preparations for slipping the warship's cable had not been properly carried out, so the *Wachusett* went off course, hitting the *Florida* a glancing blow on the starboard side that carried away the mizzenmast, crushed the bulwarks, and smashed in the quarter boat on deck. Small-arms fire cracked out from both ships. Then the *Wachusett* backed away and fired her two biggest guns.

A call for surrender caused the subordinate officers in charge of the *Florida* to go into a huddle. They decided that the ship was in no condition to fight, and the lieutenant commanding went aboard the *Wachusett* to turn over his sword and the *Florida's* ensign.

Collins sent a prize crew aboard the captured ship and took her under tow. The harbor forts fired at him as he ran out, and he was followed for a while by a Brazilian sloop of war towed by a paddle-wheel gunboat. But the *Wachusett* had no trouble getting away.

Collins kept his prisoners in double irons, but when he reached St. Thomas on October 31 he was so eager to be rid of them that he allowed 18 of them to escape in the coal barge that was bringing fuel to the *Wachusett*. Two weeks later he brought his celebrated prize into Hampton Roads, where he was greeted with a wave of popular acclaim that was as great as that which had been lavished on Wilkes when he took Mason and Slidell off the *Trent*.

The *Wachusett*, a Brazilian warship, and the *Florida* at anchor in Bahia Harbor.

The *Florida* sinking while under the protection of the guns of the USS *Atlanta*.

The Mysterious End
of the FLORIDA

Like the Confederate Commisioners taken off the *Trent*, the possession of the *Florida* proved to be embarrassing to the United States Government. Although it did not directly concern them, the English press and people raised a great outcry against the seizure of a ship in neutral waters. Brazil lodged a formal protest, and the United States had to apologize for the unauthorized action of its glory-seeking naval officer.

Collins was brought before a court of inquiry which rendered a verdict of guilty just two days before Appomattox. The Navy Department refused to accept the decision, and Collins was made a captain, a rank he lost a few years later when his ship was wrecked in the Bay of Bengal while he was playing chess.

A few days after the *Florida* was brought into Hampton Roads to be anchored there, she was struck by the steam transport *Alliance,* which carried away her jibboom and figurehead and then raked her along the side. The crippled raider was moved to Newport News where she was anchored near the area in which the *Cumberland* had been sunk. There she was placed under the protection of the guns of the captured Confederate ironclad *Atlanta* (Bulloch's old ship, the

Fingal). The *Florida* was leaking badly and the steam and hand pumps had to be kept going day and night. On November 28 the water was gaining so fast that a tugboat was brought up to tow her into the shallows, but she went down 15 minutes after the tug arrived. She settled on the bottom in nine fathoms of water, with her masts rising above the surface. Rumors began to spread that the troublesome ship had been deliberately scuttled.

It was a time for rumor and talk of conspiracy. A Confederate attempt to burn a number of hotels and public buildings in New York had been made on November 24, and three days later General Ben Butler's headquarters boat, the *Greyhound,* was blown up by a bomb concealed in the coal bunkers. Butler and Admiral David Dixon Porter, who were then planning the expedition against Fort Fisher, escaped uninjured but with their easily triggered tempers raging. The *Florida* was Porter's responsibility, and his narrow escape from Confederate saboteurs did not make him feel kindly disposed toward the unwanted raider or the Army transport that had collided with her. He instructed a court of inquiry to "ascertain . . . whether the collision was accidental or through bad management or done purposely."

The court established the fact that high seas and strong winds had contributed to the collision, and found that there was "nothing to show that the accident was designed." The court also stated that in its

The wreck of the *Florida* guarded by a Federal monitor.

opinion the officer on the *Florida* had done everything possible to save her when she was about to sink.

In 1885, when Porter's book, *The Naval History of the Civil War,* appeared, it stated that "an engineer was placed on board [the *Florida*] . . . with two men to assist him in looking after the water cocks, but strangely enough she sank." No one was in a better position to know all the facts in the case than the Union admiral in charge of the area where the *Florida* was anchored. Porter went on to say that the sinking was the best thing that could have happened and that both the Secretary of State and the Secretary of the Navy never asked any questions and were glad to have the white elephant off their hands.

Brazil, however, was far from being pleased. The United States Government wanted to make amends to the aggrieved nation, although many people felt that she deserved what had happened because she had permitted the *Alabama* to take on coal at Bahia and burn three American ships within the range of the guns in the forts.

In July 1866, nearly two years after the *Florida* had been captured and long after the war was over, the USS *Nipsic* went under orders to Bahia. On July 23 (the Emperor's birthday), the little wooden gunboat was dressed with the Brazilian colors flying at the main. A few minutes before noon, the American flag was hauled down from the foremasthead and the Brazilian flag was run up while a salute of 21 guns was fired with great ceremony. The Brazilian warship *Dona Januaria* returned the salute, gun for gun, with the American flag displayed at the main.

The scholarly naval historian, James Russell Soley, said of Collins' action that "the capture of the *Florida* was as gross and deliberate a violation of the rights of neutrals as was ever committed in any age or country. It is idle to attempt to apologize for it or to explain it; the circumstances were such that the question does not admit of discussion. All that can be said is that it was the independent act of an officer, and that it was disavowed by the Government. In the words of the Secretary of State, it 'was an unauthorized, unlawful, and indefensible exercise of the naval force of the United States within a foreign country, in defiance of its established and duly recognized Government.' "

The United States was so eager to forget the incident that Welles gave orders for the prisoners from the *Florida* to be released from Fort Warren if they would leave the country in ten days. To this they gladly agreed, and took ship for England, where their captain and some of their officers had long since arrived from Brazil. They reached Liverpool in time to help man the new Confederate ironclad *Stonewall,* which needed a trained fighting crew.

(1) An Enfield, British-made double-edged officer's navy cutlass. (2) The scabbard for it. (3) A Roman-type double-edged navy cutlass marked CSN; made in New Orleans in 1861.

Swords and Seals of the Confederate Navy

The Great Seal of the Confederate States of America was authorized by Congress in April 1863. Mason then had it made in England. It was brought safely through the blockade and arrived in Richmond on September 4, 1864. But the iron press for making an impression from it never got past Bermuda, where it is still supposed to be in private hands. The original seal is now in the Confederate Museum in Richmond.

Less is known about the history or the present whereabouts of the seal of the Confederate Navy Department (ILLUSTRATED ABOVE). Impressions made from it are occasionally seen affixed to official documents. Unlike the Naval Ensign, Pennant, and Jack (as well as the Confederate Flag), all of which ordinarily carried 13 stars, the seal has only seven.

England also made many swords, sabers, cutlasses, and other edged weapons for the Confederacy. Although the cutlass was the traditional weapon used when boarding a ship, few actual wounds were ever inflicted by it during the Civil War. The day of the bayonet and the sword had already passed. Of the 2272 men in the Union Navy killed by Confederates, nearly all died from gunshots; 308 drowned in battle.

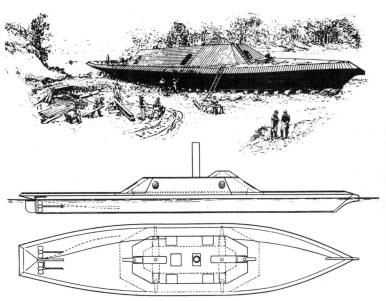

Inside the *Albemarle's* casemate when the *Sassacus* struck.

WAR ON THE CAROLINA SOUNDS IN 1864

The Confederates bitterly resented their loss of the Carolina Sounds early in 1862 (SEE PAGE 68) and made a number of attempts to regain control of those waters. By this time they had learned how to build ironclads under the most adverse circumstances. During the winter of 1863–64 they constructed one on the muddy shores of the Roanoke River, and named her the *Albemarle*. Another, called the *Neuse* after the river on which it was built, had a less remarkable career.

On April 17, 1864, the newly completed *Albemarle* was taken backward down the flooded river, using chains dragging from the bow to guide her course. The next evening she was stopped about three miles above Plymouth (SEE MAP ON PAGE 69), where obstructions were supposed to make the river impassable. A sounding party sent out during the night reported that there were ten feet of clearance over the obstructions because of the unusually high water. The ironclad ran past the Federal forts in the darkness and came upon two armed side-wheel steamers chained together to trap the Confederate ship between them. But the *Albemarle* approached so quickly that they did not have time to maneuver. She rammed into one of them, the *Southfield,* thrusting her prow so far into the wooden hull that she had trouble backing off. The other Federal ship, the *Miami,* fired harmless broadside after broadside at the armored sides of the ironclad, which could not swing her guns far enough around to reply. A battle with small arms at close quarters took place until the *Albemarle* succeeded in breaking away. The *Southfield* sank, but the *Miami* got away to Albemarle Sound, carrying with her the body of her captain, who had been killed by a shell fragment.

A scale model of the *Albemarle* showing details of construction.

Plymouth, which had been attacked simultaneously by Confederate forces, promptly surrendered, and the *Albemarle* had uncontested control of the area.

Federal preparations to destroy or capture the new ironclad were made with frantic haste. When the *Albemarle* came down the river on the afternoon of May 5, a fleet of nine ships was waiting to attack her and two small steamers as she entered the bay. The Union plan was to use a net to foul the ironclad's propellers and blow her up with a spar torpedo. The larger ships were to run in to fire, then load as they came around and discharge their guns when they closed in again.

The *Albemarle* started shooting as she approached the Federal ships. Firing then became general, and a thick pall of smoke hung over the water. In the confused melee that followed, one of the Confederate steamers was forced to surrender. The ironclad seemed invincible; heavy missiles hit her sloping sides without any perceptible effect. Finally, the USS *Sassacus,* a large side-wheel steamer armed with a three-ton bronze beak, made ready to ram the *Albemarle* at the vulnerable spot where the iron-sheathed casemate joined the hull.

Waste and oil were thrown into the fires of the *Sassacus* to bring up steam quickly. Four bells were sounded; the big paddle wheels revolved faster and faster, churning the water into foam, and the long wooden hull sped swiftly toward the Confederate ironclad. The men on the *Sassacus* were ordered to lie down to avoid being thrown off their feet when the collision came. Space between the two ships narrowed rapidly. Then the bow of the Union vessel crashed into the side of its adversary, lifting the heavy ironclad partly out of the water for a moment. The *Sassacus* kept her paddle wheels going as she pushed against

the *Albemarle*. The two ships struggled together like snorting sea monsters. A lucky shot from one of the Brooke rifles of the ironclad went through the wooden side of her attacker to pierce her starboard boiler and release a howling blast of superheated steam that scalded and blinded the men in the engine room. Guns and small arms kept firing through the dense clouds of smoke and steam. Sailors stationed in the rigging of the *Sassacus* threw grenades down, hoping to drop one through a hatchway or the smokestack.

The *Albemarle* succeeded in pulling away. She steamed off, leaving her wounded attacker still shrouded by escaping steam. But Federal gunners on the *Sassacus* kept sending 9-inch shots ricocheting across the water. They bounced over the Confederate ship, which seemed to be more than ordinarily lucky in battle. Other Union vessels followed the Confederate ironclad, but they maintained a respectful distance, firing their guns while too far away to be effective. A desultory action was kept up until night closed in. By that time the *Albemarle* had reached the protection of the narrower waters of the Roanoke River.

In reporting the battle, the commander of the *Sassacus* said that "the *Albemarle* is more formidable than the *Merrimack* or *Atlanta,* for our solid 100-pounder rifle shot flew into splinters against her iron plates." The *Sassacus* did not sink, but it was obvious that the wooden ships which the Federal Navy had in the Carolina Sounds were wholly inadequate to deal with the makeshift ironclad that had been built in a swamp. The Federals could not bring in an armored ship because it would draw too much water to get over the Hatteras bar. Nor was there time to build one inside the sounds. The Union Navy had to devise a new and ingenious method of attack.

The *Sassacus* rams the *Albemarle*, and the two ships are locked together in combat.

Lieutenant Cushing blows up the *Albemarle*. (The illustration gives the ship too many guns and smokestacks.)

Blowing up the ALBEMARLE

The Federal Navy was very much aware of the menace of the *Albemarle* although the ironclad lay idle for months. On May 25, five volunteers from the USS *Wyalusing* carried two 100-pound torpedoes overland to the Roanoke River, put them in the water connected together by a cable, and guided them downstream by swimming with them. But the swimmers were seen as they neared the ram and were driven away by rifle fire.

On July 5 the young officer who had acted so bravely when he commanded the *Ellis* on the New River in November 1862 (SEE PAGE 71) was called to Hampton Roads. There, William B. Cushing gladly undertook the dangerous mission. He had lost a brother at Gettysburg, and the commander of the *Miami*, who had been killed in the battle between that

ship and the *Albemarle* on April 19, had been a good friend of his. Besides, Cushing enjoyed taking on risky assignments. Like Charles W. Read, his counterpart in the Confederate Navy, he specialized in them.

After several plans had been discussed and discarded, it was decided to make the attack by using a small steam launch armed with a boat howitzer and carrying a spar torpedo. Since it took time to get everything ready, the actual assault did not begin until October 27. It was raining when the little launch steamed up the river in the darkness with Cushing and 13 men. And it was well after midnight when the launch reached Plymouth, where the *Albemarle* was moored to a wharf. Cushing at first thought he could land and make a surprise attack from the rear, but a sentry heard the launch approach and challenged him loudly. There was nothing to do but go straight in. Cushing tells the story himself: "Ordering all steam, [we] went

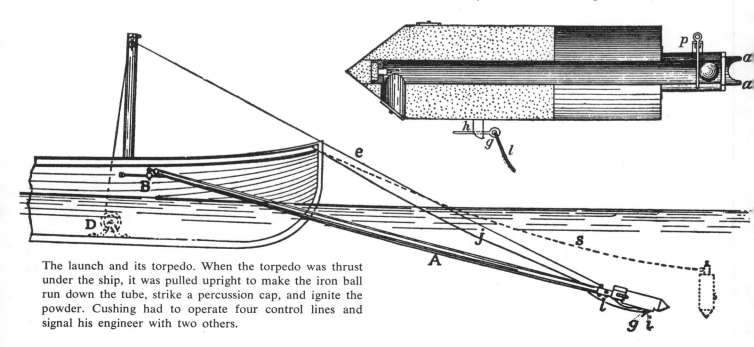

The launch and its torpedo. When the torpedo was thrust under the ship, it was pulled upright to make the iron ball run down the tube, strike a percussion cap, and ignite the powder. Cushing had to operate four control lines and signal his engineer with two others.

at the dark mountain of iron in front of us. A heavy fire was at once opened upon us, not only from the ship, but from men stationed on the shore. This did not disable us, and we neared them rapidly. A large fire now blazed upon the bank, and by its light I discovered the unfortunate fact that there was a circle of logs [chained together] around the *Albemarle,* boomed well out from her side, with the very intention of preventing the action of torpedoes. To examine them more closely, I ran alongside until amidships, received the enemy's fire, and sheered off for the purpose of turning a hundred yards away and going to the booms squarely . . . trusting to their having been long enough in the water to have become slimy—in which case my boat under full headway would bump up against them and slip over into the pen with the ram. This was my only chance of success, but once over the obstruction my boat would never get out again. As I turned, the whole back of my coat was torn by buckshot, and the sole of my shoe was carried away. . . .

"In a lull of the firing, the captain hailed us, again demanding what boat it was. All my men gave comical answers, and mine was a dose of canister from the howitzer. In another instant we had struck the logs and were over, with headway nearly gone, slowly forging up under the enemy's quarterport. Ten feet from us the muzzle of . . . an 8-inch cannon looked into our faces, and every word of command on board was distinctly heard.

"My clothing was perforated with bullets as I stood in the bow, the heel-jigger in my right hand and the exploding-line in the left. We were near enough then, and I ordered the boom lowered until the forward motion of the launch carried the torpedo under the ram's overhang. A strong pull of the detaching line, a moment's waiting for the torpedo to rise under the hull, and I hauled in the left hand [line]. . . .

"The explosion took place at the same instant that

100 pounds of grape at 10 feet range crashed among us, and the dense mass of water thrown out by the torpedo came down with choking weight upon us.

"Twice refusing to surrender, I commanded the men to save themselves; and, throwing off a sword, revolver, shoes, and coat, struck out from my disabled and sinking boat into the river. It was cold . . . and the water chilled the blood, while the whole surface of the stream was plowed up by grape and musketry. My nearest friends, the fleet, were twelve miles away; but anything was better than to fall into rebel hands, so I swam for the opposite shore. As I neared it a man, one of my crew, gave a great gurgling yell and went down."

Cushing reached a swamp near Plymouth, but he was so exhausted that he could not drag himself out of the mud until daylight came. Then he hid in the swamp, stole a boat and paddled for ten hours to reach the Federal fleet. Only one other man from the launch escaped; the others were either drowned or captured.

President Lincoln asked Congress to give a vote of thanks to Cushing and thus make it possible for him to be automatically promoted for distinguished conduct.

The Confederate naval historian J. T. Scharf, commenting on the loss of the *Albemarle,* said: "Thus, by negligence and carelessness on the part of the Confederates, and by the enterprise and gallantry of the Federal detachment, the ram . . . which had successfully stood the solid shot and shell from the Federal gunboats, was destroyed by a launch and thirty brave men, and with the weapon the Confederates had perfected and appropriated as peculiarly theirs."

Another Confederate ram being built on the Neuse River was destroyed by a Federal raiding party, and the ironclad *Neuse* was also captured and destroyed.

With its last three rams in this area gone, the Confederacy lost control of the Carolina Sounds and was thus placed in a poor defensive position when Sherman came through there early in 1865.

The *Albemarle* photographed at the Norfolk Navy Yard after she was raised and towed there in April 1865— too late to be of any use to her captors. The two women standing on deck give an idea of the ironclad's size.

This engraving of the ironclad *Sphinx* (later the CSS *Stonewall*) was published in *Le Monde Illustré* on September 17, 186

THE FATE OF
THE FRENCH-BUILT SHIPS

The Confederates were bitter about the way Napoleon III had invited them to build ships of war in France and then, when the North began winning victories, had refused to let them have the six ships they were building in Bordeaux and Nantes (SEE PAGE 162). But there was nothing they could do about the Emperor's perfidy. Nor could they do anything about five of the six ships; two corvettes had been sold legitimately to Peru, and Prussia had bought the other two as well as the ironclad *Cheops*. But there was a possibility that they might still be able to get the ironclad *Sphinx*. She had been sold to Denmark, but now that the war with Prussia was over, the Danes no longer had any immediate need for the armored ship.

In November 1864, Bulloch was approached by Lucien Arman's agent, a man named Henri Arman de Rivière, who said that he could get possession of the *Sphinx* if the Confederate Government would pay him a commission of 375,000 francs for his services. A month before, Bulloch had said that De Rivière was "without scruple or principle" and that he "declined having anything to do with him."

But the Confederate Navy had such urgent need of the ironclad that Bulloch was reluctantly forced to make a deal with De Rivière. An agreement was drawn up between them on December 16. After that, events moved swiftly. The fully armed *Sphinx* had already gone to a Swedish port to be sold nominally to a Swedish citizen. It then went under the Swedish flag to Copenhagen, where it was now lying. De Rivière's job was to persuade the Danish Government to reject the ironclad as unsatisfactory. It would then be re-

turned to its French builders—who, of course, would deliver it to the Confederates.

Captain Thomas Jefferson Page, CSN, was sent to Copenhagen in December to take command of the *Sphinx.* Everyone in the plot was optimistic about getting the ship, for De Rivière was going to report so bad a performance record for the ironclad that the Danes would not want her.

Meanwhile, Bulloch set the stage for the arrival of the armored ship, which had been renamed the *Staerkodder* by the Danes (it would be called the *Olinde* on its return to France). The *City of Richmond* was to put a trained crew from the *Rappahannock* and the *Florida* on board; a lieutenant was sent to Nieuwe Diep to arrange for coaling; and a list of coded phrases was drawn up so information could be sent secretly. Among the phrases were seemingly innocent ones like "No coffee in the market" which really meant "Detained at Nieuwe Diep," or "Coffee is bought" which more hopefully signified "Difficulty removed. Sail tomorrow."

It all sounded like a comic-opera plot, but it was deadly serious. The elaborate machinery of the scheme

got ponderously under way as soon as De Rivière obtained permission from the Danes to take the *Sphinx* back to France. And that, oddly enough, was the only thing that was to be easy to accomplish.

The ship which had turned in a deliberately calculated poor performance record in order to deceive the Danes proved in reality to be a poor performer. The weather was very bad, and the ironclad was held up by a blinding snowstorm off Elsinore. Winter gales kept howling along the entire route, and the *Sphinx-Staerkodder-Olinde* rolled in them as if she were as unseaworthy as the enormous block of stone that had given her her original name. Captain Page reported that the only Confederate European-built ironclad to reach the sea was leaking water through an opening near the rudderpost. Last-minute alterations made by a Danish engineer sent to the French shipbuilder's yard may have been responsible, but there was no doubt that the mighty *Stonewall,* as the ironclad was soon to be renamed, was badly constructed.

She was to meet her tender, the *City of Richmond,* near Belle Île off the southern coast of Brittany. It took the supposedly fast twin-screw armored ship eighteen days to make the run from Copenhagen to Belle Île. Even then her troubles were not over, for another storm arose soon after she reached her destination (SEE PAGE 246).

A section of the *Sphinx* showing the engine, various compartments, the protruding steel ram, and the massive 300-pounder Armstrong rifle mounted in the bow.

BLOCKADE-RUNNING IN 1864

During the early part of the war, ships had little trouble entering or leaving any Confederate port. The turning point came in 1862 when the footholds the Federal forces had established along the Atlantic coast made it harder for blockade-runners to come and go. And the loss of New Orleans made matters worse. The Union Navy kept growing, and as it grew, it was able to station more ships outside the more important Confederate ports. The rate of capture rose, but the price of cotton in Europe went up with it, so the business of blockade-running remained very profitable. Many fast, shallow-draft ships continued to be built in Britain for the trade, but the quality of their construction went down. Time was so important that eager owners frantically urged the builders to turn out their ships quickly in order to get them into service while the chance for high earnings was still good.

The Federal blockading fleet was learning how to strengthen its grip on the seacoasts of the Confederacy. Some of the ships were equipped with Drummond lights to spot blockade-runners at night. And their guns became larger, with ever increasing range. The blockading fleet *looked* so impressive that it seemed impossible for anything to get past it. But the blockade-runners, taking advantage of every bit of "bad" weather (bad, that is, for other ships, but good for those that wanted to hide in fog or darkness) kept dashing in and out of such well-guarded ports as Charleston and Wilmington. They were so amazingly successful that charges were made that officers in the Federal fleet were being bribed to let them through.

The Union Navy sent ships overseas to watch the exits from British ports in an effort to capture the blockade-runners on the high seas near the beginning of their run. They also patrolled Funchal where ships often took on coal before crossing the Atlantic. And they became so numerous around the Bahamas that the blockade-runners had to shift much of their business to Bermuda for a while.

The Navy adopted a new technique in an attempt to prevent trading with the Mexican port of Matamoras. United States courts had ruled that Matamoras was beyond their jurisdiction so nothing could be done legally against ships that put in there. Nevertheless, determined Federal naval officers continued to seize suspected vessels and send them north as prizes even

A photograph of a Federal fleet blockading a Confederate port in 1864.

though they knew they would eventually have to be freed. But the long voyage to an American port and the even longer court proceeding kept such ships out of service for a while.

Because many small ports were still open on the Gulf, a new and seldom-mentioned type of blockade-running developed there. This was the use of swift centerboard schooners to bring in cargoes from the Bahamas, Cuba, and even from faraway Mexico. The shallow inlets and bays along the Gulf Coast could easily be entered by these sailing vessels, and once inside, they were safe from pursuit by deep-draft naval ships. Florida, which was then largely unsettled between St. Augustine and Key West, had many such inlets on both shores.

Because the men who owned and operated the blockade-runners found it more profitable to bring in high-value, small-bulk goods like personal luxuries or drugs and medicines than much-needed food, arms, ammuni-

On November 26, 1864, while a Union fleet was being assembled to attack Fort Fisher, Harper's *Weekly* published the picture shown above. Evidently impressed by the drama of the scene portrayed in the American paper, a French artist working for *Le Monde Illustré* copied the picture with only slight changes. His version (at left) is reversed because he engraved it on wood just as it appeared in Harper's. When it was printed everything was turned around, but he was clever enough to make sure that his men were right-handed.

tion, and machinery, the Confederate Government had to take steps to control the trade. It began to operate its own blockade-runners, and in February 1864 passed laws prohibiting the importation of luxuries or unnecessary goods. From a third to a half of the cargo space on privately owned runners was to be reserved for the Government. But it was easier to pass such laws than to enforce them—especially on incoming ships. Since luxury goods took up little space and brought high rates of profit, they continued to arrive even though they had to be smuggled in.

The Confederacy accomplished much more with its Government-owned ships. The Ordnance Bureau had been running a fleet of such vessels to bring in war materials. The *R. E. Lee, Merrimac,* and *Cornubia* made many trips without a loss, encouraging Richmond to consider acquiring others.

Bulloch, who had bought the *Fingal* for the Government early in the war, was very much in favor of the Government owning blockade-runners. Beginning in January 1863, he wrote a series of letters to Mallory urging him to authorize such a fleet. He needed money to meet his contract terms for cruisers, and he believed that the best way to get funds was for the Government to export large quantities of cotton and use the proceeds to pay for the fighting ships. He pointed out that the blockade-runners could be armed and sent out to capture transports and make group raids on the Federal fleet patrolling Confederate ports. Bulloch obtained a blockade-runner in October 1863, when he bought the twin-screw steamer *Coquette.* He purchased her only because he needed immediate transportation for some marine engines that were ready to be shipped into the Confederacy. Six months later, orders came through to start building a fleet of Government blockade-runners.

Since about 600,000 small arms, cannon of all sizes, ammunition, uniforms, raw material, and food for the Confederate armies were brought through the blockade, it must be considered as one of the Confederacy's most successful war efforts. It would have been impossible to continue hostilities without the goods delivered by the blockade-runners. Whatever such supplies cost, they were worth it to a nation without the facilities for manufacturing its own weapons in quantity.

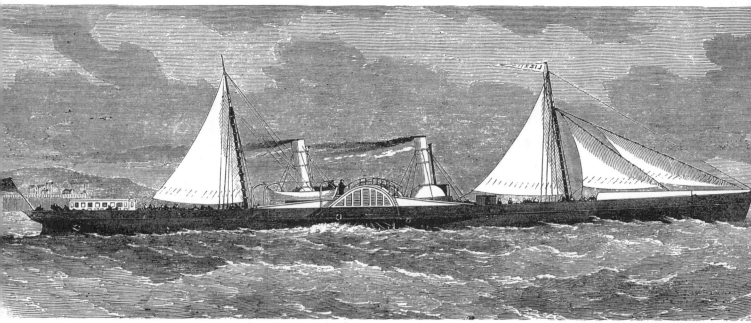

The blockade-runner *Lizzie* under full steam.

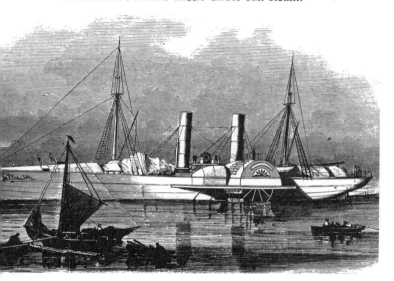

The *Wando* in Boston Harbor after her capture.

The *Lilian* running through the blockade to Wilmington.

Blockade-Runners: 1864 Models

The blockade-runners shown here all have one thing in common—they represent the highest development of this type of ocean racer. The shipbuilders in England and Scotland who produced these vessels made no secret of what they were doing. Their ships' trial runs were conducted openly, and the results were proudly published, because it was good publicity for a yard to establish a new speed record with one of its blockade-runners. The British were trying to get as much shipbuilding work as they could, and they wanted to attract the attention of the entire world.

Many of the yards specializing in fast steamers were located on the Clyde. The 230-foot *Lizzie* was launched at one of them near Renfrew in the summer of 1864. She made a record of 22 mph on her first run, which exceeded the speed expected of her by her builders and owners. Driven by two 150-hp engines designed "on the builder's patent diagonal oscillating principle," her feathering paddle wheels were her main source of motive power, for her masts and sails were unusually small.

The *Colonel Lamb,* built at Liverpool and launched during the same summer, was 280 feet long—the largest steel ship built up to that time. In a race between this new blockade-runner and the *Douglas,* which was one of the fastest ships on the Mersey, the *Colonel Lamb* (named after the commander of Fort Fisher)

The USS *Richmond* on patrol duty in rough seas.

The steel-hulled *Colonel Lamb* racing at Liverpool.

The captured *Ella and Annie* renamed the USS *Malvern*.

was four miles ahead of her rival at the end of two and a half hours.

The blockade-runner *Ella and Annie,* after her capture by the Union Navy, was renamed the *Malvern.* Because of her speed, Admiral Porter chose her for his flagship. She carried President Lincoln up the James River to Richmond after the city was evacuated in April 1865. The *Wando* was another blockade-runner unlucky enough to fall into the hands of the Federal Navy. She was commissioned under the same name as an armed steamer at Boston on December 22, 1864. The *Lilian* was commanded by Maffitt of *Florida* fame. She, too, was eventually captured and commissioned in the U. S. Navy under her own name.

The first four Government-owned blockade-runners to be constructed late in the war as a result of Bulloch's urging were the *Owl, Bat, Stag,* and *Deer*. They were all built on the same plan as paddle steamers 230 feet long, drawing seven and a half feet of water. They could carry 800 bales of cotton in addition to the coal needed to run from Wilmington to Bermuda. They were to be followed by ten others of various sizes and specifications. Construction of four other steamers intended to be armed for harbor defense was also begun, but only one of these ships was finished and that one was too late to be of any use.

As an example of what the blockade-runners had to contend with at this time, a picture of the heavily armed U.S. sloop of war *Richmond* is shown as she appeared on patrol duty off Mobile early in 1864.

Way Stops to Confederate Ports

Nassau and Bermuda were much more than convenient coaling stations for the blockade-runners. Early in the war, when cargoes were brought directly from England to Confederate ports, it was quickly established that the ships carrying them could legally be seized by the Federal Navy. Nor was it enough merely to put in briefly at Bermuda or Nassau, for a long-recognized ruling of British prize courts (called the Doctrine of Continuous Voyage) still made the ships subject to capture. The temporary stop at the islands did not break the continuity of a voyage which was obviously intended to terminate at a Confederate port.

In an effort to get around this legal barrier, large British oceangoing ships were used to bring cargoes from England to the islands. There title to the goods was changed to a new owner, and the merchandise was transferred to small fast shallow-draft blockade-runners which took the cargoes into a Confederate port. In this way, the risk was reduced to only a small part of the voyage, and that part was covered by ships designed especially for the work.

United States courts soon ruled that the entire voyage was a subterfuge and that the ships and cargoes were therefore still subject to seizure. But the idea of transferring cargoes to smaller, faster vessels made such good economic sense (because the blockade-runners cost much less than the bigger ships) that the practice was continued.

Trade boomed in the two island ports, and the people there, with profits piling up rapidly, were so enthusiastically pro-Confederate that Federal officials were sometimes booed and even attacked in the streets.

At first, Nassau was the most-often used port. Then, during the year 1863, Bermuda was the chief base of operations. After that, Nassau again became more popular. The Confederate Government stationed agents in these and other Caribbean ports to expedite the flow of goods. Havana also was used as a way station, but British ports were generally preferred.

Before the war, both Nassau and Bermuda had been sleepy, unimportant little places where the natives dwelt in semipoverty. But with the coming of the blockade-running trade, the island towns blossomed into lively, free-spending seaports where the sudden flush of prosperity changed the living habits of the entire population.

Frank Vandiver describes wartime Bermuda in his *Confederate Blockade-Running Through Bermuda:* "Life in Bermuda took on a note of high gaiety as the blockade-runners flocked to the islands. Mrs. Norman Walker [wife of the Confederate agent] maintained a perennial open house for the South's supporters and the Bourne's 'Rose Hill,' overlooking St. George's harbor, ebbed and flowed tides of Confederate agents and naval officers. The young girls of the

Unloading cotton from blockade-runners at Nassau.

A view of Nassau made while it was at the height of its blockade-running activities early in 1864.

islands arranged many social functions to which the young officers were invariably invited, and many of them were so fortunate as to receive invitations to some of the old homes on the islands. They found that 'St. George's became not only a harbor of refuge, but a pleasant resting place after the excitement and fatigue of an outward voyage.' Crates marked 'merchandize' jammed W. L. Penno's warehouse. . . . Kegs of 'nails' and cases of 'combustibles' filled J. W. Musson's warehouse, and that of Bourne, himself, bulged with gray cloth, shoes, blankets, and commissary stores. St. George's, along with most other cities booming with war business, had its bad spots. The vast numbers of sailors crowding the streets of St. George's were out for a good time while on shore leave. They had plenty of money that came easily with running the blockade, and they were not afraid to spend it rapidly. Bermuda boasted excellent rum and many good places to drink. St. George's offered, in addition, the diversion of the famous 'Shinbone Alley,' at the base of the road to Barrack Hill. Here the sailors could spend their nights and their money for all types of diversion, and consequently here they congregated."

Life in Nassau was very much the same as in Bermuda, but perhaps even livelier, judging from contemporary accounts.

Despite the convenience of using these island way stops, some ships continued to run into Confederate ports with cargoes from England. One of them, a new blockade-runner named the *Condor,* went first to Halifax in September 1864 and then attempted to enter the Cape Fear River to reach Wilmington. She carried two distinguished passengers. One was James B. Holcombe, Confederate Commissioner to Great Britain, who boarded the ship at Halifax after leaving Niagara Falls where he had made an unsuccessful effort to negotiate peace. The other was the romantic-looking Confederate spy, Mrs. Rose O'Neal Greenhow. While

in London she had published a book about her experiences and was bringing with her the money it had earned, about $2000 in gold which she carried in a leather bag.

Word of the *Condor's* destination had been telegraphed from Halifax to Washington, and the Federal fleet had been alerted. When the blockade-runner tried to enter New Inlet in heavy weather on October 1, the USS *Niphon* was waiting for her.

In the chase, the *Condor* nearly collided with the hull of a blockade-runner which had been wrecked the night before, and in trying to avoid the unexpected obstacle, ran aground. The guns of Fort Fisher held back the Federal warship, but huge waves quickly broke up the stranded ship. Mrs. Greenhow insisted on being put ashore in a small boat which quickly overturned. Its rowers succeeded in getting to the beach, but Mrs. Greenhow was drowned. The heavy bag of gold she had chained to herself probably contributed to her death. Her body was washed ashore and was found by a Confederate sailor who appropriated the gold but later, conscience stricken, turned it over to the authorities.

ROSE O'NEAL GREENHOW, the Confederate spy who helped win the Battle of Bull Run by sending secret dispatches to Beauregard. She spent six months in Old Capitol Prison and was then allowed to go to Richmond. The Confederate Government gave her $2500 from secret service funds and sent her to England where she wrote and published her book. On her return to America, she was drowned at Cape Fear.

Federal monitors close in on a blockade-runner that ran ashore near Charleston on February 2, 1865.

The wreck of the blockade-runner *Colt*.

End Game

By the middle of September 1864, the Confederacy was far advanced with its plan to build and operate its own blockade-runners. The *Owl* was already at sea; so was the *Bat,* although this unlucky ship was captured at Wilmington on her first voyage. The *Stag* and the *Deer* were almost ready to sail, and ten others were under construction. These ships had to be registered in the names of private British owners, for Lord Russell had stated publicly that any blockade-runners known to be the property of the Confederate Government would be considered as transports and would have to enter British ports on the same basis as the

A blockade-runner stranded on the beach. Painted by D. J. Kennedy in 1864.

A New York-made board game based on blockade-running.

men-of-war of belligerent powers. In most cases, the Government did not hold more than a two-thirds interest in the ships, but that would have been enough to make them come under this ruling.

Meanwhile, private blockade-runners were still doing a good business and would continue to do so until the ports of Charleston and Wilmington were closed. Several blockade-runners, unaware that Wilmington was no longer in Confederate hands after its capture on January 15, 1865, tried to enter that port. The Federal occupation forces gladly guided them into the trap by using the customary range lights.

After the loss of these two major seaports, the Confederacy no longer needed the large blockade-runners being built for it. Only ships drawing six feet of water or less could enter the shallow inlets and rivers still in Confederate hands. On February 24, 1865, Mallory issued orders to sell the unwanted ships at a loss.

By this time the great blockade-running adventure was over. But in those days of poor communications, a few would-be adventurers kept putting out to sea. On April 27, 1865, the *Windsor Forest* left Liverpool with a cargo of munitions consigned to a government that no longer existed. She was probably the last blockade-runner, although one cannot be sure. Records on the subject are voluminous in England and America, but the complicated story of blockade-running has never been thoroughly explored. A definitive study of it is one of the most-needed projects in Civil War naval history.

FLAG OFFICER

CAPTAIN

COMMANDER

LIEUTENANT

PURSER

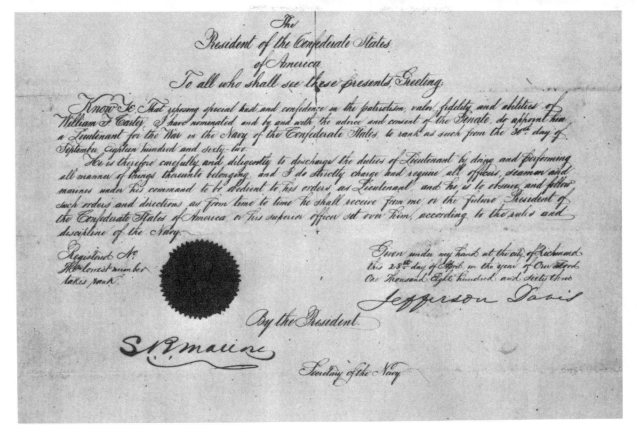

An officer's commission signed by Jefferson Davis and Stephen R. Mallory.

RANK AND UNIFORMS
IN THE CONFEDERATE NAVY

The Confederate Navy had to be made into a working organization overnight. There was no time for the orderly but time-consuming processes by which men and ships are usually integrated into a fighting unit. Even uniforms were problems, for the cloth came from abroad. For naval officers, uniforms were steel gray, lined with black silk serge, and decorated with gold lace and brass buttons.

A Flag Officer, who was next to an Admiral in rank, wore four stars on his shoulder straps and three stripes plus a looped stripe on his sleeves. Then came a Captain with three stars and one less sleeve stripe. After him came a Commander with two stars and one sleeve stripe plus a looped stripe. A Lieutenant wore only one star and one looped sleeve stripe. Officers below these in rank who were entitled to shoulder straps wore them without stars, either with leaves or blank.

The officers listed above also wore cap ornaments with a device showing a foul anchor in an open wreath of live oak leaves surmounted by the proper number of stars to indicate rank.

By 1864 the Confederate Navy had 753 officers and 4460 enlisted men. There was always a shortage of younger officers. The number of acting midshipmen was limited by law to 106. Training was given on the school ship *Patrick Henry* stationed in the James River below Richmond or on ships in service.

Officers' salaries, established in 1861, ranged from $800 for passed midshipmen to $6000 for an admiral. As Confederate currency depreciated in value, fixed salaries naturally bought less and less. This was not so bad on a ship where food and shelter were provided, but in other circumstances it was. An officer traveling overland on duty was allowed 10 cents a mile for all out-of-pocket expenses, but a 15-day round-trip journey from Richmond to Mobile actually cost $450 in 1864, yet only $216 could be repaid as compensation.

Enlisted men received $283 a year in 1864. No one got rich in the Confederate Navy. Some officers and men in the Union Navy got large sums of prize money, but this was seldom true for Confederate seamen because their Government collapsed before most claims could be paid.

THE BOMBARDMENT OF FORT FISHER   Frank Vizetelly, the British artist who was sent to the South to cover the war for *The Illustrated London News,*

1865

On January 1, 1865, the Confederacy had less than four months to go. Many realized that the end was very near, but they kept fighting until their Government ceased to exist. Those who were on ships far away at sea had no way of knowing what was happening at home, so they continued to act as fighting men for the Confederacy long after the armies had surrendered. The fall of North Carolina's Fort Fisher on January 15, 1865, closed the South's last major seaport. Once it was gone, there was no longer any way of getting supplies from abroad, and the day of the blockade-runner was over.

made this dramatic sketch of the interior of Fort Fisher as it appeared while under fire from the Union fleet.

1865.

JANUARY								JULY						
Sun.	M.	T.	W.	T.	F.	Sat.		Sun.	M.	T.	W.	T.	F.	Sat.
1	2	3	4	5	6	7		..	..	..	..	..	..	1
8	9	10	11	12	13	14		2	3	4	5	6	7	8
15	16	17	18	19	20	21		9	10	11	12	13	14	15
22	23	24	25	26	27	28		16	17	18	19	20	21	22
29	30	31	..	..	..	..		23	24	25	26	27	28	29
..	..	..	..	..	..	..		30	31	..	..	..	..	..

FEBRUARY								AUGUST						
..	..	..	1	2	3	4		..	..	1	2	3	4	5
5	6	7	8	9	10	11		6	7	8	9	10	11	12
12	13	14	15	16	17	18		13	14	15	16	17	18	19
19	20	21	22	23	24	25		20	21	22	23	24	25	26
26	27	28	..	..	..	..		27	28	29	30	31	..	..

MARCH								SEPTEMBER						
..	..	..	1	2	3	4		..	..	..	..	..	1	2
5	6	7	8	9	10	11		3	4	5	6	7	8	9
12	13	14	15	16	17	18		10	11	12	13	14	15	16
19	20	21	22	23	24	25		17	18	19	20	21	22	23
26	27	28	29	30	31	..		24	25	26	27	28	29	30

APRIL								OCTOBER						
..	..	..	..	..	..	1		1	2	3	4	5	6	7
2	3	4	5	6	7	8		8	9	10	11	12	13	14
9	10	11	12	13	14	15		15	16	17	18	19	20	21
16	17	18	19	20	21	22		22	23	24	25	26	27	28
23	24	25	26	27	28	29		29	30	31	..	..	..	..
30	..	..	..	..	..	..		..	..	..	..	..	..	..

MAY								NOVEMBER						
..	1	2	3	4	5	6		..	..	1	2	3	4	
7	8	9	10	11	12	13		5	6	7	8	9	10	11
14	15	16	17	18	19	20		12	13	14	15	16	17	18
21	22	23	24	25	26	27		19	20	21	22	23	24	25
28	29	30	31	..	..	..		26	27	28	29	30	..	..

JUNE								DECEMBER						
..	..	..	1	2	3		..	..	..	..	..	1	2	
4	5	6	7	8	9	10		3	4	5	6	7	8	9
11	12	13	14	15	16	17		10	11	12	13	14	15	16
18	19	20	21	22	23	24		17	18	19	20	21	22	23
25	26	27	28	29	30	..		24	25	26	27	28	29	30
..	..	..	..	..	..	..		31	..	..	..	..	..	..

FORT FISHER

One by one the Confederacy's seaports had fallen; from Port Royal and New Orleans to Mobile, they had been taken by Federal attacks. Only a few in Texas were still open at the end of 1864, but they were too far away to be of much use. Charleston was still in Confederate hands, but it was heavily blockaded and was destined to be evacuated on February 17 when Sherman's army cut off its communications to the interior. Only Wilmington remained, and that highly important gateway to the South was now to be the object of an intensive amphibious assault.

The great series of fortifications guarding the two entrances to the Cape Fear River were the strongest of all Civil War defenses. By this time, engineers had learned the value of earthworks, which were far superior to more costly masonry construction. A parapet 25 feet thick protected the big guns which were mounted in barbette. Only the bombproofs and magazines were covered; everything else was open to the sky. But the fort was made secure by underwater torpedoes, and the beaches and sand dunes around it had been heavily planted with land mines.

The first expedition against Fort Fisher was planned by Grant as early as September 1864. He put Admiral David Dixon Porter and General Benjamin Butler in charge of the combined operation. The two men had no use for each other, and Porter had urged that Butler not be put in command of the infantry attack. But Butler wanted to salvage his reputation, which had suffered by his blundering at Bermuda Hundred. He came up with a seemingly ingenious scheme of blowing up the fort by sending a ship loaded with gunpowder close to the shore and exploding it there. Grant had no use for the idea, but he allowed Butler to go ahead.

The 295-foot screw-steamer *Louisiana,* disguised with an extra false funnel to look like a blockade-runner, was packed with 215 tons of gunpowder which was to be triggered off by clockwork mechanism. Late in the night of December 23, the ship was first towed and then run in under her own power to within a few hundred yards of the shore. The clockwork was set to go off at 1:30 A.M., but the officer in charge did not trust it. He set fire to the giant floating torpedo before abandoning it. His doubts were confirmed, for the clock did not explode the dangerous cargo. Twenty-two minutes later, when flames reached the gunpowder, the ship blew up.

The explosion made a great deal of noise and lighted the sky with a bright glare, but it did little if any damage to the fort. When the Federal fleet moved in the next morning, a Confederate flag was flying over the long lines of earthworks.

The fleet that appeared before Fort Fisher on December 24 was the largest ever assembled under the American flag during the Civil War. Ironclads, monitors, wooden frigates, and gunboats of all kinds came on inexorably. Every ship was powered by steam.

At 12:40 P.M., the fleet drawn up in arcs of concentric circles, let loose its 619 guns against the fort's 44 guns and three mortars. The Confederates were so short of ammunition that they had to hoard it, firing each gun once every 30 minutes, while the attacking fleet could hurl 115 shells a minute. The Union bombardment was so heavy that it filled the heavens with thunder. Yet it was oddly ineffective against the almost indestructible earthen walls. On the first day, the mighty torrent of shot and shell dismounted only three or four of the well-protected Confederate guns. It did, however, blow up two of the fort's magazines and destroy part of the quarters. Yet casualties in the fort were slight. They were worse on the Union ships, because six of their notoriously undependable 100-pounder Parrott guns exploded.

On Christmas Day, General Godfrey Weitzel landed 2500 of Butler's 16,000 troops. A desultory infantry attack was made; then Butler, who was cruising up and down the beach in a tugboat, agreed with Weitzel that the fort had not been reduced sufficiently by the naval guns to be ready for a land assault. And a storm was coming up. Butler ordered the men withdrawn and hurriedly left the scene himself. About 700 of the troops had to be taken back to the transports by the Navy.

The first attempt to capture the Confederate stronghold was an utter failure. General A. H. Terry was then put in Butler's place. Terry, a Connecticut clerk of the court, was also a volunteer officer. But there the similarity between him and Butler ended. Terry was a natural-born soldier who remained in the Army after the war. Under him, the troops who had accomplished little under his predecessor's command became efficient fighting men.

The next attempt to take the fort was scheduled for mid-January 1865. Colonel William Lamb, the Confederate commander of the besieged stronghold, had repaired some of the damage done in the December attack. But he was short of men to hold the defenses against a land assault. He telegraphed for rein-

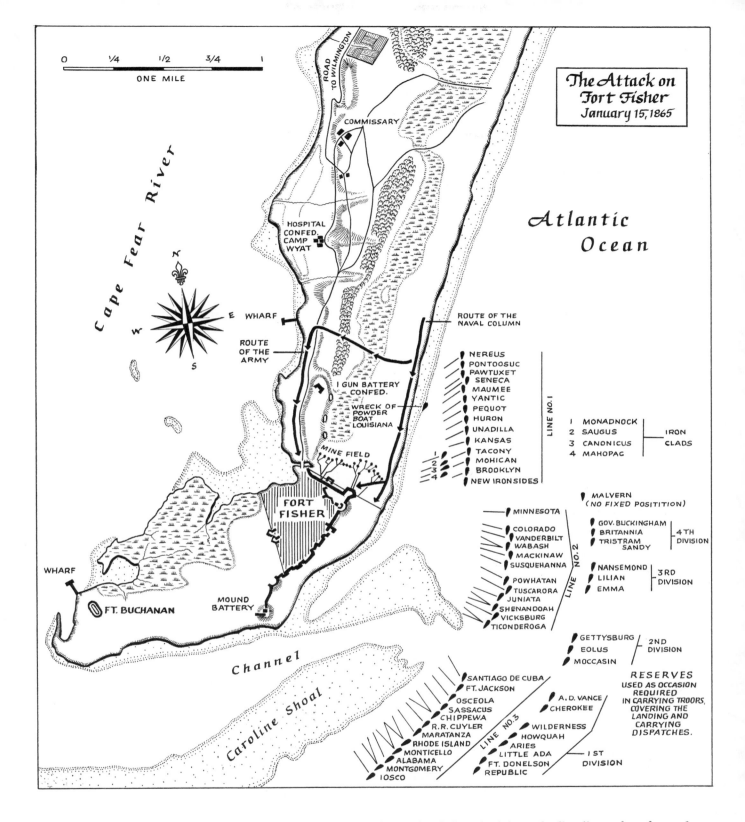

The Attack on Fort Fisher
January 15, 1865

forcements and got a few. On January 12, he saw the Union fleet returning with even more vessels and guns than it had had before.

At 7:30 A.M. the next morning, the furious bombardment began. During the first attack, firing from the Federal fleet had been badly directed and poorly aimed. Now it was precise and devastating. It went on, day and night, on January 13 and 14 with no letup. The Confederates had no chance to repair damage. Colonel Lamb said that the ships "bowled their

11- and 15-inch shells along the parapet, scattering shrapnel in the darkness. We could scarcely gather up and bury our dead without fresh casualties. At least 200 had been killed and wounded in the two days since the fight began." And now, on January 15, the great assault was about to begin.

At dawn on January 15 the Federal fleet stepped up its firing. Smooth water helped the gunners' aim, and the big shells slammed into the fort with dreadful effect. Hour after hour, the shore was lashed by a storm of metal. By noon, the defenders had only one gun left on the side facing the sea, and they were in desperate need of ammunition and reinforcements. About 700 men had come to their assistance during the previous day and night, but the garrison was rapidly being reduced by the killing fire from the fleet. Knowing the importance of the key fort, the Confederates sent in another 350 men just before the Federal land attack began.

By 2:30 P.M. some 8000 Union soldiers and sailors, provided with more than 600,000 rounds of ammunition were ready for a determined assault on the north wall of the fort. A party of 100 sharpshooters equipped with Spencer repeating carbines ran close to the work

On the morning after the surrender, one of the fort's powder magazines was accidentally blown up with great loss of life.

and hastily dug themselves in. They kept the parapet under fire while the main body of troops moved up.

A young Union lieutenant who was later to become a famous admiral ("Fighting Bob" Evans) describes the assault of the naval battalion: "At three o'clock the order to charge was given, and we started for our long run of 1200 yards over the loose sand. The fleet kept up a hot fire until we approached within about 600 yards of the fort and then ceased firing. The rebels . . . manned the parapet and opened on us with 2600 muskets. . . . Under the shower of bullets the marines broke . . . and did not appear again . . . in the assault. . . . About 500 yards from the fort the head of the column suddenly stopped, and . . . the whole mass of men went down like a row of falling bricks. . . . The officers called on the men, and they responded instantly, starting forward as fast as they could go. At about 300 yards they again went down, this time under the effect of canister added to the rifle fire. Again we rallied them, and once more started to the front under a perfect hail of lead, with men dropping rapidly in every direction. We were now so close that we could hear the voices of the rebels. . . . The officers were pulling their caps down over their eyes, for it was almost impossible to look at the deadly flashing blue line of parapet, and we all felt that in a few minutes more we should get our cutlasses to work and make up for the fearful loss we had suffered.

"At this moment I saw Colonel Lamb, the Confederate commander, gallantly standing out on the parapet and calling on his men to get up and shoot the Yankees. I considered him within range of revolver, so took a deliberate shot at him. As I fired, a bullet ripped through the front of my coat across my breast, turning me completely around. I felt a burning sensation, like a hot iron, over my heart, and saw something red coming out of the hole in my coat. . . . But that was no place to stop, so I went on at the head of my company. As we approached . . . the stockade, I was aware that one particular sharpshooter was shooting at me, and when we were a hundred yards away he hit me in the left leg, about three inches below the knee. The force of the blow was so great that I landed on my face in the sand. . . .

"About this time the men were stumbling over wires which they cut with their knives. They proved to be wires to the torpedoes over which we had charged, but they failed to explode. My left leg seemed asleep, but I was able to use it. The stockade . . . was very near, and I determined to lead my company . . . through a break in it and then charge over the angle of the fort. . . . I managed to get through the stockade . . . when my sharpshooter friend sent a bullet through my right knee. . . . I tried to stand up,

A British-made rifled Armstrong 150-pound gun captured at Fort Fisher. It is now at West Point.

The interior of Fort Fisher photographed after its surrender. Note the two dismounted guns in the water.

but it was no use; my legs would not hold me, and besides this I was bleeding dreadfully. . . . I heard someone say. 'They are retreating!' and . . . I saw our men breaking from the rear of the columns. . . .

"Just as our men began to break, the army made their charge and were able to make a lodgment on the northwest portion of the works before the rebels . . . saw them. When they discovered them, they went at them with a savage yell, and for seven hours fought them desperately. . . .

"From my new position I could see the army slowly fighting its way from one gun to another. It was a magnificent sight. They knew their business thoroughly. . . . At ten o'clock that night they won a victory that will live as long as heroic deeds are recorded. . . . The Confederates were doing . . . all that human courage could do, but they were wearing out, and the arrival of fresh brigades on our side discouraged them."

It was after dark when the last bit of desperate resistance from the fort flickered out. With the fall of the great stronghold, the port of Wilmington could no longer be used by blockade-runners, and the Confederacy's vital supply line to Europe was cut forever. To accomplish this, the Federal fleet fired more than 40,000 shells. The defenders of the fort had a supply of only 3600 rounds for their guns to use during both attacks.

JOHN BULL'S OCCUPATION GONE
John Bull (*Coster-monger*). "My heyes!—Market shut up!—and I've got to trundle my combustibles and other wegetables back 'ome again!" From Harper's *Weekly*.

The Confederate fleet tries to pass the obstructions in the James on January 23, 1865.

FINAL OPERATIONS ON THE JAMES

A number of Confederate naval vessels had been bottled up for a long while on the James by a Federal fleet that barred their way down the river (SEE PAGE 202). When the Federals prepared their attack on Fort Fisher they commandeered nearly every ship on the east coast. The Confederates saw their chance to break through. And by good fortune, the James was running unusually high in mid-January 1865. A naval expedition was organized to go to City Point and attack Grant's base of supplies there.

Lieutenant Charles W. Read of *Clarence-Tacony-Archer* fame (SEE PAGE 140), now released from Fort Warren and serving with the James River Squadron, reported on January 15 that the floodwaters were washing out the obstructions which the Federals had placed across the river. A week later he told General George E. Pickett that he thought the ships could get through. Pickett sent him to Lee who advised him to go to Richmond and urge Mallory to dispatch the fleet immediately.

At 7 P.M. January 23, the ironclads *Virginia No. 2, Richmond,* and *Fredericksburg,* the wooden gunboats *Hampton, Nansemond, Drewry,* and *Beaufort,* the converted tug *Torpedo,* and three small torpedo launches under Read's command started down the river. Flag Officer J. K. Mitchell was in charge of the little fleet. It quickly ran into trouble. The *Torpedo* went aground at eight thirty; at midnight the *Virginia* got stuck on a shoal near Trent's Reach while sending out a boat to cut a way through the obstructions which the Federals had hastily repaired after the flood had destroyed part of them. The *Torpedo* pulled clear, but there was no moving the heavy ironclad. Mitchell had no choice but to wait for water to rise in the tidal river.

Read went down to help in the work of cutting a passage through the obstructions. The *Fredericksburg* went through the opening that was soon made, but she found herself alone. The *Richmond* had grounded farther upstream, and so had the gunboat *Drewry* as well as one of the torpedo launches. It was difficult navigating the treacherous James in the dark.

Read was sent down again to recall the *Fredericksburg,* which was then ordered to stay near the *Richmond* and cover the grounded ships. Federal gunners and sharpshooters, alerted to what was going on, brought in a powerful Drummond light to illuminate the river. With its rays to guide them, they fired shells and Minié balls at the stranded vessels. The crew of the helpless wooden *Drewry* was removed to the shelter of the ironclad *Richmond* just before dawn. Soon after daylight, a shell hit the gunboat's magazine which blew up and tore the ship to pieces.

Federal guns along the shore now began to concentrate their fire on the *Virginia.* Her iron sides fended off the shells, but her vulnerable smokestack and other exposed parts were riddled with holes or shot away. The other ships also got their share of the firing, but there was nothing they could do except to wait for the tide to rise. To make matters worse, the double-turreted monitor *Onandaga* came up and began to use her 15-inch guns on them.

By 10:30 A.M. the water was high enough for the *Virginia* to get afloat. She headed upstream, followed by the rest of the severely damaged ships and finally reached the shelter of Chaffin's Bluff.

Another expedition was sent out on February 10, when about one hundred men with the indestructible Lieutenant Read in command tried to take several torpedo boats mounted on wagon wheels overland to a point below City Point and then go up the river to

The people of Richmond flee from the burning city and cross Mayo's Bridge on April 2, 1865.

attack the Federal base. A lieutenant named Lewis who had a long record of service in both the Confederate Army and Navy was sent ahead to reconnoiter. The wagon-boat party then went through the wooded backcountry in bitter cold weather which was followed by a blinding sleet storm that drove the half-frozen sailors to the shelter of a deserted farmhouse. A Confederate prisoner of war who had escaped from Fort Monroe came to tell them that they had been betrayed, that their trusted scout was waiting with a Union regiment to capture them when they crossed a certain ford. It was decided that the entire party hide in the woods with the boats while Read investigated the situation. He returned a day later as "cool and collected as ever" and said that they would have to hurry back to Richmond. Federal cavalry was already searching the woods for them. A local guide showed them how to take a shortcut by wading waist-deep through the icy waters of the Appomattox River. They reached Richmond safely, but 75 of the men were so ill from exposure that they had to be hospitalized.

A few days after this episode, Mallory gave Read a note authorizing him to draw £10,000 from Bulloch in London to go on a cruise. The mysterious cruise never materialized, for Read was in Louisiana less than six weeks later.

On February 10, Raphael Semmes was made a rear admiral and on the eighteenth was placed in charge of the James River Squadron. It was an unhappy command, quickly destined to failure as was everything about the ill-fated naval defenses of Richmond at that late day.

When Grant closed in on the Confederate lines around Petersburg and that city and Richmond had to be abandoned, Semmes received an order from Mallory on April 2 to destroy his ships and join General Lee's forces in the march toward Danville.

It was a bitter order for the man who had sailed the *Sumter* and the *Alabama* on the oceans of the world. But he dutifully called together the captains of his ships and broke the news to them. While they made their plans for the night, flag-of-truce boats kept passing up and down the river between Richmond and City Point with their decks filled with prisoners who had just been exchanged. When Confederate prisoners saw the flag on Semmes's *Virginia,* they cheered it, not realizing that in a few days it would not represent a nation but only a lost cause.

At nightfall Semmes led his fleet up to Drewry's Bluff, where he intended to sink the ironclads quietly and proceed in the gunboats to Richmond. Shortly after dark he saw the north side of the James aglow with flames from fires started by Confederate soldiers as they abandoned their trenches and burned everything of value. Soon afterward he could see the glare of the great conflagration that was consuming the heart of the Confederate capital. Since there was no longer any need for concealment, he decided to blow up the three ironclads.

His men had to be made ready for the long march ahead of them. Hammocks, blankets, arms, and provisions were distributed and packed for individuals to carry. The sailors from the ironclads were put on board the gunboats, and the rams were then set on fire. The little wooden fleet headed upstream toward the burning city, leaving the three armored ships behind them in flames.

Blowing up the rams in the James River fleet on April 2, 1865.

BLOWING UP THE RAMS

Semmes describes the scene on the river near Richmond that night: "An explosion, like the shock of an earthquake, took place, and the air was filled with missiles. It was the blowing up of the *Virginia,* my late flagship. The spectacle was grand beyond description. Her shell rooms had been full of loaded shells. The explosion of the magazine threw all these shells, with their fuses lighted, into the air. The fuses were of different lengths, and as the shells exploded by twos and threes, and by the dozen, the pyrotechnic effect was very fine. The explosion shook the houses in Richmond and must have waked the echoes of the night for forty miles around. . . . Owing to a delay [at the bridge], the sun—a glorious, unclouded sun, as if to mock our misfortunes—was now rising over Richmond. Some windows, which fronted to the east, were all aglow with his rays, mimicking the real fires that were already breaking out in various parts of the city. In the lower part of the city, the schoolship *Patrick Henry* was burning, and some of the houses near the Navy Yard were on fire. But higher up was the principal scene of the conflagration. Entire blocks were on fire here, and a dense canopy of smoke, rising high in the still morning air, was covering the city as with a pall. The rear guard of our army had just crossed as I landed my fleet at Manchester, and the bridges were burning in their rear. The Tredegar Iron Works were on fire, and continual explosions of loaded shell stored there were taking place."

Semmes then put his 500 sailors and their baggage on shore. While the wooden gunboats were being set on fire and pushed out into the stream, he learned that all the trains had been seized by the Government and had long since departed. He told his steam-engine experts to put a train together from the odds and ends of railroad stock left in the yards. These resourceful men soon had a small locomotive ready, but it was not powerful enough to pull a long line of cars loaded with sailors, baggage, and frantic citizens who insisted on crowding on board. Another engine

The destruction of the ram *Webb* below New Orleans on April 24, 1865.

Destroying the ram *Savannah* when that city was evacuated in December 1864.

was found in the shops. By the time it got steam up, Yankee soldiers could be seen pouring into the streets of Richmond across the river. The makeshift train finally got off. It reached Danville late the next night. When Semmes joined Jefferson Davis and his Cabinet, he was made a general as well as an admiral so he would not be outranked by the Army officers attached to the Government. His command was transformed into an artillery brigade, but it was never to see action. Semmes and his men surrendered with Joseph E. Johnston's army on May 1.

The sailors from the shore batteries along the James did not fare as well as the men from the fleet. They had come north from Charleston and Wilmington after those cities were evacuated. Now they were made part of the rear guard of Lee's army as it marched toward Appomattox. They fought bravely in the Battle of Sayler's Creek on April 6, and were among the several thousand Confederates who surrendered there.

Semmes's rams were not the only ones which had to be destroyed during the last days of the Confederacy. The *Savannah* was blown up in December 1864 when the city after which she was named was evacuated. So were the ironclads *Charleston, Palmetto State,* and the *Chicora* at Charleston in February 1865. There were still others. And at Richmond the powerful ironclad ram *Texas,* in a still unfinished condition, was captured.

Most remarkable of all, however, was the fate of the wooden steam ram *William H. Webb.* The indefatigable—and ubiquitous—Charles W. Read got himself transferred back to the Mississippi theater of war where his adventurous career had begun. On March 31, 1865, he assumed command of the *Webb* at Shreveport. He took the ship down the Red River, eluded a Federal monitor and two ironclads sent to block his way, and ran past New Orleans flying the American flag as a disguise. The USS *Hollyhock* was waiting for him 25 miles below the city. The dauntless young lieutenant burned the *Webb* and tried to escape overland but was captured with 25 of his men on April 26, seventeen days after Lee surrendered the Army of Northern Virginia at Appomattox.

The riddled smokestack of the *Virginia No. 2.*

243

THE WATERS GIVE UP
THEIR HIDDEN WEAPONS

When the war ended, the officers of the Federal Navy had their first good chance to see how truly ingenious the Confederates had been in underwater warfare. The evacuation of Charleston threw several abandoned Davids into their hands, and they also fell heir to vast quantities of the various kinds of torpedoes which had been used in that area. They gathered an impressive collection of them at the Charleston Arsenal where they were carefully labeled and studied.

After Fort Fisher fell, Confederates on the Cape Fear River used up their supply of 200 torpedoes by letting them drift downstream in the hope that they would strike Federal ships and destroy them. One did some damage to the gunboat *Osceola;* another blew up a cutter from the *Shawmut.* Fishing nets were then placed across the river to prevent more torpedoes from coming down.

Long after the Battle of Mobile Bay, torpedoes remaining in the waters there damaged or sank a number of Union ships that were unlucky enough to run into one of them. And when Richmond was evacuated, the James River was known to be heavily mined. But it was essential for Federal ships to reach the former Confederate capital so minesweeping operations were started immediately. Armed men were sent along the banks to find and cut any suspicious-looking wires leading into the water and also to capture any torpedo operators who might still be around. Meanwhile, boats dragged the river to locate unattached contact mines.

Richmond was occupied by Federal troops early on April 3. The next day, while the city was still in flames, Admiral Porter took President Lincoln up the already cleared river to visit the vanquished Confederate capital. They saw many large torpedoes that had been pulled out of the water and left on the banks, and they passed through narrow gaps in the obstructions that had blocked the channel. It was a dangerous voyage, but nothing untoward happened, and the President reached the city without harm.

On the following day, two Confederate torpedo experts were brought to Porter's ship, the *Malvern,* then at Richmond with the President on board. They were asked to point out the location of still-unfound torpedoes in order to make the river safe for navigation again. They cooperated in the final work of clearing the James and were then allowed to go free.

As late as June 6, 1865, a Federal gunboat, the *Jonquil,* was seriously injured by the explosion of a stray torpedo in the Ashley River near Charleston.

Even more remarkable Confederate devices for underwater warfare were being developed when the war ended. Maury sailed from England after Appomattox with thousands of dollars' worth of torpedo equipment which he hoped to bring into a Texas port. When he reached Havana, he realized that there was no point in trying to continue the war, so he left everything there and consigned it to Bulloch. Among his inventions was a system of firing torpedoes by using cross bearings to determine exactly when a ship was in the field of destruction. Then two operators could explode the mine at just the right moment. He had also devised a method of instantly bringing up a deeply sunk torpedo to a desired distance under the surface. And he made an electrical gauge to test the condition of torpedoes in the field without firing them.

Confederate torpedoes and heavy ordnance in the Charleston Arsenal.

The Federal torpedo boat *Spuyten Duyvil* (right, with flag) blowing up obstructions in the James River immediately after the evacuation of Richmond.

One of the Davids found on shore after Charleston was evacuated. The tall smokestack shows that the non-submersible vessel was powered by steam.

The photographs above and below, evidently taken during the winter of 1864, show a Federal station on the James where charges from captured torpedoes were removed by men trained to do this dangerous work. In the lower picture an Army officer with high riding boots discusses the job with a Navy officer. Both the Confederate and Union armies used torpedoes, sometimes planting them underwater without informing their navies where they had put them.

THE *STONEWALL* BEGINS
HER BRIEF CAREER

When the *Stonewall* reached her rendezvous off the southern coast of Brittany on January 24 (SEE PAGE 123), Captain Page knew that he did not like his expensive new ironclad. He wrote to Samuel Barron, the flag officer in charge of Confederate naval operations in Europe: "You must not expect too much of me; I fear that the power and effect of this vessel have been too much exaggerated." And a young officer in the expedition said in a letter to a friend: "What a devil of a scrape we have gone and got ourselves into with this *Stonewall;* but you can not laugh at us, for I . . . knew what was coming of her and felt the sacrificial knife . . . as soon as I saw B[ulloch] yield to Rivière and his confederates."

The French agent left the ship on January 26 and was paid his commission. Bulloch had the doubtful consolation of knowing that the Confederate Government had already realized a profit of $200,000 on the sale of the four corvettes. The ironclad purchased by Prussia also brought a profit, but these were only bookkeeping figures, for everything was soon to be swept away in the grand debacle after Appomattox.

The *Stonewall* weathered a frightful storm on January 29 and 30 and then limped into El Ferrol, Spain, for repairs. While she was there, Page was in communication with Barron and Bulloch. What he told Bulloch inspired him to write to Richmond that "the preparation and outfit of the ship [shows that] we have been cheated and deceived by some of the parties in a manner which clearly justifies my original distrust of them." It is interesting to note that the singular culprit—De Rivière—has now become plural.

While repairs were being made to the *Stonewall,* the U.S. frigate *Niagara* arrived off El Ferrol on February 11 and was soon joined by the *Sacramento.* Page hurried off to Paris to consult Captain Barron. He and Bulloch both arrived in that city on February 22. It was a poor time to expect much of Barron, for he and several other Confederate officers had been ordered to return to Richmond. Bulloch, however, was now to be in full charge of European operations, and Page got instructions from him in writing. He was to take the ironclad across the Atlantic to Bermuda, recoal there, and then strike at Port Royal, where the Union Navy was supposed to be sending a fleet to support Sherman. By this time Sherman was nearly two hundred miles beyond Port Royal, but Bulloch had no way of knowing that.

Page returned unhappily to his ship. During his absence, the two Federal warships had moved closer to the *Stonewall.* All the trouble he had had while bringing his leaking command through heavy seas from Denmark to Spain was nothing compared with the dilemma that faced him now. He carried written orders to cross the Atlantic and attack an American port which he had every reason to believe was heavily guarded. And two menacing-looking Union warships were barring his way to the sea.

Page boarded the *Stonewall* at El Ferrol on March 16. The next day the masts were dismantled, and the ship was made ready for what her captain despairingly called an "unequal engagement." Oddly enough, Captain T. T. Craven of the USS *Niagara* was having the same kind of doubt about a battle between the two wooden frigates and the seemingly formidable ironclad ram. The *Stonewall's* heavy armor, huge bow gun, and underwater beak made her look like a dangerous adversary. An uninformed observer would certainly have put heavy odds on the Confederate battleship. The Spaniards thought she was sure to win. Only the Confederates knew how serious her shortcomings were.

Bad weather closed in again to lash the two Federal ships grimly patrolling the exit from the great triple bay lying between La Coruña and El Ferrol. Twice Page headed his ship out to sea and then came back when he saw how strong the storm was outside. From bitter experience he knew that the *Stonewall* might have a chance if she fought in calm waters, but that she was difficult to maneuver in rough seas.

After he returned for the second time, the Spanish authorities told Page that he must leave El Ferrol for good. The American minister to Madrid was exerting pressure, and the local Spaniards were probably bored with a ship that had long been inactive. They wanted to see her fight.

At 10:30 A.M. on March 24, the *Stonewall* left

The *Stonewall* sketched while under sail in Danish waters.

The *Stonewall* photographed after the end of the war.

El Ferrol, accompanied by a Spanish frigate to make sure that there was no violation of Spanish territory. Page tells the story of his departure: "I remained off the harbors of Ferrol and Coruña (where lay the Yankee men-of-war, the *Niagara* and *Sacramento,* with steam up, in full view) until 8:30 P.M., but neither of them made a move from their anchors. . . . To suppose that these two heavily armed men-of-war were afraid of the *Stonewall* is to me incredible; and yet the fact of their conduct was such as I state. . . . Finding earlier in the day that they declined coming out, there was no course for me to pursue . . . but to . . . go on my way. . . . I suppose their object will be to encounter us somewhere at sea, where we may have such weather as to weaken the power of the *Stonewall.* But how Captain Craven can excuse himself for not meeting her yesterday . . . I cannot conceive. Unless he has a reason beyond his control, his commission would not be worth much in most navies. This makes our course more complicated than ever, and recent events seem to place us truly in a quandary. Would that there were some power to advise and direct. It is thought . . . by some of the officers . . . that as the *Stonewall* had been dismantled to lower masts (our spars had been left on shore) we should thus be forced to sea without them, and consequently without the means of crossing the Atlantic."

Page, however, had no intention of crossing the Atlantic yet. He ran down to Lisbon where he found the Portuguese even less cordial than the Spaniards. They told him to leave within 24 hours. Since his twin nemeses *Niagara* and *Sacramento* had followed him and were again outside the bar, the news was most unwelcome.

Page wrote to Bulloch from Lisbon on March 27 to say that he had decided to go to Nassau rather than Bermuda because he could get coal at Tenerife and then expect to have good weather from there to the Bahamas. His letter shows that the captain was questioning the usefulness of his mission. He expressed his thoughts freely to his superior: "The change in our affairs at home since the period at which you had every reason to believe the *Stonewall* would have done most effective and important service has made her comparatively inefficient, and so decidedly deprived her of striking the vital blow and doing the enemy the heavy damage that she would have done that I cannot but entertain serious doubts as to the propriety of her pursuing the course that has been marked out for her."

Speaking of the ever present Federal warships, he said: "If this vessel is thus to be pursued in every port into which she may find it necessary to enter, you see at once what her condition must inevitably become. She cannot run to sea and there remain, as could the *Alabama* and *Florida,* and this the enemy must be as well aware of as we are."

Then he added a troubled postscript: "6 o'clock P.M.—I have opened this to say that the *Niagara* and *Sacramento* are off the bar, and I suppose will come in. I should have been off this evening, but the pilot thinks it too late to attempt going out. These ships are dogging us to take an opportunity most favorable to them. The wind is strong from the north—very much against us; but we must go out tomorrow, as we are ordered out. We must encounter them. We have just sent up our spars; I wish they were down."

Meanwhile, the Portuguese authorities requested the two Federal captains to anchor their ships near the fortified island tower Belém, which they did.

Captain Thomas Jefferson Page

The Portuguese artillery-tower Belém.

The *Stonewall* leaving Lisbon, March 28, 1865.

The Ship That Was Too Late

In accordance with the request of the Portuguese Government, the *Stonewall* left the port of Lisbon about 10 A.M. on March 28. International law required that the *Niagara* and the *Sacramento* allow her a 24-hour start. At three fifteen that afternoon, lookouts from the tower-fort Belém saw the *Niagara* raise her anchor and start moving away from the position to which she had been assigned. There was much excitement in the port, where it was believed that the Federal warship was about to go in pursuit of the *Stonewall*. Three shots were fired from Belém's guns. Craven ordered his flag to be hauled down as a sign that the warning was noted and understood. He also turned the ship to face away from the harbor exit. He said later that he simply wanted to move to a better anchorage, but the Portuguese, incensed because he had not given them notice of his intentions, continued to fire, striking his ship three times before they stopped the guns.

Much protest and a formal apology followed, all of which took time. The *Niagara* was not able to leave Lisbon until April 6 when goodwill salutes of 21 guns were fired mutually from the fort and the ship. By that time, the *Stonewall* was far out on the ocean.

But the lucky break that enabled the ironclad to leave Lisbon without being followed by her pursuers was the only one that luckless ship was to have in her short career in the Confederate Navy. She went to Tenerife for coal and then lumbered slowly across the Atlantic while the Confederacy's military forces melted away and its Government fled from Richmond. She anchored briefly outside Nassau on May 6 and seems not to have been told what was happening. On May 11, the day after the Confederacy's President was captured by a Northern cavalry patrol, she entered Havana, which was to be her last port of call as a Confederate ship.

The Federal Navy had been alerted as to her whereabouts, and ships streamed into Havana to make sure that the motionless ironclad did not make trouble. Among them were the monitors *Canonicus* and *Monadnock,* which had been in the line of battle at Fort Fisher. They were towed to Havana, the first instance of monitors leaving their sheltered home waters. The admiral in charge of the squadron sent to Cuba was unimpressed by the *Stonewall*. He wrote to Gideon Welles that he thought "the *Canonicus* would have crushed her, and the *Monadnock* [with two turrets] could have taken her beyond a doubt."

But no such test of strength had to be made. Although Page would rather have sunk his ship than

The Union ironclad ram *Dunderberg* as she looked when she finally got to sea after the war was over.

let her fall into Yankee hands, he turned her over to the Spanish authorities in Cuba. He did this in order to raise $16,000 to pay off his crew, and although the nearly new warship was worth a great deal more than that, he refused to accept anything but the cash needed to cover the payroll.

On May 19, the only ironclad ever to carry the Confederate flag on the high seas was surrendered to the Captain General of Cuba for the Queen of Spain to decide who was her rightful owner. Two months later the Spanish Government ceded the vessel to the United States. There was no other claimant.

Since ironclads were in surplus supply at the end of the war, the United States sold the *Stonewall* to Japan. Under the successive names *Kotetsukan, Adzumakan,* and *Adzuma,* the former Confederate warship—which had never fired a shot in battle while under the Confederate flag—spent many years in Japan's growing young navy.

Two other Civil War ironclads also proved to be useless to the navies that built them. One was the giant Union armored ram *Dunderberg* which was launched on July 22, 1865, after the war was over. She is described on page 169.

The other was a Confederate ironclad built in great secrecy in Glasgow by James and George Thompson under a contract originally made by the Confederate agent George Sanders. Since Commander James H. North supervised her construction after Sanders returned to Richmond, the ship is commonly associated with his name. While under construction she was known by her dockyard number as the 61, although she was sometimes called the *Santa Maria,* to make people think she was destined for a Latin country.

Work on this 270-foot, heavily armored double-turreted fighting ship was begun early in 1862. The usual trouble the Confederates had with the British Government over getting ships obviously designed for war out of the country held up her construction. When it was feared that the big ironclad might be seized late in 1863, North transferred title to her builders. They sold the ship a month later to Denmark for £40,000, which the Confederacy still owed them. Since the ironclad was to cost £182,000, the Danes got a great bargain. They bought her, however, under the proviso that the builders—acting, of course, for the Confederate Government—could repurchase her for repayment plus the costs laid out for delivery. Under the name *Danmark* she served until 1902.

This shadowy vessel, which did not become a reality until the Danes bought her and made her existence public, was a powerful fighting ship. She was often referred to in veiled terms—sometimes only as "Lieutenant North's ironclad"—in Confederate correspondence. If the South had obtained possession of her in June 1863, when she was due for delivery, her armed strength turned against Northern ports and ships might have made a difference in the outcome of the war.

The mysterious Glasgow-built Confederate ironclad No. 61 which became the Danish naval ship *Danmark.*

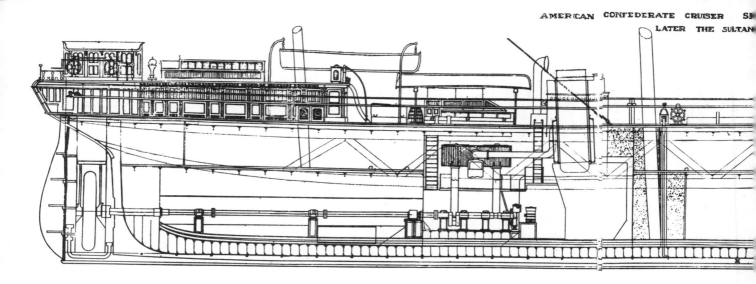

The original builder's plans for the *Sea King*, later the *Shenandoah*. She was planked with wood over steel frames and was

THE *SHENANDOAH*— LAST CONFEDERATE RAIDER

By the summer of 1864 the Atlantic had been swept so clean of Yankee ships that the Confederates had to look elsewhere. Bulloch received orders from Richmond to obtain and outfit a cruiser to go to the Pacific and from there to the Arctic to prey on the New England whaling fleet in those waters. In the autumn of 1863 he had seen a suitable full-rigged ship with

auxiliary steam power, which was about to leave on her maiden voyage to Bombay. It is said that he put an observer on board her to report on her qualities during the run. At any rate, he bought her when she returned the next year. Named the *Sea King*, she was called the *Shenandoah* when she was commissioned in the Confederate Navy.

The Federal spy system was now so efficient that a letter to Gideon Welles informed him in April 1864 (while the *Sea King* was still on her Bombay cruise for private owners) that the Confederates were going to buy the ship and send her to the Pacific to attack the whaling fleet.

Despite the fact that his plans were known, Bulloch was able to get the *Sea King* out of England on October 8, 1864, by the usual method of having her leave the port of London unarmed while a tender, in this case the *Laurel,* carried guns and ammunition to equip her at sea.

The *Sea King* and the *Laurel* met at Funchal, Madeira, on October 18 and transferred the guns and supplies. Lieutenant James I. Waddell took over the ship from her temporary English captain and tried to persuade the crew to sail with him. The crewmen were strangely reluctant. They knew about the fate of the *Alabama,* and they also knew that the Federal Navy had become very strong. It had been rumored that Semmes was to command the new cruiser, and this too made the men hesitant, for Semmes was known as a hard-driving captain who took great risks. Only

LIEUTENANT JAMES I. WADDELL

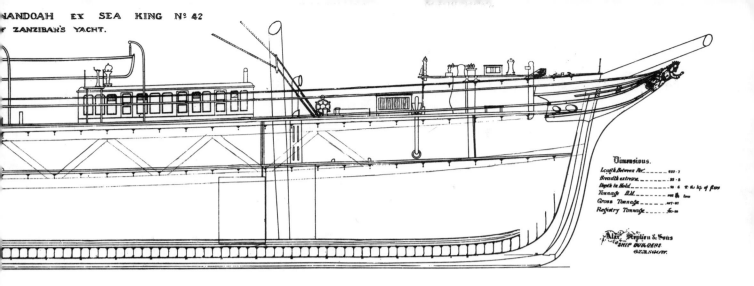

Dimensions.

Length Between Pp. _____ 232·7
Breadth extreme _____ 32·5
Depth in Hold _____ 20·6 ♯ the top of floor
Tonnage B.M. _____ 900 ♯ tons
Gross Tonnage _____ 1017·93
Registry Tonnage _____ 50·90

Alfr. Stephen & Sons
SHIP BUILDERS
GLASGOW.

designed for long cruises.

20 men (some of them from the *Alabama*) were willing to go, while 42 had to be put ashore at Tenerife. Acting on instructions, they spread word there that the *Sea King* had been wrecked on a desolate island called Las Desertas and that they had been rescued by the *Laurel*.

Waddell had to sail shorthanded. But he succeeded in enlisting enough men from the ships he captured to bring his fighting strength up to 51 men and 22 officers before the year was over.

He left Madeira on October 19 and made his first capture on October 30 when he took the bark *Alina* of Searsport, Maine, and scuttled her. He sailed on, capturing other ships. On December 16 he passed the Cape of Good Hope and reached Melbourne, Australia, on January 25, 1865. There he had to wait until February 18 to get his propeller repaired.

The Australian people seemed friendly, but the Government was not. During the stay, 18 men deserted, and threats were made against the ship. Waddell was told that some Yankee sailors were planning to hide themselves below and capture the ship at sea. Actually 42 men of various nationalities did come on board secretly, but that was because they wanted to enlist.

The *Shenandoah* sailed on, passing through violent storms and sometimes skirting the shores of Pacific islands where natives came out in their canoes to trade. She went on for weeks, looking for the whalers.

She came across four of them at Ascension Island (Ponape) in the eastern Carolines. Waddell anchored his ship in the narrow entrance to the harbor and sent out four boats to board them. The whalers' officers were so surprised that they offered no resistance.

The sail plan of the *Sea King-Shenandoah*.

The Last Confederate Raider's Last Voyage

The *Shenandoah* arrived at Ascension Island on April 1. During the next 13 days—days that saw the surrender of General Lee at Appomattox and the flight of the Confederate Government from Richmond—Waddell burned the four whalers and invited one of the native rulers to visit his ship. King Ish-Y-Paw came with 70 war canoes and was presented with 70 muskets. Waddell also gave the King a sword which he buckled around his naked waist. He was very proud of it, but it got in his way when he went below to inspect the engine room and marvel at the giant machines that tirelessly did the work of the hundreds of men who paddled his war canoes.

The King then invited Waddell to visit the royal residence. It proved to be a small and simple cane-and-vine structure built on piles to be out of the reach of the highest tides. It was furnished only with mats, two chairs, a box, and an old trunk which was offered to the guest as a seat of honor. Waddell found the Queen ugly, and hastily declined the gift of a royal princess.

He made arrangements to leave 130 prisoners on the island and departed on April 13, bound for northern seas and better hunting beyond the Arctic Circle. On May 23 he entered the Sea of Okhotsk and sailed along the coast of Kamchatka. Eight days later, he burned the New Bedford whaler *Abigail* on the edge of a wide field of floe ice.

The *Shenandoah* reached the Bering Sea on June 16. Neither ice nor fog prevented Waddell from finding the New England whaling ships he had crossed the world to track down. From June 22 to June 28 Waddell completely destroyed the Yankee whaling fleet in the Arctic. He captured 24 ships and burned all but four, which he used as cartels for hundreds of prisoners.

One of the captains taken prisoner on June 22 said that the war was over. Since he could not produce documentary evidence to prove it, Waddell refused to believe him. But the next day, when he captured a ship from San Francisco which had some newspapers with fairly recent telegraph dispatches received at that city, he had good reason to be troubled. They said that the Confederate Government had moved to Danville, that Lee had surrendered to Grant, but that most of the Army of Northern Virginia had joined Johnston's army in North Carolina. They also printed a proclamation from President Davis announcing that the war was to be carried on with renewed vigor. Waddell therefore decided to continue his work of destruction. He took 19 more ships during the next five days. He burned all but four which he placed under bond to carry his numerous prisoners to the nearest port.

The *Shenandoah* then turned southward, passed through the Bering Strait, plowed through an ice field by ramming her way under steam, and kept going down the west coast of North America. Waddell was planning to run into San Francisco Bay at night and board the Federal ironclad *Camanche,* which he knew had been shipped there (SEE PAGE 164), and demand ransom from the city.

Before doing so, however, he wanted recent news from there. He kept on going until he met the British

The CSS *Shenandoah,* long out of communication with land, destroys a fleet of New England whaling ships in the Arctic Ocean more than two months after the war was over. She is the bare-masted vessel at the left.

The *Shenandoah* anchors in the Mersey on November 6, 1865, ending a 58,000-mile cruise on which she captured 38 ships and destroyed 32 of them valued at $1,172,223. She also took 1053 prisoners.

bark *Baracouta* on August 2. She had left San Francisco 13 days before and carried newspapers which convinced Waddell that the war was really over and that further attempts at destruction were useless. He ordered the battery to be struck below and the crew disarmed.

The *Shenandoah* had sailed more than 40,000 miles by this time, but Waddell decided to make the long run of 17,000 miles or more to reach Liverpool. Some of his officers preferred to go to Cape Town, and for a while mutiny threatened. But most of the ship's personnel stood by their captain, and the former raider continued the lengthy voyage under sail. For two months she avoided all ports and other ships, proceeding silently on her lonely way.

On November 5 the *Shenandoah* entered St. George's Channel and picked up a pilot to guide her up the Mersey to Liverpool. The next day she anchored near HMS *Donegal,* hauled down the Confederate flag, and surrendered to the British authorities. Everyone went ashore for good on November 10, and the only Confederate ship ever to circumnavigate the globe was turned over to the United States consul to be sold at auction.

The historic raider then passed into the possession of the Sultan of Zanzibar. She was wrecked on a coral reef in the Indian Ocean in 1879.

THE OLD *RIP* OF THE "SHENANDOAH."

CAPTAIN WADDELL (AS RIP VAN WINKLE). "Law! Mr. Pilot, you don't say so! The war in America over these Eight Months? Dear! dear! who'd ever a' thought it!"

The End

INDEX